£16·50

A HISTORY OF WOMEN PHILOSOPHERS

£3

A History of Women Philosophers

A History of
Women Philosophers

Volume 1

Ancient Women Philosophers

600 B.C. – 500 A.D.

Edited by
MARY ELLEN WAITHE
University of Minnesota

1987
MARTINUS NIJHOFF PUBLISHERS
A MEMBER OF THE KLUWER ACADEMIC PUBLISHERS GROUP
DORDRECHT · BOSTON · LANCASTER

Distributors

for the United States and Canada: Kluwer Academic Publishers, P.O. Box 358, Accord Station, Hingham, MA 02018-0358, USA
for the UK and Ireland: Kluwer Academic Publishers, MTP Press Limited, Falcon House, Queen Square, Lancaster LA1 1RN, UK
for all other countries: Kluwer Academic Publishers Group, Distribution Center, P.O. Box 322, 3300 AH Dordrecht, The Netherlands

Library of Congress Cataloging in Publication Data

Ancient women philosophers, 600 B.C.–500 A.D.

   (A History of women philosophers ; v. 1)
   Bibliography: p.
   Includes index.
   1. Women philosophers. 2. Philosophy, Ancient.
I. Waithe, Mary Ellen. II. Series.
B105.W6A53 1986   180'.88042   86–8675

ISBN 90-247-3348-0 (Hardback)
ISBN 90-247-3368-5 (Paperback)

Copyright

PRINTED IN THE NETHERLANDS

ocrates   Pericles Aspasia   Plato   Anaxagoras   Alcibiades Archimedes

Phidias Sophocles   Antisthenes   Ictinus Polygnotus

'Aspasia's Salon'

Photograph of fresco over portal of the main building of the University of Athens,
Greece. With the kind permission of Professor Michael P. Stathopoulos, Rector of the
University of Athens.

Contents

Introduction to the Series

Two events led to the creation of our four-volume series on the history of women philosophers. The first occurred on a sweltering October afternoon in 1980 when I sought comfort in the basement library of City University of New York's Graduate Center. I came upon a reference to a work by Aegidius Menagius, *Historia Mulierum Philosopharum*, published in 1690 and 1692. I had never heard of any women philosophers prior to the 20th century with the exceptions of Queen Christina of Sweden, known as Descartes' student, and Hildegard von Bingen, who lived in the 12th century. Two months later, the second event occurred. I went to the Brooklyn Museum to see Judy Chicago's *Dinner Party*, a sculptural history of the achievements of women. Part of the exhibit consisted of posters listing the names, nationalities and dates of birth of accomplished women, together with brief descriptions of their accomplishments. Some of those listed were identified as "philosophers."

It took sixteen months to obtain a copy of Menagius' book. (A modern English translation of *Mulierum* by Beatrice Zedler, a participant in the Project on the History of Women in Philosophy, is available through University Press of America.) Although Menage footnoted his sources, the abbreviation conventions used by him made it difficult to duplicate his research. Little did I know then about the existence of reference works giving commonly used abbreviations for early scholarly materials. My problem was compounded by the need to locate editions of the source materials that would have been available to Menage. As it turns out, many of the women he listed as philosophers were astronomers, astrologers, gynecologists, or simply relatives of male philosophers. Nevertheless, the list of women alleged to have been philosophers was impressive.

I contacted Judy Chicago's Through the Flower Corporation, explaining my interest in their research materials about the women identified as philosophers in *Dinner Party*. Unfortunately, Through the Flower had no funds with which to index their archival material, which had by that time been placed in storage. Armed only with Chicago's list of names, I attempted to locate information about the women philosophers. By the end of 1981 I had concluded that the accomplishments of some one hundred or more women philosophers had been omitted from the standard philosophic reference works and histories of philosophy. Just check sources such as *The Encyclopedia of Philosophy*, and the histories of philosophy by Copleston, Zeller, Bury, Grote and others. If the women are mentioned at all, it is in passing, in a footnote.

I. CREATING THE PROJECT ON THE HISTORY OF WOMEN IN PHILOSOPHY

I decided to attempt to restore women's contributions to the history of philosophy, and initially believed that the subject would make an interesting article for, say, the *Journal of the History of Philosophy*. But the sheer volume of information I collected made it obvious that the "article" would be a book-length one. At my husband's suggestion, I took steps to do what Judy Chicago had done: create a team of experts to collaborate with me in this endeavor. I placed a notice in the SWIP (Society for Women in Philosophy) Newsletter and received a half-dozen responses from philosophers offering encouragement, research, writing and translation skills. Frequently, the letters named women philosophers unmentioned by Menage or Chicago. The list grew, and as it grew, the purpose of the Project became clearer. We would help restore women's contributions to the history of philosophy through a program of careful research and scholarship. The purpose of the research was to rediscover previously lost works of women philosophers and make information about those works available in a format that would be useful for students as well as scholars. We would do this in a way that reflected the highest standards of scholarship: meticulous documentation of sources, careful translations of original writings by women philosophers, and critical analysis of our findings. The philosophy student will find the essays to be clear, well-written and understandable. The scholar, whether historian, philosopher or classicist will find apparatuses of translations, meticulous footnoting and a comprehensive bibliography. By providing the educator with new material for the classroom teaching of the history of philosophy, and women's history, we hope to generate a new awareness of women's contributions to our intellectual heritage. By providing the scholar with access to previously unknown or unavailable philosophical writings by women, we hope to encourage further research in this area.

II. CRITERIA FOR SELECTION OF WOMEN PHILOSOPHERS

Prior to announcing the formation of the Project on the History of Women in Philosophy, I mentioned to a male colleague that I had located some writings by Pythagorean women philosophers. He replied that he had heard of some ancient women philosophers, "but, weren't they just writing about — heh, heh — home economics?" Concerned that what I had found wasn't *really* philosophical, I re-read the materials. I could see how a superficial glance at the first few lines of some of the letters or fragmentary works could leave an impression that the Pythagoreans did write about home ecnomics. Their topics included child-rearing and the role of women in ancient society. But a closer, complete reading of the materials I had located belied such a conclusion. These philosophers were analyzing how the Pythagorean concept *harmonia* applied to the structure and running of the state, and to the structure and running of the family, viewed as a microcosm of the state. They discussed how a woman might apply that principle in raising children to become just, harmonious individuals, and how a woman might apply that principle in other areas of her daily life. This wasn't home economics, this was applied ethical theory, complete with a psychology of moral development, a theory of familial obligation, and much, much more. Yet the question suggested by my colleague's comment was relevant: what criteria would I use to identify works that were *really* philosophical?

I could not presume to undertake the task of re-defining the discipline of philosophy, so I chose a purely *ad hoc* device for identifying philosophical works: use a definition of "philosophy" that has been an accepted definition of philosophy for some identifiable historical period. Unfortunately, this *ad hoc* device, uncontroversial though it may at first seem, begs an important feminist question. If traditional philosophy has always been an essentially male enterprise, by selecting works of women that fit those traditional definitions, am I not merely selecting works by women who "thought like men" or who "did what men did"? Perhaps. Examining the question whether philosophy as we have come to know the discipline, defines essentially masculist enterprises that necessarily excluded women, is a worthwhile undertaking. But it is far beyond the expertise of this philosopher, and beyond the immediate task of the Project. The women were engaged in precisely the same kind of philosophical enterprises that have historically characterized male philosophers.

In spite of what I've just said, there are differences between the enterprises that typically characterized male philosophers, and those characteristic of at least some female philosophers. While both males and females have inquired into the basic principles of science, mathematics, and human behavior, when women philosophers examined the principles underlying human behavior, they frequently did so from the perspective of a woman. Aesara of Lucania said that human nature provided the standard for law and justice in the home as well as in the city. Theano II applied the principle of *harmonia* to a woman who was coping with an unfaithful husband, and attempted to show how this principle could help such a woman decide what she ought to do and how she ought to act. Phintys and Perictione applied the principle to the question "how ought women act in public and private life?" Mary Astell and Anna Maria van Schurman applied Lockean and Leibnizian philosophy to the question whether women were capable of rational learning, and argued forcefully for the education of women. Harriet Taylor Mill and Mary Wollstonecraft were among those women philosophers arguing for the economic, social, and political rights of women. Yet, the majority of women philosophers' writings do not reflect concern with the nature, status, and rights of women.

Diotima's discussion of love adopts a masculine perspective, and Hypatia's commentaries on the algebraic theory of Diophantus and the astronomical theory of Ptolemy are as gender-neutral as would be those of any male philosophers. Hildegard von Bingen develops a cosmological theory and a philosophy of medicine. Oliva Sabuco de Nantes Barrera's philosophy of medicine includes a theory about physical diseases that are rooted in psychological causes which, she argues, are themselves the products of personal moral conflict or of the failure to exemplify certain virtues. Anne Conway's *Principles* influence Leibniz, and it is from her that he gets the term "monad." Hortense Allart de Meritens' *Novum Organum ou Sainteté Philosophique* is an attempt to understand natural religion as an object of scientific inquiry. Shikibu Murasaki traces the effects of competing concepts of free will and determinism in the development of social and political philosophy characteristic of feudalistic Japan. Indeed, the philosophical topics and theories of the women philosophers are every bit as diverse and interesting as are those which characterize "traditional" male philosophers.

III. RESEARCH METHODS AND MATERIALS

Research about the history of women philosophers has proceeded in several stages: first, creating a compendium of names, nationalities, and dates of birth of women alleged to have been philosophers. Second, confirming or disconfirming the allegations. In the first stage of research, names appearing in Menage's and Chicago's lists were checked in general encyclopedias, history books, encyclopedias and histories of philosophy, religion, astronomy, mathematics, science, etc. Some of these entries would name other women alleged to be philosophers; names which would then be added to the list. Books about "famous ladies" and "notable females" were read in full, yielding more new names, and frequently, biographical sketches and bibliographical information. As word of the Project spread, new information about previously unknown women philosophers was received. Some of the information came from scholars who were later to become collaborators in the Project; some came from well-wishers impressed by the scope

and significance of our work. The same basic method of research
was used for the compendium-creating stage for all four volumes.
But the methods of research for the second stage — confirming
that the woman actually was a philosopher — varied somewhat
with each volume's research. Verifying information about pre-17th
century women was much more difficult than verifying information about modern and contemporary women philosophers. In
order to locate reliable sources about the ancient and pre-modern
philosophers, we frequently relied on "free association" of the
names with names of male colleagues, male relatives, subject
headings for topics the women wrote about, or with names of
schools of philosophy and locations with which the women were
associated.

For example, information about Hypatia rarely resulted from
mentions of her name in indices, tables of contents, bibliographies,
or card catalogues. Rather, it came from searches for mention of
Theon, her father, Synesius, her pupil, Diophantus, Apollonius
Pergaeus, and Ptolemy, whose works she commented on, neo-
Platonism, astronomy and mathematics, subjects she taught or
wrote about, and the Library and Museum of Alexandria, with
which she was affiliated.

Different philosophers presented special research challenges.
For example, it is usually assumed that Diotima is a fictitious
character created by Plato. Since the Project was interested in the
history of actual women who were philosophers, I had assumed
that Diotima would not be included among those philosophers.
Yet, there was little discussion in the philosophic literature of the
question "was Diotima a fictitious creation of Plato, or was she
really a philosopher who had the conversation with Socrates
reported in the *Symposium*?" Other disciplines, especially classics
and archeology, have considered this issue, and in following
sources outside philosophy I came across two different types of
evidence bearing upon it. First, it appears that in the 15th century
a scholar suggested that it was "silly" to think that a woman
would have been a philosopher. Second, there is ancient archeological evidence which classicists and archeologists have interpreted as support for the claim that Diotima was indeed a historical person. The question whether she was the same person as she
who had that conversation with Socrates described in the *Sym-*

posium is not conclusively proven. It is important to note, however, that it is not conclusively *disproven* either. The evidence is not conclusive, but it is very persuasive, and is made even more persuasive in that it enables us to explain this otherwise anomalous Socratic/Platonic dialogue. I have included Diotima in our first volume partly to spur further investigation by scholars.

Fortunately, there are many resources which contain the surviving fragments of the Pythagorean women philosophers. Stobaeus' *Eclogarum Physicarum* and *Florilegium* are the oldest sources, with Theodoret's *De Vita Pythagoras* and Diels' *Epistolographi Graeci* sources for Theano II's letters. Gregory of Nyssa's *Vita Makrina* and *De Anima et Resurrectione* are the primary sources of material about the life and philosophy of his famous sister. The famous Roman Empress-philosopher Julia Domna was widely commemorated in her time. Historical information about her life and her political stature is discussed in the numismatic, archeological, and philatetic literature. The moral and legal philosophy of the philosophic circle which she fostered is discussed in Roman Law sources and histories of the later Roman Empire.

The second stage of research about women philosophers of the Medieval, Renaissance, and Enlightenment periods did not require us to go quite so far afield of philosophy as did our research for philosophers discussed in Volume 1. Most of the women philosophers of the medieval period were affiliated with religious institutions. Religious history sources, theological publications, library card catalogues of holdings of the successor institutions to medieval monasteries, as well as the extensive collections of the Vatican Libraries proved useful resources. Migne's *Patrologie Latine et Grecque* is an extremely valuable, if difficult to use source of original works and correspondence for the entire medieval period and beyond. The Pontifical Institute of Medieval Studies in Toronto possesses a wealth of source material, including established texts of original works of Juliana of Norwich, Hildegard von Bingen and the correspondence of Heloise and Abelard.

State archives proved useful for locating works by Oliva Sabuco de Nantes Barrera. Sabuco de Nantes had been categorized as a "medical theorist" and as a "poet/playwrite." The first identification was no doubt made because her moral psychology provides the theoretical basis for her understanding of physical illness. The second identification was probably due to her writing style: she wrote in dialogue form. Would Xenophon have been so cast? Unfortunately, parts of her *Nueva Filosofia de la Naturaleza del Hombre* were excised by the Spanish Inquisition. The work has been preserved as part of Spain's national archives of literature and is widely available in its original, late medieval Spanish.

Fortunately there has been recent renewed interest in the works of Christine de Pisan, the first person ever known to have been self-supporting as a writer, and in Anne Conway. Modern English translations of Pisan's *Cité des Dames* (deliberately modelled after Augustine's *City of God*) have recently been published. A Modern English edition of Anne Conway's *Principles of the Most Ancient and Modern Philosophy* appeared in the past decade. Renewed interest in these philosophers, especially Pisan, made our research easier. This was in part due to the useful biographical and bibliographic information presented in the contemporary editions. Verification of previously-achieved research results was thereby simplified. Unfortunately, Pisan's most remarkable philosophical writings, on political theory, remain untranslated. Like Pisan, Sabuco de Nantes has usually been characterized as a literary, rather than as a philosophical writer. This means that most secondary literature focusses on discussions of her style, language, and thematic representations. Its philosophical merits are equally worthy of discussion and are examined in detail in the second volume to this series.

Sor Juana Inez de la Cruz, another philosopher treated solely as a literary figure, is also widely published and widely discussed in the secondary literature. Like Pisan and Sabuco de Nantes, her philosophy has been ignored. Instead, she is widely known as a late medieval poet. Like Teresa of Avila and Juliana of Norwich, de la Cruz was a religious mystic. Like them she is ignored in the philosophical literature. Although the second stage of our research led us afield of philosophy, it did not take us far afield from the history of philosophy literature. Rarely, however, did that literature include any substantial information about those philosophers. More fruitful was research in church history, theology, history of medicine, on the one hand, and Spanish, French, British, and Mexican literary history on the other.

As we progressed to the modern era and the second stage of research for Volume Three. *Modern Women Philosophers*, we found that the card catalogues of both national and university libraries were increasingly reliable. Commentary articles about women philosophers began to appear in computerized databases, and journals containing those works were more easily obtained. When we had sought original or early editions of works by the ancient and medieval through enlightenment women philosophers we frequently faced understandable reluctance of libraries to lend rare copies of centuries-old volumes. When material could be borrowed, it usually could not be photocopied. Rarely were such restrictions placed on access to works of the modern era. For once we knew that a woman was reputed to have been a philosopher, and knew when and where she lived, there were often several resources for obtaining copies of her works. Her correspondence and estate papers had often been catalogued and secondary or commentary literature was referenced in standard hisorical (but not philosophical) sources. Where indices were lacking, we thumbed through volume after volume of early scholarly journals, proceedings of learned societies, and other sources. The *Journal des Scavans* (1665-1697, 1816 --), *Acta Eruditorum* (1682-1786) and other early journals were frequently valuable. The *Women's History Microfilm Collection* contains many works by women philosophers including Anne Conway, Catharine Trotter Cockburn, Anna Maria van Schurman, Mary Wollstonecraft and others. Modern English editions of the works of these and other women philosophers are available. The works of Margaret Fuller Ossolli, Mary Wollstonecraft and Harriet Taylor Mill are frequently taught as part of women's history courses. The collected works of Julie Favre, although not available in English, can be obtained for scholarly use through university libraries. Christine Ladd Franklin's work on perception, as well as her logical writings co-authored with Pierce, have been published in philosophical journals at the turn of the century. Likewise, Sophie Bryant's work on symbolic logic.

No longer did the second stage of our research take us as far afield of philosophy as archeology, numismatics, and philately. In part, shifts in academic disciplines as primary sources of research materials reflected changes that extended far beyond philosophy

itself. Just as the medieval through enlightenment periods reflected a change from intellectual interests in religion and the
study of the classics to the study of political theory, new literary
forms, and modern science, so the primary academic disciplines
from which material about women philosophers came also changed.
And just as the modern era reflected a change from intellectual
interests in political theory and basic science to a new focus on the
rights of the disenfranchised, and the relationship between philosophy of mind and the new medical discipline, psychology, so the
primary academic disciplines from which material about women
philosophers came also changed. For the first time, that information came from philosophy journals and histories of philosophy,
from archives of philosophy departments in major universities, and
from proceedings of philosophical professional associations.

Our final volume, *Contemporary Women Philosophers* utilized the
usual philosophical source materials for the second stage of
research. But we also relied upon permission from the families or
executors of the estates of women philosophers to study unpub-
lished materials. These private sources provided the means with
which to complete the research on Gerda Walther, Edith Stein and
Hedwig Conrad Martius. Other 20th century women philosophers,
such as Simone Weil and Simone de Beauvoir, have long tran-
scended the philosophical literature and made their way into the
popular literature. Philosophers such as Charlotte Perkins Gil-
man, Antoinette Blackwell and Monique Wittig are widely known
in the feminist literature, while Lizzie Susan Stebbing is widely
known among 20th century philosophers.

There are some philosophical reflections about this Project that I
would like to share. What has struck me as fundamentally serious
is the ramification that the contents of these four volumes will
have for philosophy itself. Three kinds of important questions are
immediately raised: first, "What *is* the history of philosophy?";
second, "Have philosophers failed at that most basic task of
philosophy — to question one's basic assumptions thereby to
discover the truth?"; and third, "Might we come to a different
understanding of the nature of philosophy itself as a result of an
acquaintance with women's thought?"

The very existence of what in retrospect appears to have been not terribly well hidden (after all, all the writings of the Pythagorean women excepting the letters were preserved by Stobeaus) suggests that philosophers have been more than careless about knowing the history of their discipline, and certainly not very inquisitive about it. Perhaps these volumes have only scratched the surface: are there many more works by women philosophers to be found? Probably. How well integrated into the philosophical circles of their times were these women? Were they listened to by men who styled themselves philosophers? Did they influence them, and in what ways did male philosophers take their views into account? How might our history have read were there truly no women philosophers (as most of us had come to believe)? How might our history now read were we to attempt to integrate the contributions of women with those of men?

In addition to noting these fundamental questions about the history of the field, we must realize that its literature is wanting the availability of full-length translations and modern editions of the works of women philosophers. We certainly cannot hope accurately to reconstruct our history until we have had the opportunity to study and discuss these works. That process of philosophizing among ourselves about the meaning of certain works requires years. The lasting impact that the women make will come only when we have been long steeped in their ideas and have learned to see them in relationship to each other and to that other world of philosophy – the one we thought was purely male. But having full-length modern translations only provides scholars with good reading. What about our students, what about the larger academic community? Articles about individual women philosophers will slowly swell the volumes of general-readership encyclopedias and other reference works. Historians, classicists, and members of other related professions will be unwilling to rely on the standard histories of philosophy, and on other philosophy reference materials. It could be difficult to reconcile other scholarly professions to relying on information coming from a field that has consistently failed to acknowledge and avail itself of the contributions made to it by a particular group. This brings me to the second question: Have philosophers failed at that most basic task of philosophy: questioning one's basic assumptions?

I was never going to include Diotima in these volumes. Everyone knew that she was a fictitious character in a platonic dialogue. Then, I decided to try and find out. After all, what if everyone were wrong? So I tried to find discussions in the literature on the question of Diotima's historicity. Since this was something everyone knew not to be the case, it seemed to be something that would have been frequently mentioned. How else would every philosopher know this to be the case? But there was no discussion of it in the mainstream philosophical literature that I recall. But surely, this knowledge must have come from somewhere. And here's where I got introduced to Classical Studies, a wonderful field of inquiry — literary archeology. It was the pursuit of the Diotima question in the classics literature that made clear the nature of philosophy's failing. The kinds of basic philosophic questions — you know, the ones we ask of freshmen in "What is Philosophy?" courses — are ones we've never asked ourselves. Have we asked of our literature "is it complete?" Have we asked of our history "is it true?" We have not, and this, I submit is a very serious flaw, because we like to style ourselves as experts in asking the right questions, and in questioning all our basic assumptions. We are philosophers, and questioning, doubting, is what we are supposed to do well. In this one area, we haven't done it at all while other disciplines have done it for us — although not as well as we might have done it had we done it.

And now to my third question: "Might we come to a different understanding of the nature of philosophy itself as a result of our acquaintance with the ideas of women?" In what ways did women philosophize differently than men? Were they concerned about particular areas in or problems of philosophy which men showed little interest in? The most striking difference between the ways in which men philosophized and the ways in which women philosophized are evident respecting the texts by the Pythagorean women philosophers. Whereas men who philosophized about ethics tended to attempt to construct ideal theories, for use in ideal states or ideal worlds, the Pythagorean women were concerned with applications of the prevaling ethical theory to everyday life. They concerned themselves almost exclusively with analyzing the ways in which the normative principle of *harmonia* can be applied to the living of everyday life. They are particularly concerned how best to implement that principle in fulfilling their preordained social roles as women. Consequently, their concerns are to show other women how to run just, harmonious hoseholds, how to raise just, harmonious children, how to preserve harmony in a marital relationship, and how to interact with servants so as to preserve harmony at home. That was women's job, to preserve harmony at home and to raise just, harmonious individuals. Men's job was to establish harmony in society and to create a just state. If we except the Pythagorean women, we find little differences in the ways men and women did philosophy. Both have been concerned with ethics, metaphysics, cosmology, epistemology and other areas of philosophic inquiry. An acquaintance with the contributions women have made to the history of philosophy cannot help but force us to reconsider that history in light of the new materials introduced in this and subsequent volumes of this series.

MARY ELLEN WAITHE

Acknowledgements

So many individuals have contributed to this volume and all deserve more thanks than space permits. The person who has done the most to see this volume to completion is my husband, Lloyd Waithe. Not only was the creation of the Project on the History of Women in Philosophy his idea, but he has consistently supported my efforts to administer the Project, to write much of this first volume, and to edit this series. In addition, he has translated Hypatia's *Commentary on Diophantus' Arithmeticorum.*

Erika Linke, a talented and dedicated librarian, spent many hours teaching me how to do the research which ultimately culminated in this volume. She worked tirelessly to obtain rare copies of works containing the materials translated here. D. Burnham Terrell, Naomi Schoeman, Edward Lee, and Project members Wolfgang Gombocz, Alice ter Meulen, Beatrice Zedler, Sr. Prudence Hope Allen and Vicki Lynn Harper are among many who have contributed bibliographic material. Ann-Sofie Winter of the Abo Akademis Bibliotek generously sent complementary copies of Holger Thesleff's *The Pythagorean Texts of the Hellenistic Period* and *An Introduction to the Pythagorean Writings of the Hellenistic Period.* Project members Beatrice Zedler and Sr. Prudence Hope Allen donated copies of their own works on women philosophers.

Project member Rhoda Burger collaborated with Vicki Lynn Harper in early drafts of the translation of the fragment by Aesara of Lucania. Project member Linda L. McAlister summarized Kranz' discussions of the historicity of Diotima. Elisabeth M. Lewis translated a lengthy article without which the Hypatia chapter could not have been written. Vicki Lynn Harper, Elizabeth Belfiore, John Pepple, Theofanis Stavrou and Sandra Peterson all offered translations of the troublesome phrase with which Theon attributes Book III of the *Commentary on Ptolemy's Syntaxis Mathematica* to Hypatia.

Karen Warren convinced us to approach the Society for Women in Philosophy and the Minnesota Philosophical Society which afforded early opportunities to present some of our work. James Nelson of St. John's University and Elizabeth Stich of the College of Saint Scholastica afforded opportunities to share with their faculties the research skills that will ultimately contribute to others discovering additional works by women philosophers. Duane Cady of Hamline University provided an opportunity to teach a course on the history of women philosophers. In addition, Marquette University, the College of Saint Olaf and many other institutions that are home to Project members have expanded their curricula to include teaching of the history of women philosophers. Project member Nancy Weber copy edited earlier drafts of several chapters and made useful suggestions regarding the writing and organization of the text. Librarian Mary Schwind edited and verified entries in the bibliography. Leslie Martens permitted use of word processing equipment, Therese Pash provided patient instruction in its use, and David Born contributed many hours of badly-needed technical assistance. To these and all others who have made the completion of this volume possible, I offer heartfelt thanks and deep appreciation.

MARY ELLEN WAITHE

Chronological Table

					B.C.
600	500	400	300	200	100

Themistoclea

Theano
of Crotona

Diotima of
Mantinea

Axiothea
of Philasia

Damo

Aspasia
of Miletus

————————Aesara of Lucania————

Arignote

————————Theano II————

————————Perictione II————

Myia

?

Hipparchia

Cleobulina
of Rhodes

Lasthenia
of Mantinea

Arete
of Cyrene

Phintys
of Sparta

[—Perictione I—]
?

Pythagoras	Socrates	Plato	Epicurus	Didymus	Cicero
	Euclides	Crates	Aristotle	Occellus	
		Aristippus			

A.D. 100	. 200	300	400	500
Julia Domna		Makrina		
			Asclepigenia of Athens	
			Hypatia of Alexandria	

Antipater	Porphyry	Plutarch	Proclus	
Numenius	Plotinus	Iamblichus	Themistius	
		Philostratus		

Introduction to Volume 1

MARY ELLEN WAITHE

If we trace the history of philosophy to Hesiod, we know that philosophy, at least in its written form, was engaging men since at least the 8th century, B.C. Verbal philosophizing no doubt predates Hesiod, but without a record of that oral history, we do now know by how much. There is a record that Pythagoras received his aesthetic principles from a woman priestess-philosopher, Themistoclea, but there are no further details to be found about her. Theano of Crotona, wife of Pythagoras of Samos, was from an aristocratic, Orphic family. There is a document attributed to her, in which she discusses Pythagorean metaphysics, and there are records of her apothegms from which we can sketch her views on marriage, sex, women, and ethics. Little more is known about Theano, except that her daughters Damo, Myia and Arignote were also reputed to be among the original Pythagorean philosophers. Other women, including Phintys of Sparta, Aesara of Lucania, Perictione, Perictione II and Theano II were Pythagoreans, but they lived several centuries after the members of the original Pythagorean community.

The recent philosophic tradition has assumed that Diotima was not a historical person who held the dialogue with Socrates on the nature of erotic love that is reported in Plato's *Symposium*. This Platonic dialogue, however, has long puzzled Plato scholars because several of the views that are attributed to Diotima appear not to be consistent with Plato's own views. We introduce the textual and archeological evidence for a view that challenges traditional claims concerning Diotima's historicity, and trace the origins of the suggestion that Diotima was not a historical person to a 15th century humanist.

A History of Women Philosophers / Volume 1, ed. by Mary Ellen Waithe
©Martinus Nijhoff Publishers, Dordrecht – Printed in the Netherlands

The two surviving fragments from Phintys' *On the Moderation of Women* reflect the Pythagorean assumption that there are some essential differences between men's and women's natures. Phintys notes that although some virtues are common to both (courage, justice, and wisdom) temperance or moderation is more common to women. She acknowledges that the limitations on women's social roles reflect an understanding of the nature of women's souls. Thus, the normative principle of *harmonia* is to be satisfied within the context of the specific social roles permitted women.

The surviving fragment from Aesara of Lucania's *Book on Human Nature* presents a natural law theory which claims that through introspection into the nature and structure of the human soul we can discover the natural philosophical foundations for all of human law, including the technical structure of moral law and positive law. Her natural law theory concerns three applications of the moral law: individual, private morality, the moral basis of familial institutions, and the moral basis of social institutions.

Although two fragments from *On the Harmony of Women* and a fragment *On Wisdom* are both identified as authored by a woman named Perictione, it does not appear that both ought to be attributed to the same Perictione. And, although Plato's mother was named Perictione, we cannot know with confidence whether either author is Plato's mother. The fragments from *On the Harmony of Women* constitute an application of the normative principle of *harmonia* to the harsh realities of women's social roles. They give a realistic assessment of how a woman, faced with the fact that her freedom of action is limited by society, can fulfill her duty to act virtuously. The fragment *On Wisdom* provides a teleological analysis of the nature and purpose of philosophy, and distinguishes philosophy from other theoretical disciplines.

Two writings survive of Theano II: they are letters to Euboule, and to Nikostrate, both preserved by Theodoret in his *De Vita Pythagoras*. In her letter to Euboule, Theano II explains that because young children are unable to understand how to apply the principle of *harmonia*, they must be guided and disciplined. Theano II's assumption that the responsibility for this rests with the mother because it is woman's special virtue to be able to create justice and harmony in the home, is consistent with the views of womens' place expressed by Phintys and Perictione. The special virtue of women obligates them also to behave justly towards their husbands, even when husbands treat them unjustly. This view is expressed in Theano II's letter to Nikostrate, and has its roots in her views of women's responsibility for maintaining harmony in a marriage. She notes that compounding one injustice with another is not the way to restore order and harmony, but the way to create further discord. Only by acting honorably and justly, can the woman demonstrate her moral superiority to the man and thereby set the example for him to emulate.

Successor to the school of philosophy originally founded by her father Aristippus, Arete of Cyrene headed the Cyrenaic school of hedonistic philosophy following his death. Since her father was present at Socrates' death, we may assume that Arete was a contemporary of Plato. This school of philosophy held that the most important human intellectual enterprise was the search for happiness. They rejected the scientific disciplines as irrelevant to that search. The sole criterion of morality was present experience of pleasure, a moral principle defended on both empirical and epistemological grounds. Philosophers were uniquely suited to the pursuit of pleasure because they were better suited to exercizing rational control of that pursuit. The hedonistic ethics which Arete and the other early Cyrenaics promoted was a philosophic hedonism, and not merely an advocacy of profligate living.

Known throughout the Later Roman Empire as "The Philosopher Julia," this Roman Empress of the Severan dynasty devoted herself to the study of philosophy and sponsored a philosophical circle consisting of mathematicians, sophists, lawyers, physicians, historians, and other learned academicians. She is best known as a proponent of "the second sophistic," a school of philosophical rhetoric devoted to discussions of the philosophic treatment of subjects like justice, cosmology, as well as to discussions of neo-Pythagorean and neo-Platonic philosophies.

Makrina lived in Neocaesarea in the 4th century, A.D. Her deathbed discussion with her brother, Gregory, Bishop of Nyssa, on the nature of the soul was recorded by him in the dialogue *De Anima et Resurrectione* shortly following her death. Makrina came from a family in which both men and women were intellectuals, and was educated by her mother. A student of Greek philosophy, Makrina was also a Christian, and extremely knowledgeable about Christian philosophy. Although nothing is directly known of her views on the question of the equality of the souls of men and women, from her discussions of the nature of the soul and of human creation, it is clear that Makrina found no essential differences between the souls of men and those of women. According to Makrina, the capacity for rational thought is the essential characteristic of the soul. The passions are not essential features of the soul. Hence, she argues, even if, as gnosticism and early Christian philosophy maintained, women were morally inferior to men, this is not due to essential differences in the natures of men's and women's souls, but to choices made by individual women. In her view, both men and women are made "in the image and likeness of God." Makrina rejects the idea that humans are reincarnated as animals and plants in punishment for their sins.

Hypatia lived in Alexandria, at a time when it was the western world's center of scientific and philosophic achievement. It was at that time the site of tremendous social, political, religious, and academic turmoil. The daughter of the Alexandrinian Museum's most famous mathematician, Theon, Hypatia allegedly exceeded his mathematical abilities while attaining a reputation as Alexandria's most eminent neo-Platonic philosopher. The Christian Roman government honored her achievements with her unprecedented appointment to a paid public position as head of the Plotinian school. Although she taught philosophy, including the works of Plato, Aristotle and their successors, she apparently did not write philosophy. Rather, philosophy provided her with the theoretical foundations with which to assess the merits of the most powerful mathematical, geometrical, and astronomical theories of her time. She became known for her commentaries on the mathematical and astronomical theories of Ptolemy, (exceeding even Pappus' reputation in this regard) for her contribution to algebraic theory through her commentary on Diophantus' *Arithmeticorum*, and for her commentaries on the solid geometry of Apollonius Pergaeus' *Conic Sections*. Her written work is largely unknown to modern scholars, many of whom have repeated the unfounded claims of the Suda *Lexicon* that all of her works perished. Rather, historical mention of Hypatia has usually been limited to mention of her untimely and gruesome death at the hands of a mob of monks.

Asclepigenia of Athens was a younger contemporary of Hypatia, but while Hypatia applied her knowledge of Platonic and Aristotelian philosophy to the great mathematical and scientific questions of her day, Asclepigenia applied her knowledge of Plato and Aristotle to the great religious and metaphysical questions raised by Christian ethical theory. The pagan philosophers sought to understand the mysteries of the cosmos and to intervene with the gods to change human fate. Christianity on the other hand represented an acceptance, even a welcoming of tragedy and fate in this life and promised salvation and consolation in the next. It was in this context that the philosophy taught by Asclepigenia sought the greatest good. Pagan philosophers like Asclepigenia reacted to dissatisfaction with life's fates by understanding and mastering the "secret" principles of metaphysics which controlled the universe and applying magical and theurgic principles to affect those fates. Thus Asclepigenia stood in marked contrast to the philosophers of the Alexandrinian school of Hypatia who sought the Absolute through mastery of metaphysics, cosmology, mathematics, and science. The philosophers of the Athenian school, and in particular, Asclepigenia's pupil Proclus, sought the Absolute through contemplation of the mysteries of metaphysics, cosmology, mysticism, magic, and theurgy.

1. Early Pythagoreans:
Themistoclea, Theano, Arignote, Myia, and Damo

MARY ELLEN WAITHE

Pythagoreanism represented an active and popular school of philosophy from the end of the 6th century B.C. through the 2nd or 3rd centuries A.D. The original or "early" Pythagoreans included the immediate members of his family and other successors who headed Pythagorean societies or cults in parts of Greece and southern Italy. Early Pythagoreans are to be distinguished from "late" Pythagoreans of the 4th and 3rd centuries B.C. and from the "neo Pythagoreans" of the 1st century B.C. through perhaps the 3rd century A.D. The early Pythagoreans included Themistoclea, Theano, Arignote, Myia and Damo. With the possible exception of Themistoclea, these women were members of Pythagoras' family. Late Pythagoreans, including Phintys, Aesara of Lucania, Perictione, (possibly) Perictione II, and Theano II can better be described as philosophers in the Pythagorean tradition. They probably lived *circa* 4th-2nd centuries B.C.[1]

I. THEMISTOCLEA, ARIGNOTE, AND DAMO

The ancient sources indicate that women were active in early Pythagorean societies and may have played a central role in the development of early Pythagorean philosophy. Diogenes Laertius[2] reports that:

> Aristonexus asserts that Pythagoras derived the greater part of his ethical doctrines from Themistoclea, the priestess at Delphi.

A History of Women Philosophers / Volume 1, ed. by Mary Ellen Waithe
©*Martinus Nijhoff Publishers. Dordrecht − Printed in the Netherlands*

Early Pythagoreans viewed the cosmos or universe as orderly and harmonious. Everything bears a particular mathematical relationship to everything else. Harmony and order exist when things are in their proper relationship to each other. This relationship can be expressed as a mathematical proportion. One of the "sacred discourses" is attributed to Pythagoras' daughter, Arignote.[3] According to Arignote:[4]

> ... the eternal essence of number is the most providential cause of the whole heaven, earth and the region in between. Likewise it is the root of the continued existence of the gods and daimones, as well as that of divine men.

Arignote's comment is consistent with one attributed to her mother, Theano of Crotona in that all that exists, all that is real can be distinguished from other things through enumeration. The eternal essence of number is also directly related to the harmonious coexistence of different things. This harmony can be expressed as a mathematical relationship. In these two ways, number is the cause of all things: without it we could not enumerate, delineate, and distinguish among things, and it expresses the orderly relationships among things.

II. THEANO OF CROTONA

Theano was the daugther of Brontinus, a Crotona orphic and aristocrat. She first became the pupil of Pythagoras of Samos, and later his wife. In a document attributed to a larger work by her, *On Piety,*[5] she alludes to the metaphysical concepts of imitation and participation. The text is translated by Vicki Lynn Harper:[6]

> I have learned that many of the Greeks believe Pythagoras said all things are generated from number. The very assertion poses a difficulty: How can things which do not exist even be conceived to generate? But he did not say that all things come to be from number; rather, in accordance with number — on the grounds that order in the primary sense is in number and it is by participation in order that a first and a second

and the rest sequentially are assigned to things which are counted.

Theano is saying that when we ask what is the nature of an object, we can reply either by drawing an analogy between that object and something else, or we can define the object. According to her, Pythagoras meant to express an analogy between things and numbers. This is the concept of imitation: things are like numbers. By its participation in the universe of order and harmony, an object, whether corporeal or not, can be sequenced with all other objects and can be counted. Things can be counted in accordance with number, the primary sense of which is ordering.

The document attributed to Theano of Crotona appears to have been unknown to Aristotle who said that the Pythagoreans:[7]

> ... construct natural bodies out of numbers, things that have lightness and weight out of things that have not weight or lightness...

If we read Theano's "things" to mean "corporeal, or physical objects," as I think we must, given her use of the term "generate," she is claiming only that corporeal things do not come into existence from number itself because number is non-corporeal. Rather, it is number that enables us to distinguish one thing from another. By enumerating things as first, second, etc., we tacitly claim to be able to specify the physical parameters of the thing: it begins here, it ends there, and between the beginning and the end is one object. Thus in enumerating we also delineate objects. We can tell that something is an object because we can count it.

An apothegem attributed to Theano concerns two well-known Pythagorean doctrines: the immortality of souls, and the transmigration of souls. Theano confirms that the Pythagoreans believed in "divine justice" in the afterlife and in the transmigration of souls after death into a new body which was not necessarily human. From this apothegem, we get a picture of a process of transmigration through which harmony can be restored to the universe when a person has disrupted that harmony by violating the moral law during their lifetime. Theano connects morality with cosmology by showing why there should be no doubt about the immortality of the soul:[8]

>If the soul is not immortal, then life is truly a feast for
>evil-doers who die after having lived their lives so iniquitous-
>ly.

In a principled, harmonious universe, everything has its own place
and performs its own functions according to some law: the laws of
physics, of logic, or of morality and religion. Evil or immoral
actions are contrary to law, and contribute to disorder and discord.
According to Theano, if the soul is not immortal, then those who
contribute to disorder not only get a kind of free ride throughout
life at the expense of those whom they have wronged, but they
also disrupt the orderliness of the universe. If balance and harmony in the universe is to be restored, souls must be immortal.
Then the immoral can restore order by accepting the punishment
of being reborn as something less than a human being and by living
that later life as required by the moral law.

Stobeaus quotes several apothegems by Theano which reveal
Pythagorean attitudes toward women. A wife's sexual activity is to
be restricted to pleasing her husband — she is not to have other
lovers. In the context of marriage, chastity and virtue are not
identified with abstinence. When Theano was asked how many
days following sexual intercourse are required for a woman to
once again be considered "pure," her reply was that if the activity
was with the woman's own husband, she remains pure, but if it
was with someone else, she can never again become pure.[9] When
asked what duties are incumbent upon a married woman, her
response is "to please her husband."[10] Theano viewed romantic
love as nothing more than "the natural inclination of an empty
soul."[11] These quotes can perhaps best be understood in the light
of the writings of the later Pythagorean philosophers, Phintys,
Theano II, Perictione, Aesara of Lucania and Perictione II. From
their writings we see that Pythagorean doctrines are to be applied
to personal and to family life. Women, whose special virtue is
temperance, bear the responsibility for maintaining law and justice
(or harmony) within the home. According to Aesara of Lucania[12]
the home is a microcosm of the state. Consequently women bear a
large responsibility for creating the conditions under which
harmony and order, and law and justice can exist in the state. A
woman who doesn't understand this is likely to contribute to

disorder, discord, and chaos. When we read Theano's apothegems in this context, we can better appreciate the force of her comment:[13]

> Better to be on a runaway horse than to be a woman who does not reflect.

III. MYIA

Myia is mentioned as one of the daughters of Theano and Pythagoras.[14] She was married to an athlete, Milo (sometimes referred to as Milon, Mylon, or even Meno) who came from her mother's native Crotona. It was in her home that Pythagoras was burned to death. Like the other women Pythagoreans, she writes about the application of the principle of *harmonia* in the daily life of a woman. Her letter to Phyllis discusses the importance of filling the needs of a newborn infant in accordance with that principle. Her point seems to be that a newborn naturally desires that which is appropriate to its needs, and what it needs is moderation: neither too little nor too much food, clothing, heat, cold, fresh air, etc. What is interesting about her letter is the suggestion that the newborn naturally desires moderation in everything, and that it benefits most from moderation. For these reasons, the new mother must select a nurse that is temperate, also. The nurse must not be given to excesses of sleep or drink, and must moderate her husband's sexual appetite (presumably because pregnancy will prevent lactation). She must "do all things well at the appropriate time." She must be attuned to the well-being of the child, and temper her own needs so that her nurturing of the newborn will contribute to its being well-raised.

Text of Myia's letter to Phyllis[15]

> Myia to Phyllis: Greetings. Because you have become a mother, I offer you this advice. Choose a nurse that is well-disposed and clean, one that is modest and not given to excessive sleep or drink. Such a woman will be best able to judge how to bring up your children in a manner appropriate

to their free-born station — provided, of course, that she has enough milk to nourish a child, and is not easily overcome by her husband's entreaties to share his bed. A nurse has a great part in this which is first and prefatory to a child's whole life, i.e., nurturing with a view to raising the child well. For she will do all things well at the appropriate time. Let her offer the nipple and breast and nourishment, not on the spur of the moment, but according to due consideration. Thus will she guide the baby to health. She should not give in whenever she herself wishes to sleep, but when the newborn desires to rest; she will be no small comfort to the child. Let her not be irascible or loquacious or indiscriminate in the taking of food, but orderly and temperate and — if at all possible — not foreign but Greek. It is best to put the newborn to sleep when it has been suitably filled with milk, for then rest is sweet to the young, and such nourishment is easy to digest. If there is any other nourishment, one must give food that is as plain as possible. Hold off altogether from wine, because of its strong effect, or add it sparingly in a mixture to the evening milk. Don't continually give the child baths. A practice of infrequent baths, at a mild temperature, is better. In addition, the air should have a suitable balance of heat and cold, and the house should not be too drafty or too closed in. The water should be neither hard nor soft, and the bed-clothes should be not rough but falling agreeably on the skin. In all these things nature yearns for what is fitting, not what is extravagant. These are the things it seems useful to write to you for the present: my hopes based on nursing according to plan. With the help of god, we shall provide feasible and fitting reminders concerning the child's upbringing again at a later time.

The reader may be impressed, as I was, at the extent to which this advice of temperance is carried out by Myia herself: she ends the letter with the statement that "these are the things it seems useful to write to you for the present..." There is moderation even in the giving of advice, for she promises more later on, when it will be "fitting" to remind Phyllis of other details of harmonious childrearing! This closing statement summarizes what it is that the

Pythagorean women see themselves *really* doing through their letters and texts. There is something task-oriented about Myia's letter, and those of Theano II, as well as the fragments by Perictione I and Phyntis. It is their task as women philosophers to teach to other women that which women need to know if they are to live their lives harmoniously and, as Aesara of Lucania suggests, create justice and harmony in their souls and in their homes. Likewise, it is the task of men philosophers to teach to other men that which men need to know if they are to live their lives harmoniously, creating justice and harmony in their souls and in the state. This task orientation in part explains, and in part merely describes the reasons for the "realistic" approach to moral philosophy that the women take, as well as the "ideal" approach to it that men take. They take different approaches because their tasks are different. Their tasks are different because the natures of men and women differ.

NOTES

1. See Ch. 4, Authenticating the Fragments and Letters.
2. Diogenes Laertius, *Lives of the Eminent Philosophers*, R.D. Hicks, transl. Cambridge: Harvard University Press, 1942. V, 341.
3. Armand Delatte, *Études sur la litterature Pythagoricienne*, Bibliothèque de l'École des Hautes Études, 217, Paris, 1915.
4. Peter Gorman, *Pythagoras, A Life*, Boston: Routledge & Kegan Paul, 1979, p. 90.
5. Thesleff, Holger, "Pythagorean Texts of the Hellenistic Period," *Acta Academiae Aboensis, Humaniora*, Ser. A. Vol. 30, 1, p. 125 (1965) Stob., 1.10.13, 125 Wa.
6. Harper adopts the reading γεννᾶν. ὁ δὲ (Heeren), following Thesleff.
7. Aristotle, *Metaphysics* 1090a22.
8. Clement of Alexandria, *Stromata*, IV.7.
9. Stobaeus, *Eclogae Physicae Dialecticae et Ethicae* (Hense) IV, 586.
10. *Op. cit.*, 587.
11. *Ibid.*
12. Variously spelled "Aisara" and "Aresas," the latter sometimes confused with a male of that name who was not the same as our Aesara.
13. Stobaeus (Meineke) *Florilegium*, 268.
14. Clement of Alexandria, *Stromata*, IV, 19., Suda *Lexicon*, s.v. "Myia," "Theano." Iamblichus, *Life of Pythagoras*, 30 and 36.
15. Thesleff, *op. cit.*, 123-4; Hercher, *Epistolographi Graeci*, 608. Translated by Vicki Lynn Harper.

2. Late Pythagoreans:
Aesata of Lucania, Phintys of Sparta, and Perictione I

MARY ELLEN WAITHE
with translations and additional commentary by
VICKI LYNN HARPER

Aesara of Lucania, Phintys of Sparta and Perictione I can be distinguished from the early Pythagorean women who were members of Pythagoras' family and the original Pythagorean cults. The late Pythagoreans probably lived no earlier than *circa* 425 B.C. and some possibly as late as *circa* 100 A.D.

I. AESARA OF LUCANIA

Only a fragment survives of Aesara of Lucania's *Book on Human Nature*, but it provides a key to understanding the philosophies of Phintys, Perictione and Theano II as well. Aesara presents a familiar and intuitive natural law theory. She says that through the activity of introspection into our own nature — specifically the nature of a human soul — we can discover not only the natural philosophic foundation for all of human law, but we can also discern the technical structure of morality, positive law, and, it may be inferred, the laws of moral psychology and of physical medicine. Aesara's natural law theory concerns laws governing three applications of moral law: individual or private morality, laws governing the moral basis of the institution of the family, and, laws governing the moral foundations of social institutions. By analyzing the nature of the soul, Aesara says, we will understand the nature of law and of justice at the individual, familial, and social levels.

A History of Women Philosophers / Volume 1, ed. by Mary Ellen Waithe
©*Martinus Nijhoff Publishers, Dordrecht – Printed in the Netherlands*

1. *Text of* On Human Nature[1]

From *On Human Nature* by Aesara,* Pythagorean of Lucania:

Human nature seems to me to provide a standard of law and justice both for the home and for the city. By following the tracks within himself whoever seeks will make a discovery: law is in him and justice, which is the orderly arrangement of the soul. Being threefold, it is organized in accordance with triple functions: that which effects judgment and thoughtfulness is [the mind]**, that which effects strength and ability is [high spirit],*** and that which effects love and kindliness is desire. These are all so disposed relatively to one another that the best part is in command, the most inferior is governed, and the one in between holds a middle place; it both governs and is governed.

God thus contrived these things according to principle in both the outline and completion of the human dwelling place, because he intended man alone to become a recipient of law and justice, and none other of mortal animals. A composite unity of association could not come about from a single thing, nor indeed from several which are all alike. (For it is necessary, since the things to be done are different, that the parts of the soul also be different, just as in the case of the body [the organs of touch and]**** sight and hearing and taste and smell differ, for these do not all have the same affinity with everything.)

Nor could such a unity come from several dissimilar things at random, but rather, from parts formed in accordance with the completion and organization and fitting together of the entire composite whole. Not only is the soul composed from several dissimilar parts, these being fashioned in conformity with the whole and complete, but in addition these are not arranged haphazardly and at random, but in accordance with rational attention.

*   Αἰσάρας FP., ᾽Αρεσᾶ Th., ᾽Αρέσα Heeren.
**   ὁ νόος add. Heeren.
***   ἁ θύμωσις add. Heeren.
****   ἄψιος ὄργανα καὶ add. Wachsmuth.

For if they had an equal share of power and honor, though being themselves unequal — some inferior, some better, some in between — the association of parts throughout the soul could not have been fitted together. Or, even if they did have an unequal share, but the worse rather than the better had the greater share, there would be great folly and disorder in the soul. And even if the better had the greater and the worse the lesser, but each of these not in the proper proportion, there could not be unanimity and friendship and justice throughout the soul, since when each one is arranged in accordance with the suitable proportion, this sort of arrangement I assert to be justice.

And indeed, a certain unanimity and agreement in sentiment accompanies such an arrangement. This sort would justly be called good order, whichever, due to the better part's ruling and the inferior's being ruled, should add the strength of virtue to itself. Friendship and love and kindliness, cognate and kindred, will sprout from these parts. For closely-inspecting mind persuades, desire loves, and high spirit is filled with strength; once seething with hatred, it becomes friendly to desire.

Mind having fitted the pleasant together with the painful, mingling also the tense and robust with the slight and relaxed portion of the soul, each part is distributed in accordance with its kindred and suitable concern for each thing: mind closely inspecting and tracking out things, high spirit adding impetuosity and strength to what is closely inspected, and desire, being akin to affection, adapts to the mind, preserving the pleasant as its own and giving up the thoughtful to the thoughtful part of the soul. By virtue of these things the best life for man seems to me to be whenever the pleasant should be mixed with the earnest, and pleasure with virtue. Mind is able to fit these things to itself, becoming lovely through systematic education and virtue.

Aesara's soul is tripartite in structure. Its three parts are the mind, spiritedness, and desire. The mind affects judgment and thoughtfulness. Here, "thoughtfulness" should be understood in the purely analytic sense, not the affective sense. Spiritedness affects strength and ability. Desire affects love and "kindliness." These three parts form a "composite unity of association." God intends the three parts of the soul to function together according to a rational principle, the principle of appropriate proportion. The appropriateness of the proportion of one part of the soul to another depends upon what the task at hand is, i.e., upon what Aesara calls the different things to be done. As such, the principle is not only mathematical, rational, and divine, but also functional.

2. *The Nature of Law and Justice*

What can we infer about the nature and structure of law and of justice from Aesara's analysis of the nature and structure of the soul? First, we can infer that both law and justice are products of a rational, mathematical, divine, and functional principle — that of appropriate proportion. Second, both law and justice are structurally tripartite, corresponding to the structure of the human soul. Aesara's first claim, that the principle characterizes both the structure of the soul and the nature of law and justice, is a simple one. No one of the three parts of the soul, or of law and justice dominate. For example, depending upon the nature or purpose of the law, it might invoke a weakened version of the principle upon which it is based. This occurs when considerations of the other component parts of law, namely, ability of enforcement, or the many special needs of individuals, are taken into account. Were the law informed by a principle that required it to ignore these other component parts of law, much social discord could result. According to Aesara, the principle of appropriate proportion supercedes any particular legal principle. Consider as an example the competing principles behind a "flat tax" law and an "itemized deduction" tax law. The flat tax law would be based on the principle that all should bear equally the cost of governing. The itemized deduction law is based on the principle that the law should take the special needs of individuals into account when assessing how individuals should bear the cost of government. Aesara's meta-principle, the principle of appropriate proportion, would require that we establish our tax system on whatever principle would in the long run produce the least social discord.

Aesara's second claim is that both law and justice are structurally tripartite and that this structure corresponds to the structure of the human soul. Law and justice, like the mind, are thoughtful in that good law and real justice take all relevant ideas, arguments, and principles into account. Moreover, good law, and particularly, true justice are judgmental: they make decisions about matters of fact and questions of obligation and duty. These thoughtful and judgmental characteristics of law and justice correspond to the operations of Aesara's rational mind.

The strength and effectiveness of law and of the judicial system, as well as of familial rules and discipline, and personal principles and conscience, all correspond to the spirited part of Aesara's soul. Law can be a powerful deterrent and incentive. It can be powerful as an expression of the harmony and stability, the virtues and values of the individual, the family, and of the city. Law and justice, like the spirited part of the soul, are able and effective: they do in fact deter, they do in fact provide incentives, and they do in fact serve as guides to action. Law and justice stand for the values and virtues of the person, the family, and the city.

The social law, the familial law, and the personal moral law are all characterized by love, whether in the form of compassion for others, kindliness, or self-esteem. This love is analogous to that produced by the third part of Aesara's soul, desire. This affective component of law and justice is fair and is considerate of special needs and concerns. Justice is compassionate and forgiving; it is individualistic in the sense that it can take into account extenuating circumstances and reasons for non-compliance. Similarly, the harmonious family, one characterized by "a certain unanimity and agreement in sentiment" is one that is fair and considerate of the special needs of its members and is compassionate and forgiving. At the personal level, the individual who is not schizophrenic is also characterized by "a certain unanimity and agreement in sentiment." Such a person sets moral standards for herself that are in proportion to her actual abilities. She is reasonably self-forgiving and is non-obsessive about her own moral shortcomings. The social law, the familial law, and the personal moral law are all characterized by love, whether in the form of compassion for others or self-esteem, and this love is like that produced by the third part of the soul, desire.

3. *Aesara on Moral Psychology*

The fragment from *On Human Nature* recommends introspection about the nature of the human soul as a way of understanding the technical structure of three areas of human law: individual morality, laws governing the moral basis of the family, and laws governing the moral foundation of social institutions. We can also speculate how Aesara's analysis of the structure of the soul might be relevant to understanding the laws of human moral psychology and the laws of physical medicine. For example, it might be appropriate to identify Aesara's mind, the intelligent part of the soul, as corresponding vaguely to the ego. Aesara's mind rationalizes, evaluates, discovers principles, and entertains arguments. It has both inductive and deductive powers. Spiritedness is somewhat similar to the psychoanalytic concept of ego strength or will. It produces what Aesara calls "courage," "impulse," and the drive to act according to the conclusions reached by mind as moderated by desire. Desire itself may be equivalent to an instinct for pleasure as exemplified by the affective, affiliative instinct for love in its various forms, including Aesara's "kindliness," and "friendliness." However, Aesara identifies the negative affective moral emotions with the will to act according to those emotions, so we should be cautious of over-Freudianizing Aesara.

4. *Aesara and Physical Medicine*

Aesara's concept of the soul might shed light on our understanding of the laws of physical medicine. Like the soul, law and justice, the human body or "dwelling place" is a composite unity of association of several dissimilar parts. The different parts pertain to dissimilar "things to be done." The eyes do not hear, nor does the skin see, yet the various organs work together with the various parts of the soul. The mind judges and evaluates sensory information. Spiritedness provides the physical courage to act, and desire experiences the pleasures of the body. A kind of "unanimity and agreement" in sentiment exists in the body when the various parts function according to their proper proportion. Health and vigor could be defined as the proper, proportional interaction of the parts of the body. Disease and debilitation would be defined either as the failure of the parts to interact, or as their disproportionate interaction.

5. *A Note about Feminism*

Aesara's natural law theory appears to have feminist implications. If we assume, as did the Pythagoreans, that women bore the responsibility for creating harmony and justice in the home and that men had that responsibility in the city, then so-called "women's work" was the moral equivalent of "men's work." This is because justice in both arenas has the same natural foundation in the nature of the human soul. Just, harmonious cities require their component parts, households, also to be just and harmonious. Therefore, social justice depends on women raising just, harmonious individuals in those households. In the Pythagorean view, women are not peripheral to social justice, they make it possible.

6. *The Principled Structure of the Soul*

Aesara's soul is a "composite unity of association." She explains that a unity of association of the parts of the soul cannot consist of one thing only. Neither can it consist of several *identical* parts because then it would not be an arrangement of several *different* parts. Aesara illustrates her point, using the body as an example. It is a unity of association of different parts which bear a harmonious working relationship to each other. Although different senses pertain to different organs, they are interactive, forming a harmonious working relationship among themselves. A unity of association of parts cannot consist of different things that bear only a random, chance or haphazard relationship to each other. Not only must the parts be dissimilar, but they must be arranged according to a law or principle that is at once mathematical, metaphysical, and moral. The principle governs the relationship of the parts to each other as well as the functions of each part. The parts are fitted together by some rational designer, i.e., God, but according to a principle.

The principle does not permit each part of the soul an equal weight in determining the outcome of the deliberations of the soul because some parts of the soul are "better" and some are "worse" than others. It is not clear whether Aesara means this in the moral sense that the better part of the soul produces morally superior outcomes of deliberation, or whether she means this in the purely pragmatic sense that the better part of soul is better suited to the functions of the soul itself. Nevertheless, the principle arranges the parts so that the best part rules. Which part is the "best part" is determined by "the things that are to be done." Different parts of the soul are best suited to different tasks. If each part of the soul had an equal "say" we would be constantly torn between acting rationally, acting on impulse, and desire-satisfaction. We would be in a constant state of unharmonious, tumultuous schizophrenia. The mind has the ability to harmonize itself with the other parts so that impulse and desire are appropriately satisfied. The mind learns to do this through experience and through the exercise of virtue which is the pursuit of the soul's own excellence.

II. PHINTYS OF SPARTA

According to Stobaeus,[2] Phintys is the daughter of Kallicrates, and is a Pythagorean. The name Kallicrates is unknown, and Thesleff[3] prefers reading "Kallikratidas." Thucydides mentions Kallikratidas, as does Plutarch.[4] Kallikratidas was an admiral who died during the battle of the Arginusae in 406 B.C. It is only the identification of Phintys as the daughter of this admiral that permits us to identify her as of Spartan nationality, and as a somewhat older contemporary of Plato. Two fragments from her book *On the Moderation of Women* have survived. These fragments incorporate the Pythagorean assumption that the natures of men and women, although having much in common, are in some essential ways, different.

1. *Text of* On the Moderation of Women, *Fragment I*[5]

A woman must be altogether good and orderly; without excellence she would never become so. The excellence appropriate to each thing makes superior that which is receptive of it: the excellence appropriate to the eyes makes the eyes so, that appropriate to hearing, the faculty of hearing, that appropriate to a horse, a horse, that appropriate to a man, a man. So too the excellence appropriate to a woman makes a woman excellent. The excellence most appropriate to a woman is moderation. For, on account of this virtue, she will be able to honor and love her husband.

Now, perhaps many think it is not fitting for a woman to philosophize, just as it is not fitting for her to ride horses or speak in public. But I think that some things are peculiar to a man, some to a woman, some are common to both, some belong more to a man than a woman, some more to a woman than a man. Peculiar to a man are serving in battle, political activity, and public speaking; peculiar to a woman are staying at home and indoors, and welcoming and serving her husband. But I say that courage and justice and wisdom are common to both. Excellences of the body are appropriate for both a man and a woman, likewise those of the soul. And just as it is beneficial for the body of each to be healthy, so too, it is beneficial for the soul to be healthy. The excellences of the body are health, strength, keenness of perception and beauty. Some of these are more fitting for a man to cultivate and possess, some more for a woman. For courage and wisdom are more appropriate for a man, both because of the constitution of his body and because of his strength of soul, while moderation is more appropriate for a woman.

Wherefore one must discover the nature of the woman who is trained in moderation, and make known the number and kinds of things that confer this good upon a woman. I say this comes from five things: First, from piety and reverence concerning her marriage bed; second, from decency with respect to her body; third, from the processions of those from her own household; fourth, from not indulging in mystery rites and celebrations of the festival of Cybele; fifth, from being devout and correct in her sacrifices to the divine.

Of these, that which most of all causes and preserves moderation is being incorruptible with respect to her marriage, and not getting mixed up with a strange man. For, first, a woman who thus transgresses does an injustice to the gods of her race, providing not genuine, but spurious, allies to her house and family; she does an injustice to the natural gods by whom she swore, along with her ancestors and kin, to share in a common life and the lawful procreation of children. She also does an injustice to her fatherland, by not abiding among those who were duly appointed for her. Then she is wont to sin over and above those for whom death, the greatest of penalties, is determined, on account of the magnitude of injustice; to sin and to commit outrages for the sake of pleasure is unlawful and least deserving of mercy. The issue of all outrage is destruction.

2. *Women and Virtue*

According to Phintys, some virtues are common to both men and women, while some are unique to either gender. Courage, justice and wisdom are common virtues or excellences to both men and women, although in her opinion, courage and wisdom are "more appropriate" to men than to women. It is not clear what Phintys means by this. Perhaps by "more appropriate" she means "suits the kinds of activities men typically engage in." Phintys claims that temperance or moderation is more appropriately a woman's virtue. If by "more appropriate" she means "suits the kinds of activities women typically engage in," it is not difficult, given even a meagre acquaintance with women's history, to see what she is saying. Phintys shows why, for women, doing moral philosophy the way men do it — theorizing about what some ideal state or perfect world might be like — requires that women ignore the realities of their social situation. *Given* that the social order already *is* the way it is, she raises the question whether it is our moral responsibility to live our lives according to whichever moral theory best takes into account our special circumstances. Phintys says that given the kind of public life men lead in the marketplace and the seat of government, courage and wisdom are essential virtues for men. If those virtues are not exercised, the community will suffer violence, deceit and trickery from other cities, as well as from its own members. Given that the kind of restricted life women lead at home where they take personal responsibility for raising the males who will maintain harmony in the city and with its neighbors, temperance is an essential virtue. Without it, they could not be patient with children, and could not give so much of their energies to caring for others.

But perhaps this is not what Phintys was suggesting. Perhaps she is suggesting that the cultivation of the virtues of justice and wisdom in the souls of women are *limited* by the social roles permitted to each. These social roles reflect a universal (to that culture) understanding that women's souls have *this* nature and men's souls have *that* nature. The society structures its roles in such a way that men have very limited opportunities to learn much about developing the virtues of women, and *vice versa*. There are undoubtedly other, equally plausible explanations for what Phintys means by the statement that particular virtues are more appropriate to members of a particular gender. But this interpretation is attractive if we recall that according to Phintys, courage, justice and wisdom are common to both men and women. Presumably, this is why it is fitting for a woman to philosophize. But generally, the normative principle of *harmonia* is to be satisfied within the context of specific social responsibilities.

3. *Women and Justice in the Home*

Phintys describes the many injustices created by a woman who is unfaithful. When she married, she took an oath, together with her parents and all her relatives. The oath was to "the gods of her race" and the gods of nature for the purposes of securing divine allies and protection for the entire extended family. Unfaithfulness jeopardizes this protection and therefore jeopardizes her entire family. In addition to the injustice she commits toward her family when she jeopardizes their divine protection, she commits a civil offense against the country. Marriage transfers the wardship of a woman from her parents to her husband. The woman violates this wardship by "not abiding among those who were duly appointed for her." This is a crime worse than those usually punishable by death. The unfaithful woman cannot hope for mercy, either, because the usual exculpatory claims (deceit, trickery, force on the part of her lover) are unavailable: her motivation to violate the law was the basest of criminal motives: pleasure.

4. *Phintys'* On the Moderation of Women, *Fragment II*[6]

One must consider this too, that she will find no purifying remedy for this fault, so as to be chaste and loved by the gods when approaching their temples and altars. For in the case of this sin most of all, even the divine spirit is merciless. The noblest honor and the chief glory of a married woman is to bring witness of her virtue with respect to her husband through her own children if, haply, they should bear the stamp of likeness to the father who sired them. This sums up the subject of moderation with respect to marriage.

My thoughts on moderation with respect to bodily decency are as follows: The woman of moderation must be clad in white, simply and plainly dressed. She will be thus if, indeed, she does not wear transparent or embroidered robes, or those woven from silk but, rather, garments that are decent and plain white. The main thing is that she be decent and avoid luxury and display; then she will not arouse ignominious envy in other women. As for gold and emeralds, she simply will not deck herself out in them, for then she would display the characteristics of wealth and arrogance towards ordinary women.

But the well regulated city, arranged throughout with a view to the whole, must be based on sympathy and unanimity. One must even debar the craftsmen from the city, those who make such ornaments. The woman of moderation must embellish her appearance not with imported and alien ornament, but with the natural beauty of the body; washing clean with water, she must adorn herself with modesty rather than these. Thus she will bring honor to the man with whom she shares her life, and to herself.

Next, women must make public processions from the house in order to sacrifice to the founder-god of the city on behalf of themselves and their husbands, and entire households. Moreover, it is not when the evening star has risen, nor in darkness, that a woman must make her expeditions to attend the theatre or to purchase wares for the house, but rather, as market-time approaches, just so long as it is light. This she must do decorously guided by one handmaid or, at the most, two.

Next, she must offer prayers of sacrifice to the gods to the extent to which she is authorized to do so, but must refrain from secret rites at home, and celebrations of Cybele. The common law prevents women from celebrating these rites because, among other things, such religious practices lead to drunkenness and derangement. But the mistress of the house, even presiding at home, must be temperate and untouched in the face of everything.

A woman can best fulfill the principle of *harmonia* through exercise of the virtue of temperance or moderation in her personal dress, public demeanor, and religious observations. Luxury and the display of wealth and arrogance are to be avoided because they endanger the harmony of the city through the arousal of envy in other women and in the flaunting of class differences. The temperate woman will consider how the well-being of the whole city is affected by her immoderate demeanor and dress. Even craftsmen who make the kinds of frivolous frills some women affect, should be barred from peddling those items in the city. Class differences must not be paraded by allowing oneself to be publicly accompanied by too many servants.

5. *Women and Religious Observances*

From Phintys' closing comments, it is clear that the practice of religious rites can lead to a violation of the principle of *harmonia*. It is not enough that women should exercise temperance and moderation in public, and with respect to their marital relationships. It must be exercised even in the privacy of their own home at the very personal level of offering sacrifices to the gods. Too much praying, too much religious devotion, and the practice of secret rites is intemperate. This intemperance in prayer and sacrifice quickly leads to other forms of intemperance, including intoxication and mental illness. Religious practices can contribute to *harmonia*, but when the wrong kind of practices are engaged in, or when the right kind of practices are carried to excess, *harmonia* can be destroyed. It is the woman's responsibility to preserve *harmonia* through moderation even in the practice of religion.

III. PERICTIONE I

There are two documents attributed to "Perictione," the first text is apparently a fragment from a larger work entitled *On the Harmony of Women*. The second text is a brief essay, *On Wisdom*. For reasons to be discussed in the following chapter, it seems correct to identify these works as the writings of two different philosophers and to identify the author of *On the Harmony of Women* with Plato's mother. However this identification is inconclusive. I shall follow Prudence Allen[7] in identifying the author of *On the Harmony of Women* as Perictione I, and will refer to the author of *On Wisdom* as Perictione II. Perictione I seems to encourage philosophizing by women. If women exercise wisdom and self-control they can aspire to other virtues including justice and courage. She almost appears to adopt a utilitarian perspective on virtue: one exercises particular virtues in order to be able to develop other, higher virtues which will in turn bring happiness and harmony to herself and her family.

1. *Translation of the Text*[8]

> One must deem the harmonious woman to be full of wisdom and self-control; a soul must be exceedingly conscious of goodness to be just and courageous and wise, embellished with self-sufficiency and hating empty opinion. Worthwhile things come to a woman from these — for herself, her husband, her children and household, perhaps even for a city — if, at any rate, such a woman should govern cities and tribes, as we see in the case of a royal city.
>
> Having mastery over appetite and high feeling she will be righteous and harmonious; no lawless desires will impel her. She will preserve a loving disposition toward her husband and children and her entire household. As many women as become lovers of alien beds become enemies of all at home, gentry and servants alike. Such a woman continually contrives lies and deceits for her husband and fabricates falsehoods about everything to him, in order that she only may seem to excel in good will and, though she loves idleness, may seem to govern the house. To such an extent, let these things be said.

But one must also train the body to natural measures concerning nourishment and clothing, baths and anointings, the arrangement of the hair, and ornaments of gold and precious stone. Women who eat and drink every costly thing, who dress extravagantly and wear the things that women wear, are ready for the sin of every vice both with respect to the marriage bed and the rest of wrongdoing. It is necessary merely to appease hunger and thirst, even if this be done by frugal means; in the case of cold, even a goat-skin or rough garment would suffice.

To wear cloaks extravagantly purpled by dye-baths of marine shellfish, or of some other lavish color, this is great foolishness. The body wants not to shiver and — for the sake of decency — not to be naked; it requires no more. But in its ignorance human opinion hastens towards the vain and excessive. So the harmonious woman will not wrap herself in gold or precious stone from India or anywhere else, nor will she braid her hair with artful skills or anoint herself with infusions of Arabian scent, nor will she paint her face, whitening or rougeing it, darkening her eyebrows and lashes and treating her gray hair with dye; nor will she be forever bathing. The woman who seeks these things seeks an admirer of feminine weakness. It is the beauty that comes from wisdom, not from these, that gratifies women who are well-born.

But let her not think that nobility of birth, and wealth, and coming from a great city altogether are necessities, nor the good opinion and friendship of eminent and kingly men. If these should be the case, it does not hurt. But, if not, wishing does not make them so. Even if these should be alotted to her, let her soul not pursue the grand and wonderful. Let her walk also apart from them. They harm more than they help, dragging one into misfortune. Treachery and envy and malice abide with them; such a woman would not be serene.

One must revere the gods in the confident hope of happiness, obeying both ancestral laws and institutions. After these [the gods = scl. Meineke], I say to honor and to revere one's parents, for they are and effect everything equally to the gods for their offspring.

With respect to her own husband a woman must thus live lawfully and honorably: not considering anything privately, but preserving and guarding her marriage. For in this is everything. A woman must bear everything on the part of her husband, even if he should be unfortunate, or fail on account of ignorance or illness or drink, or cohabit with other women. For this error is forgiven in the case of men; for women, never. Rather, retribution is imposed. Therefore she must keep the law and not be envious. She must bear anger and stinginess, fault-finding, jealousy and abuse, and any other trait he may have by nature. Being discreet, she must handle all of his characteristics in a way pleasing to him. When a woman is loving towards her husband, and acts agreeably to him, harmony reigns; she loves the entire household and makes outsiders well-disposed towards the house.

But when she is not loving, then she wishes to see safe and sound neither the house nor her own children, nor the servants, nor any of the property but — as if she were an enemy — invokes and prays for total ruin. She even prays for her husband to die, on the grounds that he is hateful, in order that she may cohabit with other men; and whoever pleases him, she hates. But I think a woman is harmonious in the following way: if she becomes full of wisdom and self-control. For this benefits not only her husband, but also the children, relatives, slaves; the whole house, including possessions and friends, both fellow-citizens and foreign guest friends. Artlessly, she will keep their house, speaking and hearing fair things, and obeying her husband in the unanimity of their common life, attending upon the relatives and friends whom he extolls, and thinking the same things sweet and bitter as he — lest she be out of tune in relation to the whole.

Like Phintys and Theano II, Perictione adopts a different approach to ethical theory than male philosophers have. She shows no interest in an ideal theory, or in an examination of what society ought to be like. Her ethics is grounded in pragmatism. Given that society is the way it is, and given that women's roles are severely circumscribed, how might a woman satisfy the normative principle of *harmonia*?[9]

2. *Relationships and Moral Obligation*

There are certain affinities between Perictione's *On the Harmony of Women* and Phintys' *On the Moderation of Women*, discussed above. Both works focus on the social and moral status of women in society. Both begin with an acknowledgement of the *status quo* and assume that that is the basis of women's moral obligation. One is born into a family, a religion, a *polis*. These are the relationships over which a person has no control, yet they serve as the source of duty to parents, gods, and country. One marries and has a family, creating new relationships over which one has some control and for which one has additional moral responsibility. There are customary social and moral obligations that are attached to all relationships and these duties must be met if those relationships are to be harmonious.

3. *Moral Pragmatism and Faithful Wives*

Perictione I applies her moral pragmatism to the question of marital infidelity by women. Like a legal realist who holds that the key to jurisprudence is what the courts actually do, Perictione I points to the judgments that society actually makes and asserts that these are the rules in accordance with which a virtuous woman must live.[10] However unfeminist Perictione's conclusions may be, we see that they are derived from the philosophical premise that the normative principle *harmonia* is to be applied to the concrete circumstances of human life. Although her views (and those of the other Pythagoreans) present a view of woman's role which most contemporary thinkers do not share, we must understand this view as a pragmatic response to the question of moral responsibility in the face of an entrenched *status quo*.[11]

4. *Physical Beauty and the Moral Disorder of Women*

As unfeminist as her views about women's responsibilities to preserve marital fidelity are, they stand in marked contrast to the feminism of her views about personal care. She warns that excessive concern for creating the illusion of physical beauty contributes to the moral disorder of women. True beauty comes from

wisdom, not from makeup, clothing, and jewelry. Frugality and
simplicity stand in marked contrast to displays of vanity and
concerns for personal appearance in excess of those required by
basic human needs for food, clothing, shelter, and "common
decency." These comments are made all the more forceful when
we consider what must have been the personal circumstances of a
woman who could have written such a document. Clearly, she
must have been sufficiently well off to have servants and slaves,
and to have the comparative luxury of some form of an education. Indeed, the whole tone of the fragment suggests complete
familiarity with the very standard of living she identifies as immoderate or intemperate. And this is precisely her point, there is
nothing wrong with class and privilege, *per se*. What is morally
indefensible is indulging oneself in those trappings and parading
them because doing so is the first step down the slippery slope
toward "the sin of every vice." Temperance is the one virtue that
permits the development of all other virtues. Intemperance is the
one vice that makes one ready for every other vice.

5. *Virtue, Power, Class, and Oppression*

Perictione I next addressed the consequences of being born into or
attaching oneself to persons of power and position. If one is
allotted noble birth and its concomitant gifts, fine. If not, not
only won't wishing not make them so, but they are potential
obstacles to attaining virtue. Power and position tend to be
accompanied by treachery, envy and malice. These are undesirable
in themselves, and contribute to personal disharmony. Again, it is
not wrong to have these things, but pursuing "the grand and
wonderful" destroys inner harmony. Next, Perictione I exhorts
women to revere the gods and one's parents. She then enters into a
frank description of the abuses that a harmonious woman ought to
be willing suffer if she is to attain the higher goal of preserving
harmony for herself and her family. She gives a clear picture of the
limited scope within which the principle of *harmonia* can be
realistically satisfied for women. Women enter into marriage. It is
a relationship governed by law which, as it happens, gives men all
the power and authority and women none. This is the way the law
is. Laws spell out what everyone's legitimate expectations are.

Expectations that a wife should have some control over her husband's behavior, or even, some preferences of her own, are not legitimate expectations. To attempt to obtain more than the law leads you to expect is to attempt to disrupt the harmony that the law is intended to preserve. The wife must "keep the law and not be envious" that it makes the husband master of the wife, family, and property. Failing to keep the law threatens the harmony not only of the family, but of the entire household, and is deserving of retribution. Perictione is spelling out in detail the idea of harmony as a fitting together, and being part of the whole.[12] Perictione says that a woman must consider not only herself, but also her husband, children, her entire household, including the servants, relatives, friends, and foreign visitors. What she does reflects on them all and affects them all. Having created these relationships through her marriage, a woman creates obligations which must be met. If she fails to fulfill these duties she creates disharmony. In an almost too literal sense, the elements of the household will no longer fit together. If she fails to promote the good of the whole, she will be like an enemy within the gate. What would be somewhat trite admonitions against extravagance and conspicuous consumption also take on renewed importance when we recall that *harmonia* is the highest virtue.

6. *Idealism versus Pragmatism*
Comments by Vicki Lynn Harper

Perictione's aim is to specify what it takes for a woman to be morally praiseworthy in an actual society, not what the role of women might be in some hypothetical, ideal, and vastly different society. She gives only a passing nod to the idea that things might be different. Marital infidelity is forgiven in the case of a man, but never in the case of a woman. In response to this fact, Perictione merely comments that therefore it is necessary for women to uphold this law and not to envy men their apparent greater liberty. This comment, embedded in a graphic description of the abuses which a woman may have to endure, initially appears merely repellant. On reflection, however, it is impressive as a clear-eyed statement of the brute fact that the actual society in which the author lives limits or restricts the ways in which its female members can satisfy the normative principle of *harmonia*. Perictione is not speculating about what might be the case in some hypothetical, and vastly different society. Rather, she is considering how a woman can be harmonious in an actual society.

7. Women and Piety

Returning to a comment she made earlier in the text, Perictione's second fragment applies the normative principle of *harmonia* to the duties towards parents. The principle is violated whenever one fails to obey, revere, and venerate one's parents. Hating them, disobeying them, or speaking ill of them is never justified. Blind obedience is not required. If parents err, you may reason with them, presumably urging them towards right action. But disobedience and disloyalty upset the eternal harmony between generations and are therefore never justified.

8. Translation of the Text[13]

From *On the Harmony of Women* by Perictione the Pythagorean.

> One must neither speak ill of one's parents nor do them harm, but obey them in matters great and small, in every happenstance of soul and body, of inner and outer life, in peace and in war, in health and in sickness, in wealth and in poverty, in good repute and bad, in private and in public stations; one must march with them and never desert. Even in madness one must well nigh obey them. For the righteous this is wise and honorable. But if someone should despise her parents, having in mind evil of any sort, alive and dead she will be charged with sin by the gods; she will be hated by mankind and for eternity, along with the impious in their place beneath the earth, she will be assailed by evils at the hands of justice and the gods below, who are appointed as overseers of these things.
>
> The very sight of one's parents is divine and lovely, so too the veneration and care of them. Not even the sight of the sun and all the stars which the sky wears and whirls around can compare, nor indeed anything else anyone might

think to be a greater object for contemplation. I am sure the gods are not vexed when they see this occur. Thus, whether living or departed, it is necessary to revere them and never to murmur against them; even if they should act wrongly because of disease or deception, one should exhort and instruct, but in no way hate them. There could be no greater human sin and injustice than to sin against one's parents.

NOTES

1. Thesleff, *op.cit.*, 48-50, Stobaeus 1.49.27, p. 355 Wa. Translated by Vicki Lynn Harper.
2. 4.23.61, p. 588, Heeren.
3. *Op. cit.*, 11.
4. Plutarch, *Lives of the Noble Grecians and Romans*, J. Dryden transl., A.H. Clough edition, New York: Modern Library (reprint of 1864 edition), 528.
5. Thesleff, *op.cit.*, 151, Stobaeus 4.23.61, p. 588 Heeren. Translated by Vicki Lynn Harper.
6. Thesleff, *op.cit.*, 153, Stobaeus 4.23.61a, 591 Hense. Translation by Vicki Lynn Harper.
7. Allen, Prudence. *The Concept of Woman*, Montreal: Eden Press (1985), p. 142.
8. Perictione, *On the Harmony of Women*, Fr. 1, Thesleff, *op. cit.*, 142-145; Stobaeus 4.28.19, 688 Hense, translated by Vicki Lynn Harper.
9. This section is partly based on papers given by Vicki Lynn Harper in 1983 and 1984.
10. Once again, I am indebted to Professor Vicki Lynn Harper for this observation.
11. Heloise takes a similar perspective, but draws different conclusions. See Volume II of this series.
12. Again, I acknowledge my indebtedness to Professor Vicki Lynn Harper for her insights into Perictione's text.
13. Thesleff, *op. cit.*, 145, Stobaeus 4.25.50, p. 631, Heeren. Translated by Vicki Lynn Harper.

3. Late Pythagoreans:
Theano II and Perictione II

MARY ELLEN WAITHE
with translations and additional commentary by
VICKI LYNN HARPER

The name "Theano" was a popular name in antiquity.[1] It is
certain that there were at least two, and possibly more ancient
women philosophers of that name who left written records of
their views. And although "Perictione" was the name of Plato's
mother, other authors of that name have been identified. Because
there are sound philological reasons to distinguish at least two
Theanos and two Perictiones those distinctions are preserved in
this volume. While we cannot be certain whether the texts attributed to "Theano II" in this chapter ought to be attributed to
one and the same person, we can be reasonably assured that
this is not Theano of Crotona.

I. THEANO II

1. *Theano II to Euboule*

According to Theano II, a later Theano than she who was Pythagoras' wife, it is a woman's responsibility to raise her children so
that they will become virtuous, harmonious adults. If she does not
conscientiously attempt to meet this responsibility she contributes
to the personal disorder of her children's souls, and ultimately, to
the disorder of society. Phintys made precisely the same kind of
claim Theano II makes. Phintys showed why, for women, doing
moral philosophy the way men do it — theorizing about what
some ideal state or perfect world might be like — requires that
women ignore the realities of their social situation. The social
order already *is* the way it is, and Theano II raises the question

whether it is our moral responsibility to live our lives according to whichever moral theory best takes into account our special circumstances.[2]

She writes to Euboule:

> I hear that you are raising your children in luxury. The mark of a good mother is not attention to the pleasure of her children but education with a view to temperance. Look out lest you accomplish not the work of a loving mother, but that of a doting one. When pleasure and children are brought up together, it makes the children undisciplined. What is sweeter to the young than familiar pleasure? One must take care, my friend, lest the upbringing of one's children become their downfall. Luxury perverts nature when children become lovers of pleasure in spirit and sensualists in body — mentally afraid of toil and physically soft. A mother must also exercise her charges in the things they dread — even if this causes them some pain and distress — so that they shall not become slaves of their feelings — greedy for pleasure and shrinking from pain — but, rather, shall honor virtue above everything, and be able both to abstain from pleasure and to withstand pain.
>
> Don't let them be sated with nourishment, nor gratified in their every pleasure. Such lack of restraint in childhood makes them unbridled; it lets them say anything and try everything; especially if you take alarm every time they cry out, and always take pride in their laughter — smiling indulgently even if they strike their nurse or taunt you — and if you insist upon keeping them unnaturally cool in summer and warm in winter, giving them every luxury. Poor children have no experience of such things; yet they grow up readily enough — they grow no less, and become stronger by far. But you nurse your children like the scions of Sardanapallos, enfeebling their manly natures with pleasures. What would one make of a child who — if he does not eat sooner — clamors; who — whenever he eats — craves the delights of delicacies; who wilts in the heat and is felled by the cold; who — if someone finds fault with him — fights back; who — if one does not cater to his every pleasure — is aggrieved; who

— if he does not chew on something — is discontent; who gets into mischief just for the fun of it, and stutters about without living in an articulate way?

Take care, my friend — conscious of the fact that children who live licentiously become slaves when they blossom to manhood — to deprive them of such pleasures. Make their nourishment austere rather than sumptuous; let them endure both hunger and thirst, both cold and heat, and even shame — whether before their peers or their overseers. This is how they turn out to be brave in spirit no matter whether they are exalted or tormented. Hardships, my dear, serve as a hardening-up process for children, a process by which virtue is perfected. Those who have been dipped sufficiently in them bear the tempering bath of virtue as a more natural thing. So look out, dear, lest — just as vines which have been improperly tended are deficient in fruit — your children produce the evil fruit of licentiousness and utter worthlessness, all because of luxury. Farewell.

It is clear that Theano II would agree with Aesara's view that virtue is to be found in moderation of impulse and desire by the mind. But young children are unable to understand how to apply the principle of appropriate proportion and must therefore be guided and disciplined so that they will be better able to become virtuous. This is the responsibility of the mother since it is she who is able to create justice and harmony in her home, and in the children she raises.

2. *Theano II to Nikostrate*

The woman's responsibility for the creation of justice and harmony in the home requires that she behave justly towards her husband, even when he fails to act justly toward her. As Perictione I argued, women are naturally more inclined towards temperance and moderation. Consequently, the related virtues come easier to them than they do to men. The idea that a husband's injustice towards his wife cannot justify her behaving unjustly towards him has its conceptual foundations in this Pythagorean view that some virtues are peculiar to women and others to men. Theano II writes to Nikostrate:[3]

Theano to Nikostrate: Greetings. I hear repeatedly about your husband's madness: he has a courtesan; also that you are jealous of him. My dear, I have known many men with the same malady. It is as if they are hunted down by these women and held fast; as if they have lost their minds. But you are dispirited by night and by day, you are sorely troubled and contrive things against him. Don't *you*, at least, be that way, my dear. For the moral excellence of a wife is not surveillance of her husband but companionable accommodation; it is in the spirit of accommodation to bear his folly.

If he associates with the courtesan with a view towards pleasure, he associates with his wife with a view towards the beneficial. It is beneficial not to compound evils with evils and not to augment folly with folly. Some faults, dear, are stirred up all the more when they are condemned, but cease when they are passed over in silence, much as they say fire quenches itself if left alone. Besides, though it seems that you wish to escape notice yourself, by condemning him you will take away the veil that covers your own condition.

Then you will manifestly err: You are not convinced that love of one's husband resides in conduct that is noble and good. For this *is* the grace of marital association. Recognize the fact that he goes to the courtesan in order to be frivolous but that he abides with you in order to live a common life; that he loves you on the basis of good judgment, but her on the basis of passion. The moment for this is brief; it almost coincides with its own satisfaction. In a trice it both arises and ceases. The time for a courtesan is of brief duration for any man who is not excessively corrupt. For what is emptier than desire whose benefit of enjoyment is unrighteousness? Eventually he will perceive that he is diminishing his life and slandering his good character.

No one who understands persists in self-chosen harm. Thus, being summoned by his just obligation towards you and perceiving the diminuition of his livelihood [he will take notice of you,]* unable to bear the outrage of moral condemnation, he will soon repent. My dear, this is how you

* Seclusit Hercher.

must live: not defending yourself against courtesans but distinguishing yourself from them by your orderly conduct towards your husband, by your careful attention to the house, by the calm way in which you deal with the servants, and by your tender love for your children. You must not be jealous of that woman (for it is good to extend your emulation only to women who are virtuous); rather, you must make yourself fit for reconciliation. Good character brings regard even from enemies, dear, and esteem is the product of nobility and goodness alone. In this way it is even possible for the power of a woman to surpass that of a man. It is possible for her to grow in his esteem instead of having to serve one who is hostile towards her.

If he has been properly prepared for it by you, he will be all the more ashamed; he will wish to be reconciled sooner and, because he is more warmly attached to you, he will love you more tenderly. Conscious of his injustice towards you, he will perceive your attention to his livelihood and make trial of your affection towards himself. Just as bodily illnesses make their cessations sweeter, so also do differences between friends make their reconciliations more intimate. As for you, do resist the passionate resolutions of your suffering. Because he is not well, he excites you to share in his plight; because he himself misses the mark of decency, he invites you to fail in decorum; having damaged his own life, he invites you to harm what is beneficial to you. Consequently you will seem to have conspired against him and, in reproving him will appear to reprove yourself.

If you divorce yourself from him and move on, you will change your first husband only to try another and, if he has the same failings, you will resort to yet another (for the lack of a husband is not bearable for young women); or else you will abide alone without any husband like a spinster. Do you intend to be negligent of the house and to destroy your husband? Then you will share the spoils of an anguished life. Do you intend to avenge yourself upon the courtesan? Being on her guard, she will circumvent you; but, if she actively wards you off, a woman who has no tendency to blush is formidable in battle. Is it good to fight with your husband

day after day? To what advantage? The battles and reproaches will not stop his licentious behavior, but they will
increase the dissension between you by their escalations.
What, then? Are you plotting something against him? Don't
do it, my dear. Tragedy teaches us to conquer jealousy,
encompassing a systematic treatise on the actions by which
Medea was led to the commission of outrage. Just as it is
necessary to keep one's hands away from a disease of the
eyes, so must you separate your pretension from your pain.
By patiently enduring you will quench your suffering sooner.

Theano II sketches a concept of duty and obligation created by a
contractual relationship between friends. Her argument initially
creates the impression that it is a wife's lot to accept whatever ill
treatment she receives from her husband. But if we read the letter
carefully, we see that she is not simply making the traditional anti-
feminist argument for unequal treatment of women. She is not
arguing that women ought to have a subordinate place in the
family. Rather, she is saying that marriage is a relationship based
on love. The love on which marriage is founded is not the heady,
romantic love, but that which comes from reflective good judgment about the person and about the benefits of sharing a common life. The "just obligations" of marriage are more than legally
binding: they are morally binding also. The violation by one party
of the moral duties marriage imposes does not relieve the other
party of their moral duties. According to Theano II, compounding
evils with evils and folly with folly does not restore order and
harmony to a family relationship. It merely compounds the
disorder. In addition to creating further disorder within the
family, behaving unjustly towards a spouse draws notice to and
provides evidence of one's own disorderly soul.

On the other hand, a woman who refrains from behaving
unjustly towards herself, her spouse, and her family has a chance
to restore them all to harmony. Through conduct that is noble and
good, the woman's behavior stands in marked contrast to her
husband's behavior. He will notice this, and repent. Thus the
woman serves as a role model. If she behaves honorably towards
him, he will emulate her honorable behavior and behave honorably
towards her also. The woman can be more powerful than the man

in that she can be morally superior to him by behaving towards him as is required by the moral law. This is especially true when, due to his own moral "illness," he fails to obey the moral laws of decent behavior, and attempts to corrupt her also, his behavior exciting her to vengeance. Rather, by enticing him, through her exemplary behavior, to act morally, she exemplifies the moral excellence of a wife. Not only will that de-escalate the increasing discord between them, but it will, in the end, make her feel much better.

3. *Theano to Kallisto*[4]

> Theano to Kallisto: To you younger women, just as soon as you are married, authority is granted by law to govern the household.*
>
> But, to do well, instruction about household management is needed from older women: a continual source of advice. It is well to learn what you do not know ahead of time and to deem most proper the advice of older women; in these matters a young soul must be brought up from girlhood. The primary authority of women in the household is authority over the servants. And the greatest thing, my dear, is good will on the slaves' part. For this possession is not bought along with their bodies; rather, intelligent mistresses bring it about in time. Just usage is the cause of this — seeing to it that they are neither worn out by toil nor incapacitated because of deprivation.
>
> For they are human in nature. There are some women who suppose the profitable to be what is most unprofitable: maltreatment of their servants, overburdening them with tasks to be done, and depriving them of the things they need. And then, having made much of an obol's profit, they pay the price in enormous damages: ill will and the worst treacheries. As for you, let there be ready at hand a measure of food that is proportionate to the amount of woolwork produced by a day's work. With respect to the diet of your

---

*   Theano uses the terms οἱ οἰκέται (inmates of one's house), αἱ θεράπαιναι (maidservants), and ἡ δουλεία (a body of slaves) interchangeably. Here the term is "inmates of the house."

servants, this will suffice. As for undisciplined behavior, one must assist to the utmost what is fitting for you not what is advantageous to them. For it is necessary to estimate one's servants at their proper worth. On the one hand, cruelty will not bring gratitude to a soul; on the other hand, reasoning no less than righteous indignation is an effective means of control. But if there should be too much unconquerable vice on the part of the servants, one must send them away to be sold. Let what is alien to the needs [of the house] be estranged from its mistress as well.*

Let proper judgment of this take precedence so that you will determine the true facts of wrongdoing in keeping with the justice of the condemnation, and the magnitude of wrongdoing in proportion to the proper punishment. But sometimes the mistress' forgiveness and kindness towards those who have erred will release them from penalties. In this way, too, you will preserve a fitting and appropriate mode of life. There are some women, my dear, who because they are cruel — brutalized by jealousy or anger — even whip the bodies of their servants as if they were inscribing the excess of their bitterness as a memorandum. In time, some of these [female servants] are used up, utterly worked out; others procure safety by escaping; but some stop living, withdrawing into death by their own hands. In the end, the isolation of the mistress, bewailing her lack of domestic consideration, finds desolate repentance. But my dear, likening yourself to musical instruments, know what sounds they make** when they are loosened too much, but that they are snapped asunder when stretched too tight. It is the same way for your servants. Too much license creates dissonance in the matter of obedience, but the stretching of forceful necessity causes the dissolution of nature itself. One must meditate upon this: 'Right measure is best in everything.' Farewell.

---

*   More literally, "Let what is alien to the need be estranged from the (female) proper judge as well."

**   φωνεῖ Thesleff; διαφωνεῖ Hercher, p. 606, 1.22. Although both readings are consistent with the concern that loose strings on musical instruments produce dissonant sounds, they may suggest a difference in emphasis.

Commentary by Vicki Lynn Harper

I found the letter to Kallisto particularly interesting. In reading it I had the strongest impression of a live human struggle. At the same time I did not wish to beg any questions by imposing my subjective impressions on the translation. However, at the end of the letter, I felt I had to make a decision in translating the *men ... de* clauses ("on the one hand ... on the other ...").[5] Did the author intend these to have equal or unequal weight? I am convinced the latter is true, though I am also aware that some of my conviction may stem from a subjective impression of the overall tone of the text. One can point to this and this and that in the text. The question is, what do they amount to when they are taken together? At the suggestion of Maria Rogness, I offer the following account of my arithmetic.

The format of the letter, a letter of advice from an older and hence (presumably) more experienced person to a younger one, is a conventional literary device. Given the conventionality of the format, the reader may well ask: "Is the author speculating – presenting a likely story about what would be said on such an occasion – or is this the direct voice of experience?" As I worked on the translation, the uncanny feeling that I was hearing a direct voice grew ever stronger. My impression is that the author senses a tension between her role as mistress of the household (and all its possessions) and her face-to-face realization that the household slaves are persons significantly like herself. (Yes, I do believe it was written by a woman.)

Am I just hearing voices? In my translation, I used the phrase "a continual source of advice" in apposition with "older women." The Greek text for this phrase consists of the adverb ἀεί meaning "always" and the genitive plural participle παραινούντων meaning "those giving advice,"[6] and it refers back to "elders" (genitive plural) in the preceeding line. This compact expression, strikingly placed at the end of the sentence, suggested a wry and self-reflective sense of humor. Isn't it possible that the author is acknowledging that more advice from her elders is not really what Kallisto is interested in? Then there is the interesting expression which I have translated as "must be brought up from girlhood" παρθενοτροφεῖσθαι δεῖ.[7] It may merely mean that girls should be trained for their social role throughout the time they are growing up. However, the point may be that in order to prepare themselves for their responsibilities they must grow beyond girlhood. I think the author meant the latter, and that she has something significant to say about her own experience as mistress of a household.

The fact that the terms "inmates of the house," "maidservants," and "slaves" are used interchangeably means nothing in itself. But isn't it interesting that the letter begins with the ambiguous term "household inmates,", and ends with a simile that, by the logical principle of transitivity, articulates a significant likeness between the mistress and the slaves? Moreover, where the text explicitly acknowledges that the servants are slaves, the term "slaves" is used in "...good-will on the slaves' part. For this possession is not bought along with their bodies."[8] Thus it occurred to me that the author's otherwise interchangeable use of these terms might have been intentional.

Why does the author evince such concern for good-will ($\epsilon\mathring{v}\nu o\iota\alpha$) on the slaves' part? Is it simply because slaves, unlike inanimate tools, are capable of deliberate sabotage ("treacheries")?[9] Or is it for a more subtle reason? I favor the second answer. The author's concern seems to me to extend beyond a mere recognition of the fact that tools must be properly maintained in order to do their work. If one does not fuel one's lawn mower with enough oil and gas, and occasionally clean the air filter, it will not mow. So in the long run it is cost-effective to keep up a schedule of regular maintenance. The remarks in the text about profitability[10] and the recommendation to make the daily ration of food proportionate to the production of wool-work[11] may suggest such a lawn mower attitude to some readers. In that case, the psychological dimension of good will would get us no farther than the level of, say, draft horses. The live animal is more complicated than the lawn mower. It has desires as well as needs, and sometimes a disconcerting ability to do what *it* wants to do. To acknowledge this, and to offer advice on how to deal with the problem, does not mean that one regards the draft horse as significantly like oneself.

The author does insist that the servants have a *subordinate* role[12] and that, if they display "unconquerable vice," one "must send them away to be sold."[13] But here one must take into account antiquity's views on the subordination of the individual to the welfare of the community, and its most prevalent attitude towards "enemies of the house." Also, the question is not whether the author is an abolitionist, but whether there is any reason to suppose a realization on the author's part that servants are not just work animals, but persons significantly like herself.

The tale of the brutal mistress contains several textual details that may bear on the answer to this question. At first there is a plurality of brutal mistresses: the passage begins with "some women" (ἔνιαι).[14] So when I came to the feminine plural article (αἱ) "some (females)" at the beginning of the next sentence,[15] I was expecting to hear more about the mistresses. Yet, without using any noun to mark the shift, the author had turned her attention from mistresses to slaves. I found her attention to the abused slaves poignant in that it suggested an increasingly sympathetic awareness of the slaves' feelings. "Some are used up, utterly worked out": this could be compatible with the lawn mower attitude, a mere concern for cost-effectiveness, but to me it conveyed some sense of the slaves' fatigue. "Others procure safety by escaping": is this merely analogous to noting that a valuable draft horse may bolt? To me it conveyed some sense of the slaves' desperate desire for safety. Finally, "but some stop living, withdrawing into death by their own hands": here it occurred to me that suicide, as an individual and deliberate act, is distinctively human. At this point in the text the discussion returns to the mistresses but with a subtle shift in focus. Not only is the term "mistress" now in the singular – but, grammatically, the subject is not the mistress herself but the *isolation* of the mistress.[16] The syntactical construction no longer presents her directly to us as a subject. Finally, there is a fine ambiguity in the phrase I have translated as "bewailing her lack of domestic consideration."[17] Is the mistress bewailing the fact that she has not been considerate of others, or merely that she is neglected – that others are no longer considerate of her? The brutal mistress of this tale may be merely lamenting her isolation, but she inhabits a tale within a tale. The author herself seems to imply that consideration must be reciprocal. Does she also think that consideration and good will between mistress and servant must involve a mutual recognition of their humanity?

She did say earlier that slaves are "human in nature."[18] I did not find that statement impressive, but I was impressed by the simile that immediately follows the tale of the brutal mistress: Liken *yourself* to musical instruments... Your *servants* are like that, too.[19] By the logical principle of transitivity, if I am like X in some respect, and my servants are like X in the same respect, it follows that in this respect I am like my servants. Does this amount to the recognition of a *significant* likeness? I think so. The subordination in the servant's role is mirrored in the subordination of the social role of the mistress: both are instrumental to the production and maintenance of a harmonious social order. Both must stay in tune, but in both cases the intimate concern is that, if a string is stretched too tightly, it will snap asunder. If the strings are broken, is any kind of harmony possible?

4. *Spurious Texts*

Letters from Theano to Rhodope, Eukleides, Euridike and Tim(ai)onides have been alleged by Mario Meunier[20] to be spurious. Meunier bases his conclusion primarily on the fact that these letters were found in the Vatican collection. This seems an odd claim, given the many ancient documents which were discovered in the early middle ages and which subsequently found their way into the Vatican libraries. Meunier does not entertain the possibility that there was more than one Theano, as his comment dismissing the letter to Rhodope because of its mention of Plato's *Parmenides* loses its force when the likelihood that there were many Theanos is considered. Clearly, they are real letters, and that addressed to Rhodope is certainly written by an ancient woman with some background in philosophy.

Just how is it that certain writings are immediately recognizable as of female authorship? There seems to be something about the minute details of ancient domestic life, coupled with expressions of dissatisfaction even in the face of moral commitment to accepting their position as women, that makes the fact of female authorship undeniable. What is spurious about these letters is their attribution to Theano. Certainly there could have been no intention on the part of the writer of the letter to Rhodope to suggest that the author was the same Theano as she who was the wife of Pythagoras. Indeed, in view of the reported popularity of the name "Theano,"[21] there seems little reason to suspect any intent to deceive as to the identity of the writer. The "spurious" letters are included here, as well as a note by Pollux on a letter (lost) to Timareta. All have been translated by Professor Harper.

a) *Text of Letter to Rhodope*[22]

Theano to Rhodope the philosopher: Are you dispirited? I myself am dispirited. Are you distressed because I have not yet sent you Plato's book, the one entitled "Ideas or Parmenides"? But I myself am grieved to the greatest extent, because no one has yet met with me to discuss Kleon. I will not send you the book until someone arrives to clarify matters concerning this man. So exceedingly do I love the soul of the man — on the grounds that it is the soul of a philosopher, of one zealous to do good, of one who fears the gods beneath the earth? And do not think the story is otherwise than it has been told. For I am half mortal and cannot bear to look directly on the star that makes day manifest [the sun (seclusit Hercher)].

b) *Theano to Eukleides*[23]

Theano to Eukleides, the Doctor: Yesterday someone had dislocated his leg and a messenger had gone to summon you (I myself was there, for the injured party was a friend of mine), but the messenger came back with haste, declaring that the doctor himself was ailing and physically unwell. And I — I swear it! — cast away all thought of my friend's pain and thought only of the doctor's. I prayed to Panacea and to Apollo, the Renowned Archer, that nothing grievous should have happened to the doctor! Now, in spite of my despondency, I inscribe this letter to you, anxious to learn how you are: lest, perhaps, your gastric orifice is in ill plight, or your liver has been damaged by fever, or some organic harm has befallen you. Thus — disregarding innumerable limbs of my friends — shall I fondly cling to *your* dear health, my good doctor.

The letter to Eukleides, the doctor, written in the same wry sense of humor and irony as the letter to Kallisto and others, conveys an image of the unethical physician who is never available for emergencies. The author's friend has suffered a very serious, painful, debilitating injury and is in need of urgent medical care. And where is the physician? The author had previously sent a messenger, and now sends another with a letter claiming that no matter how many friends injure *innumerable* limbs, her sole concern will be with the health of the physician. The comments on the "gastric orifice" and "liver" trouble suggest that the writer knows the character of this unprofessional professional all too well. The message conveyed to the reader is that of the immoderate physician who has incapacitated himself by overeating and overdrinking to the point of being unable (or even unwilling) to fill *his* role in the order of things. Supported by the community to be available for just such situations, the doctor once again fails to fulfill his social and moral obligations. The disharmony created by the physician's indifference to the suffering of the author's friend, as evidenced by the obviously lame excuses given, leaves everything literally and figuratively out of joint. The writer's message to the physician is, all too clearly, "cure thyself."

c) *Text of Theano's Letter to Euridike*[24]

> What distress grips your soul? You are dispirited for no other reason than that your husband has gone to a courtesan and takes his bodily pleasure with her. But you should not be in such a state, oh excellent among women! Do you not see that the faculty of hearing, too, when it has become full of the pleasure of the instrument, is filled also with choral songs of music but that, when it has become sated with this, it loves the flute and listens gladly to the simple reed-pipe? Indeed, do you not see what fellowship there is among the flute and musical chords and the wonderful reverberated sound of that instrument of most honey-sweetened quality? Just as it is for you, so too is it for the courtesan with whom your husband keeps company. In his habits and nature and thought the man will be mindful of you but — if ever he shall detect a surfeit — he will (just in passing) resort to the courtesan. For,

especially in those in whom corrupting humours are stored, there is a certain love of nourishments that is not counted among goods.

d) *Pollux' Note on Theano's Letter to Timareta*[25]

'Master of the house' and 'mistress of the house' — I found both these terms in the letter written by Theano the Pythagorean woman to Timareta.

e) *Text of Theano's Letter to Tim(ai)onides*[26]

Theano to Tim(ai)onides: [Τιμωνίδη vulg., Τιμαιωνίδη cod.] What fellowship is there for you and for me? Why do you continually slander us? Or do you not know that we praise you before everybody, even if you do the opposite? Then, again, do realize that even though we praise there is no one who believes, and even though you slander there is no one who listens. And I rejoice on this account: This is how god sees it and the truth most certainly determines it to be.

II. PERICTIONE II

The apothegems of Theano and the writings of Aesara of Lucania, Theano II, Phintys, and Perictione I all suggest the advantages to a woman of being a philosopher. A woman who understands and can appreciate the ways in which her actions satisfy the principle of *harmonia* is better able to act virtuously. The suggestion of both Phintys and Perictione I is that when women live in a society that severely limits the ways in which women can fulfill this principle, there is a special need for women to be philosophers.

1. *Text of* Sophias[27]

According to Perictione II, contemplating and analyzing how all things have reference to one fundamental principle is a basic human enterprise:

Mankind came into being and exists in order to contemplate the principle of the nature of the whole. The function of wisdom is to gain possession of this very thing, and to contemplate the purpose of the things that are. Geometry, therefore, and arithmetic, and the other theoretical studies and sciences are also concerned with the things that are, but wisdom is concerned with all genera of these. Wisdom is concerned with all that is, just as sight is concerned with all that is visible and hearing with all that is audible. As for the attributes of things, some belong universally to all, some to most things, some to individual things as such.

It is appropriate to wisdom to be able to see and to contemplate those attributes which belong universally to all things; those that belong to most things are the business of natural science, while separate sciences are concerned with the more individual and particular. On account of this wisdom searches for the basic principles of all the things that are, natural science for the principles of natural things, while geometry and arithmetic and music are concerned with quantity and the harmonious.

Therefore, whoever is able to analyze all the kinds of being by reference to one and the same basic principle, and, in turn, from this principle to synthesize and enumerate the different kinds, this person seems to be the wisest and most true and, moreover, to have discovered a noble height from which he will be able to catch sight of god and all the things separated from him [god] in seried rank and order.

Harmonia is the principle "of all the things that are," including geometry, arithmetic, music, and the cosmos. It is clear, then, why the woman who understands the relationship between marital fidelity, child-rearing, parental piety, religious worship, and public demeanor on the one hand, and the nature of her soul, on the other, is better able to conform her actions to the requirements of that principle. It is clear also, that the ability to contemplate and analyze the nature of this principle as a normative principle, extends to an ability to identify it as a mathematical, metaphysical, and aesthetic principle as well. Perictione II's *Sophias* focuses on what Allen calls "a common goal for all philosophers,"[28] the attainment of wisdom through discursive reasoning about the nature of philosophy itself. As such, Perictione II recommends philosophizing for both men and women.

2. *Wisdom and Morality*

While Perictione II reminds us that the Pythagoreans considered *harmonia* a metaphysical, mathematical, and aesthetic principle, it is Theano, Aesara of Lucania, Theano II, Phintys, and Perictione I who explain how that principle can be considered the principle of all things that are. Aesara shows us that it is the principle of law, justice, and human psychology. Theano II shows us that it is the principle underlying human moral psychology and education. Theano, Theano II, Phintys, and Perictione I all show how it is the principle of public and private morality for women. Through their contributions in the form of personal letters and aphorisms, and through the surviving fragments of their larger philosophical works, we can come to a new appreciation of the role that this Pythagorean principle has played in the history of philosophy. Their discussions of its application to the concrete facts about the status of women in the ancient world provide an entirely new perspective on the history of early western philosophy, and insights into why it was necessary for women to conceive of the enterprise of moral philosophy in new ways which took into account the limitations that ancient societies had placed on the ways in which women could effectively satisfy the normative principle of *harmonia.*

NOTES

1. Blaise Nagy, "The Naming of Athenian Girls," *Classical Journal*: LXXIV (1979): 360-364.
2. Theodoret, *De Vita Pythagoras* (1598), p. 163-165. Translation by Vicki Lynn Harper.
3. Thesleff, *op. cit.*, 198; Hercher, *op. cit.*, 604, 5. Translated by Vicki Lynn Harper.
4. Thesleff, *op. cit.*, 197-8; Hercher, *op. cit.*, 605, 6.
5. Thesleff 198, lines 25-26. See my note at the end of the translation.
6. Thesleff, *op. cit.*, 197, line 28.

7. Thesleff, *op. cit.*, 197, line 30.
8. Thesleff, *op. cit.*, 197, lines 32-33.
9. Thesleff, *op. cit.*, 198, line 5.
10. Thesleff, *op. cit.*, lines 2-5.
11. Thesleff, *op. cit.*, 198, lines 5-6.
12. Thesleff, *op. cit.*, 198, lines 7-8.
13. Thesleff, *op. cit.*, 198, lines 10-11.
14. Thesleff, *op. cit.*, 198, line 17.
15. Thesleff, *op. cit.*, 198, line 20.
16. Thesleff, *op. cit.*, 198, line 22.
17. *Loc. cit.*
18. Thesleff, *op. cit.*, 198, line 1.
19. Thesleff, *op. cit.*, 198, lines 23-25.
20. Mario Meunier, *Femmes Pythagoriciennes, Fragments et Lettres* Paris: L'Artisan du Livre, (1932).
21. Nagy, *op. cit.*
22. Thesleff, *op. cit.*, 200; Hercher, *op. cit.*, 607, 10. Translated by Vicki Lynn Harper.
23. Thesleff, *op. cit.*, 196-197; Hercher, *op. cit.*, 607, 9. Translated by Vicki Lynn Harper.
24. Thesleff, *op. cit.*, 197; Hercher, *op. cit.*, 606, 7.
25. Pollux, *Onomasticon*, 10.21, translated by Professor Vicki Lynn Harper.
26. Thesleff, *op. cit.*, 200; Hercher, *op. cit.*, 606, 8.
27. Translation by Vicki Lynn Harper, from Thesleff, *op. cit.*, 146, Stob. 3.1.120, p. 86 Heeren.
28. *Op. cit.*, 151.

4. Authenticating the Fragments and Letters

MARY ELLEN WAITHE
with additional commentary by
VICKI LYNN HARPER

Thomas Taylor published his translations of the fragments of Phintys and Perictione[1] (making no distinction between Perictione I and Perictione II), but modern philosophers usually do not include the works of the Pythagorean women in their histories of philosophy. Classicists and philologists have studied many of these materials. Established texts of the fragments and letters can be found in classical and philological literature. Some of the Pythagorean women are named in Diogenes Laertius' list of philosophers, and are mentioned by Atheneus and the Suda. The texts themselves were preserved by Stobaeus, Iamblichus and Clement of Alexandria. Theodoret appends some of the letters to his *Jamblichus, De Vita Pythagoras*. Modern doxographers including Bury, Didot, Diels, Hedengrahn, Hercher, Orelli, Poestion, Thesleff and Wolf have established the texts of the fragments and letters.

In this Chapter I will analyze three hypotheses about the authenticity of the writings of the Pythagorean women. The first hypothesis is that the writings in fact come from a larger group of philosophical treatises forged by neo-Pythagoreans of the 1st and 2nd centuries, A.D. A rather intriguing second hypothesis suggests that this group of writings were textbooks produced pseudonymously by dissenting members of the Archytan school. A third, and in my view, the most plausible hypothesis, is that the words are eponymous: they were written by the named authors.

A History of Women Philosophers / Volume 1, ed. by Mary Ellen Waithe
© *Martinus Nijhoff Publishers, Dordrecht − Printed in the Netherlands*

I. THE FORGERY HYPOTHESIS

Contemporary philologist Holger Thesleff[2] gives a comprehensive philological analysis of the aphorisms and letters now attributed to Theano, the wife of Pythagoras, and to Theano II, respectively. Thesleff also provides a detailed analysis of the fragments of Aesara of Lucania, Perictione I, Phintys and Perictione II. All of these writings form part of a much larger collection of writings that has long been referred to as the "pseudoepigrapha Pythagorica." Early analysts of the collection concluded that it represented a large group of forgeries written by the notorious members of the neo-Pythagorean schools which flourished during the 1st and 2nd centuries, A.D. It was well known that members of this school put the names of early famous Pythagoreans to their own writings.

Thesleff places the apothegems and letters of Theano in a different category than the fragments of Aesara of Lucania, Perictione and Phintys because these latter differ from other Pythagorean writings in significant ways. However, he does not identify the apothegems with Theano of Crotona and the letters with Theano II as we do. Unlike the apothegems by Theano of Crotona, and unlike early Pythagorean writings by members of the original and successor Pythagorean cult-schools, the letters of Theano II, and the fragments of Aesara of Lucania, Perictione I, Perictione II and Phintys show no personal interest in Pythagoras himself. Nor do their writings mention Pythagorean secret doctrines, mysticism, symbols, music, mathematics, or religious cult initiation rites. Inasmuch as there is no reference to what any other philosopher taught or said, the writings of this group can be viewed as asserting the personal philosophic views of their authors.[3] This is not to suggest that their writings are non-Pythagorean.

If we identify the letters of Theano with "Theano II," we see that what differentiates her and the other Pythagorean women (excepting Theano of Crotona) from male philosophers is their lack of fame as philosophers. Unless Phintys is the same person as "Philtys of Kroton" or as the daughter of the admiral Kallikratidas, and unless Perictione I is the same person as Plato's mother, none of our philosophers are even mentioned in any of the philosophical, literary, or historic writings of the Hellenistic era. Fortunately, their writings have not completely vanished, but are these forged documents? Are these female names really pseudonyms for male authors?

2. *In Favor of the Forgery Hypothesis*

Two factors favor the claim that the fragments are forgeries. First, there are philologists' judgments that the writings are full of unnatural archaisms as though the writers were attempting to write in an old-fashioned, but unnatural way. Second, Eduard Zeller[4] claims that there is no conclusive evidence that Pythagorean philosophy represented an active school of philosophy during the 3rd-2nd centuries B.C. He considers the group including the fragments of Aesara of Lucania, Phintys and Perictione to be neo-Pythagorean forgeries dating from the period between the 1st century B.C. and the 2nd century A.D.[5] Zeller is not alone in his view that the fragments are of such a late date. O.F. Gruppe argues[6] that the collection was written in Alexandria by Jewish philosophers. Other historians of philosophy have accepted the attribution of "forgery" to the collection and it has been referred to as "pseudonymous" ever since. The collection has retained the label "pseudoepigrapha" even as isolated fragments of other works in the group have gradually become authenticated.

2. *Consequences of the Forgery Hypothesis*

What are the consequences of accepting the forgery theory? Consider the claim that the writings were forged around the time of Christ and that the forgers attributed their own writings to famous early Pythagoreans. The first consequence of this claim is that there must have been famous, early Pythagorean women philosophers named Aesara of Lucania, Phintys, Perictione, and Theano. If the forgeries were intended to be accepted as genuine (i.e., if they were not forged as a kind of joke that no one would take seriously), then the contents of those writings must reasonably have been expected to resemble the known philosophical positions of the famous early Pythagorean women philosophers to whom they were attributed. If this is the case, then the forged documents could not differ markedly in content from the actual philosophical positions of the real philosophers to whom they were fraudulently attributed. We would then be safe in treating these documents as genuinely representing views that were at least very close to the views of their named authors. But this wouldn't really make those documents forgeries (unless the "forgers" were attempting to sell them as valuable original editions), they would be reconstructions. Just as Plato reconstructed some of the philosophical positions held by the historical Socrates, these "forgers" reconstructed some of the philosophical positions known to have been held by the historical Aesara, Phintys, Perictione and Theano. In this case, the forgery theory does little to undermine the case for the authenticity of the fragments and letters.

Another consequence of accepting the forgery theory is that we must accept that although there is no mention of these women philosophers (Theano excepted) during nearly half a millennia of history, (from the time of Pythagoras to the time of Christ) their names and views were somehow remembered not only by their forgers, but also by their intended audiences. We are not speaking here of lapses of time sufficiently brief to enable us to rely on oral histories — say a generation or two or even three — but a minimum of five or six centuries. The forgery hypothesis invites us to rely either on there being an oral tradition in which the views of the women philosophers was preserved, or it invites us to attribute the survival of information about those views to a series of written histories, all of which were lost. Far simpler hypotheses with greater explanatory power are available. But before exploring those hypotheses, it should be mentioned that there is an additional factor that makes the forgery hypothesis questionable.

The "archaisms" in the language of some of the texts have suggested to philologists that the texts are younger than they attempt to appear. But the absence of Stoic and Cynic elements in these texts counts in favor of an earlier dating, if not of the inscripted fragments themselves, then of the ideas which those fragments contain. Those who are fond of the forgery hypothesis and who cite the presence of archaistic language in the texts, do not explain how forgers who so bungled the linguistic expressions, would so expertly prevent any Stoic or Cynic elements from creeping into the texts.

Thesleff argues that it is unlikely that such a large number of forgeries could have been taken seriously for so many centuries, but he does not question whether the fragments ought to be considered pseudonymous. Instead, he accepts, without explanation or analysis, that they are pseudonymous and argues that they should be considered to be textbooks produced by philosophers of the successor schools to Archytas of Tarentum in Italy, rather than attempts at forgeries.[7] We know that Archytas lived in the first half of the 4th century B.C. and that his Pythagorean school was probably already well-established by the time Plato visited him there *circa* 388-387 B.C.[8] prior to establishing his own Academy. Archytas' school produced a group of materials now known as the "corpus Archyteum," and Thesleff[9] surmises that the group of fragments including Aesara, Phintys and Perictione belong to that group, representing some kind of reaction to Archytas' "atticized" Pythagoreanism. Thesleff hypothesizes:[10]

> If, for instance, an author from the same philosophical environment disagreed with a doctrine attributed to Archytas, or if he for some reason did not want to write in the Tarentinian manner, he would presumably use another Early Pythagorean name. On the whole, those dissenters seem to have behaved very modestly in choosing names which nobody would find more authoritative than that of Archytas. It is very important to note that this practice cannot be called forgery either; it is just a literary convention.

1. *Consequences of the Pseudonymy Hypothesis: The 'Female Authority' View*

The consequences of accepting the pseudonymy hypothesis are similar to those of accepting the forgery hypothesis. The reader will recall that one of the objections raised above concerned the lack of evidence that there were early Pythagoreans of the same names as the named authors of our fragments. A related objection was raised concerning the lack of historical record transmitting the documents themselves. Even if Thesleff can overcome these objections, the pseudonymy hypothesis is susceptible to a third objection. Why would a male author, of Archytas' or any other school, give his work a female *nom-de-plume*? How could a male philosopher hope to give his views a ring of authority by attributing them to virtually unknown authors, and female authors at that? The only conceivable circumstance that would induce a male to write under a female pen name is that the name really was that of a famous woman philosopher. But this brings us right back to the objections raised against the forgery hypothesis. In what sense were these women famous? Our authors are virtually unknown except for Theano. Phintys and Aesara are known only by the fragments attributed to them. Perictione bears the name of Plato's mother; she was not known as a philosopher. The proponent of the pseudonymy hypothesis must be willing to claim that these women were early Pythagoreans of substantial initial fame and subsequent total obscurity who were memorialized by writers of fragments later attributed to them.

But who did write these fragments? Someone wrote them. While Thesleff may be fond of hypothesizing a peculiar literary convention of attributing one's work to virtually unknown authors as a way of giving them a ring of authority, the far simpler hypothesis is the known literary convention of putting one's own name to one's writings. Nevertheless, Thesleff may be on the right track in suggesting that these writings were authored by dissident members of Archytas' school or its successor institution.

2. Consequences of the Pseudonymy Hypothesis:
   ### The Dissident Archytan View

Could these documents represent dissident views to the school of Archytas? Most of Archytas' writings listed by Thesleff and accepted as genuine are on topics other than those discussed in the fragments by the women philosophers. Those topics range from arithmetic, to geometry, astronomy, music, and metaphysics. In contrast, the fragments by the women philosophers (excluding the spurious letter to Euridike by "Theano," which makes many analogies to Pythagorean musical theory, of which there is very little in the way of surviving documents) concern the nature of the soul, the relationship between women's and men's virtues, and moral and social aspects of women's roles in marriage, religion, and the community. A few writings usually considered not genuine examples of Archytan philosophy, the so-called Archytan pseudoepigrapha, do approach topics related to those in the fragments by women. Indeed, Perictione's *On Wisdom* is partially identical with the pseudoepigrapha *Archytas II, sophias,*[11] a series of five short fragments totalling 30 lines. Thesleff dates both Perictione's *On Wisdom* and its pseudo-Archytan counterpart to the 3rd century B.C. His hypothesis, that the writings of the women Pythagoreans may in fact be pseudonymous dissenting opinions written by members of the Archytan school rests on certain textual affinities between Perictione's *On Wisdom* and that series of fragments. That may be sufficient evidence with which to entertain the claim that the Perictione of the *sophias* lived at the same time as Archytas, but it is hardly sufficient evidence with which to claim that its author was a "dissident member of the Archytan school," or to date fragments written by others.

Only one other Archytan fragment bears the remotest relationship to the topics discussed by the women Pythagoreans. Thesleff describes this fragment as, "A short quotation in attic. – On the duty of a father to be a model for his children."[12] Thesleff's hypothesis, that the writings of the women Pythagoreans may in fact be pseudonymous dissenting opinions written by members of the Archytan school rests on two factors: similarities between Perictione's *On Wisdom* and fragments written under Archytas' pseudonym, as well as a quotation whose topic is related to one of the topics discussed by Theano II.

III. THE EPONYMY HYPOTHESIS

Thesleff's method for dating the fragments of the Pythagoreans may be unsound. Briefly, his method is this: (a) he identifies the nationality of the name of the given author; (b) he identifies the dialect of the fragment; (c) he identifies the style and subject matter of the fragment; and (d) he determines the period in which there was a coincidence of dialect, style, and subject matter in philosophic and literary circles of the place of presumed national origin of the named author. Thesleff claims that the tradition is

wrong in accepting the Pythagorean epigrapha as forgeries. Instead, he supports the position that the writings are pseudonymous. I have already questioned several aspects of his position,
including the premise that the named authors were actually early
Pythagorean philosophers whose reputations were restored by
the "forgers," and the assumption that the writings represented
dissident views of the Archytan school.

1. *The Problem with Names*

The basic flaw in Thesleff's methodology is his use of the names of
the authors to identify their nationalities. The ethnicity of an
author's name need not indicate their domicilliary nation. Scholars
travelled widely since at least the 6th century before Christ.
Children were undoubtedly sometimes named for foreign-born
ancestors. For these reasons alone, a name is insufficiently reliable
as an indicator of either domicilliary or parental nationality of the
named author. We should keep in mind that Thesleff holds that
the named authors are merely pseudonyms for the real authors.
What is merely an insufficient indicator of a nationality of a
named author becomes useless as an indicator of the nationality of
the "real" author, unless it is assumed that authors who wrote
under pseudonyms would never choose a pseudonym with an
ethnic identification different than their own. Since Thesleff
bases his dating of the fragments in part on the presumed nationality of the named author, his estimates may be quite wrong.
Indeed, his estimates are more likely to be mistaken if he assumes
that the works were written under pseudonyms, than if he assumed that the named authors are the real authors. Can a case be
made for eponymy?

2. *The Doric Language*

It is reasonable to examine the possibility that the fragments
constitute posthumous recordings of the doctrines of famous early
Pythagoreans whose teachings were handed down in a written
form later lost to us, or in the oral tradition. In support of this
view one could argue that doxographers in the Hellenistic era
attempted to reconstruct the original teachings in their presumed

original dialects. Certainly the Doric language was popular enough during the early Pythagorean period, to allow for an early dating of the texts by Aesara, Phintys and Perictione II, (the author of *On Wisdom*). According to Thesleff:[13]

> The next landmark in the official history of literary Doric prose is Philolaos of Kroton in the latter part of V cent. B.C. ... But in the 4th century, at least, Archytas of Tarentum obviously employed Doric prose; ... the later Pythagoreans seem to follow the tradition inaugurated by him. From IV cent. B.C., however, we also have some seemingly non-Pythagorean prose works in Doric: the so-called Dissoi Logoi, and the Rhetor Anonymous is very similar to that employed by the Pythagoreans.

We know from Thesleff that Doric was used, and not just by Pythagorean writers of prose but also by historians as well as other intellectual writers. It survived throughout the Doric states for centuries:[14]

> The last datable and manifest stage in the development of literary Doric prose is Archimedes' mathematical output from the latter part of II .C. His use of Doric may appear as a fairly isolated phenomenon. However, I find it tempting to regard it both as an indication of his personal Pythagorean interests and as a manifestation of the Doric vogue of the time....

He continues:[15]

> From IV cent. B.C. onwards the Attic and Koine influence grew gradually stronger. This led to the development of two kinds of West Greek Koine [Northwest Greek Koine and Doric Koine. The latter] seems to have been employed all over the Doric World from the late 4th century right down to the 2nd and even the 1st century B.C. ... The Doric states thus managed to maintain, for some centuries, a fairly homogeneous inscriptional language, probably as a conscious contrast to Attic Koine. With the Roman conquest, however,

> such national ambitions were gradually lost. ... On the other
> hand Doric was spoken at least in the Peloponnese and in
> Southern Italy throughout antiquity.

The writings of Aesara of Lucania and Phintys, as well as Perictione II's *On Wisdom* are all in Doric. However, they are free of
the Attic and Koine influences that characterize Doric prose after
the late 4th century B.C. Therefore, on the basis of language
alone, they could be dated to the late 4th century B.C. or earlier.
However, they do contain some archaic expressions which could
indicate either that they were written later, or that later copyists
interpolated the texts. These works cannot be conclusively dated;
however, we may be able to make some estimates.

3. *Perictione I's Ionic Prose*

Perictione I's fragments from *On the Harmony of Women* can be
distinguished from the group of writings by Aesara, Phintys and
Perictione II, because the fragments are written in Ionic, although
they contain occasional Doric expressions. This suggests that they
were written when the Attic and Koine influences were leading to
the popularization of Doric Koine as the language that would
eventually supplant Ionic's use in inscripted prose.

a) *East versus West*

If the fragments from Perictione I's *On the Harmony of Women*
were in fact written at a time when inscripted Doric was just
beginning to be used in prose writings instead of Ionic, then
Perictione I lived where Ionic was the language for written prose,
i.e., in "eastern" Greece, rather than in "western" Greek settle-
ments in Italy and the Peloponnese. Since it was Plato's friend,
Archytas of Tarentum who is usually credited with the popularization of inscripted Doric in western Greece, it is likely that our
author either wrote the fragments prior to the time Plato visited
Archytas, (and that the Dorisms in the text are interpolations by a
copyist), or that she wrote the fragments shortly after Doric-
language materials from the Archytan school began circulating in
Athenian academic circles.

b) *Perictione I and Plato*

Since Plato's mother, Perictione, lived in Athens prior to the popularization of Doric there, it is tempting to identify our author with that Perictione. Plato's *Epistle XII*, dated by Taylor and Burnet to 366 B.C. mentions that she is expected to die soon. This is firm evidence that she was alive approximately 22 years earlier when Plato returned from Italy. If the Dorisms in *On the Harmony of Women* can be attributed to a copyist, it is altogether possible that the author of *Harmony* is the same Perictione as she who was Plato's mother. Since there is no reason to suspect that a daughter of the house of Solon would be incapable of philosophical thinking and writing, the hypothesis that Perictione I is Plato's mother is made more attractive. Whatever the family background of Perictione I, it appears likely that she would have lived around the time of Plato, and that she was an Athenian. Professor Harper's analysis of the text of *Harmony* leads her to a different conclusion.

c) *Harper on Perictione I and Plato*

Professor Harper's analysis of the text of *On the Harmony of Women* has led her to the tentative opinion that the text post-dates the *Republic*. She notes:[16] "In the first four lines (Th. 142.18-21), where *harmonia* is analyzed in terms of several virtues, we find all four of the cardinal virtues discussed by Plato in *Republic* IV: courage ($\dot{\alpha}\nu\delta\rho\epsilon\dot{\alpha}$), self-control ($\sigma\omega\phi\rho o\sigma\dot{\nu}\nu\eta$), justice ($\delta\iota\kappa\alpha\iota o\sigma\dot{\nu}\nu\eta$), and wisdom ($\phi\rho\dot{o}\nu\eta\sigma\iota\varsigma$). It may be worth noting here that in *Republic* IV Plato uses the terms $\sigma o\phi\dot{\iota}\alpha$ and $\phi\rho\dot{o}\nu\eta\sigma\iota\varsigma$ interchangeably (see, e.g., 433b-d) and that, in his list of the four virtues at *Phaedo* 69a-b, he mentions $\phi\rho\dot{o}\nu\eta\sigma\iota\varsigma$ rather than $\sigma o\phi\dot{\iota}\alpha$. Thus I see no reason to suspect Aristotelian influence in the term. What is not reminiscent of the *Republic* in these first four lines is the term for self-sufficiency ($\alpha\dot{\upsilon}\tau\alpha\rho\kappa\epsilon\dot{\iota}\eta$ [Ionic form], Th.142.21). This term does figure prominently in Aristotle's *Nicomachean Ethics* (e.g., at 1907b7 ff. and 1177b ff.), though Plato also uses the term at *Philebus* 67a7, and it is even found in Democritus Fr. 246. (At *Republic* 369b and 387d Plato uses the adjective $\alpha\dot{\upsilon}\tau\dot{\alpha}\rho\kappa\eta\varsigma$, though clearly without any special technical meaning.) Perictione's text, however, does not elaborate on the notion of self-sufficiency in any obviously Aristotlelian way. The idea that one should not pine for or require status and riches and illustrious friends (Th.143.25ff.) spells out a general sense of self-sufficiency that accords with Plato's views and is more nearly compatible with that emphasis on the Pythagorean virtue of *harmonia* than Aristotle's sense of the term might be (Cf. *N.E.* X in which Aristotle's emphasis on self-sufficiency even clashes with his own view that man by nature is a political being). In the next sentence of our text (Th.142.21-23), the idea that benefits *result* (ἐκ τούτων γὰρ καλὰ γίνεται) from virtue is compatible with the *Republic's* classification of the fairest class of goods as that loved both for its own sake and for its results. (τὰ γιγνόμενα ἀπ᾽ αὐτοῦ, 358a2), though the idea is not strikingly unique. More striking is the tentative suggestion that a virtuous woman might benefit even a whole city − if indeed such a woman should rule − and the use of the term βασιληΐη (royal city), which is the Ionic form of the term βασιλεία that Plato applies to the best city (445d6); a city which benefits from the wise rule of guardians of either sex. Similarly, the following sentence (Th.143.1-2) about having mastery over appetite (ἐπιθυμία) and feeling (θυμός) strongly suggests Plato's tripartite soul in which θυμός and ἐπιθυμία are duly governed by the rational part of the soul (439d ff.). Finally, in the eighth line of Perictione's text, the mention of lawless desires or loves (ἔρωτες ... ἄνομοι) is paralleled in Plato's discussion of lawless pleasures and desires (παράνομοι) at 571b5 of the *Republic* and of a lawless species of desires (ἄνομον ἐπιθυμιῶν εἶδος) at 572b5.

None of this philological evidence may be conclusive, but I was continually struck by ways in which otherwise implausible points in Perictione's text might plausibly be accounted for by reference to the *Republic*. For example, the dire warning that women who indulge their desires for extravagant luxuries are prone to *every* sort of wrongdoing (Th.143.13-14) makes more sense if it presupposes Plato's psychological theory: compare Plato in Book IX of the *Republic* as he vividly describes how feeding the beast of desires can lead to the usurpation of reason's reign, and to the degeneration of the soul as a whole."

Professor Harper's analysis of the text suggests to her the

possibility that it post-dates the *Republic*. If this is the case then Perictione I may have been a reader of Plato's works, and possibly his student, "like teacher, like student." However, the similarities of the two texts could just as well favor identifying our author with Plato's mother, "like mother, like son." Alternative hypotheses cannot be conclusively ruled out either; if Thesleff is correct, and if the work was written under a pseudonym, the name "Perictione" may have been adopted by the author in order to identify it with the mother of Plato. Neither can we conclusively dismiss my hypothesis, that while Perictione I may have been the mother of Plato, she most probably was a philosopher who lived in Athens during the 4th century B.C. This hypothesis simply attributes the occasional Dorisms in the Ionic text of *Harmony* to a copyist who interpolated into the original text expressions from what had by that time become the stylish language for non-poetic intellectual writing. Whatever the true identity of its author, and whatever her relationship to Plato might have been, *On the Harmony of Women* presents intriguing challenges to the philologer and philosopher alike.

4. *Phintys'* On the Moderation of Women

The textual similarities of Phintys' *On the Moderation of Women* to Perictione's *On the Harmony of Women* strongly suggest a temporal proximity of the two works. Thesleff emends "Kallikrates" to "Kallikratidas" thus identifying Phintys the author with the daughter of Kallikratidas. Through Thucydides and Plutarch, we know Kallikratidas to be an admiral during the Peloponnesian wars who died during the battle of the Arginusae in 406 B.C. If Thesleff's emendation is correct, then Phintys would be a younger contemporary of Plato. We would also expect her to write in Doric, the language of the text because her father was a Spartan, hence Doric, and, Plutarch[17] mentions Kallikratidas' "Dorian" character. By the time Kallikratidas' daughter would have been an adult, Doric would have been the inscripted language of much of Greece. This would mean that the text should be dated to the 4th century, B.C. Thesleff dates it to the 3rd century, B.C. on the basis of archaistic expressions contained in it which suggest to him that the writer was attempting to write in an old-fashioned way.

But old-fashioned expressions in an inscripted text could also indicate interpolations by copyists, which might be attributable to the difference between inscripted Doric, whose use was already declining in the 3rd century, and the spoken Doric, which remained common.

5. *Aesara of Lucania's* On Human Nature

René Fohalle[18] attempts to date the fragment by Aesara of Lucania. While Fohalle's comments at the beginning of his article indicate that the fragment dates to the early Christian era, there is only one word in the form used used by Aesara that is never found in texts dated earlier than the earliest dating for the first seven books of the New Testament. On the basis of this one word-form, Fohalle dates this text to "the early christian era." Fohalle notes that Aristotle used the substantive form of the word, in *De Plantis*, 1,2,12. But since this work is generally accepted as pseudo-Aristotelian, the occurrence of the same root in Aesara may be meaningless. Given Fohalle's advice that a number of other words appear in Aesara's text, but not elsewhere in ancient documents, and given his comments that her style is very idiosyncratic, one occurrence of a "christian era" word seems insufficient to definitively identify the text with the Christian neo-Pythagorean period. Given that all other key-word analyses made by Fohalle date the text to the late 3rd-century B.C., it seems appropriate to date Aesara as a younger contemporary of Aristotle.

SUMMARY

In this chapter I have examined three hypotheses about the authorship of the works attributed to Aesara of Lucania, Phintys, and Perictione I. None of the hypotheses are conclusive. The forgery hypothesis requires us to conclude that there were famous early Pythagorean philosophers of the same names as the given authors whose views were more or less congruent with those presented in the texts. This hypothesis also requires us to conclude that the names and views of these early Pythagorean women were remembered for centuries either without benefit of any written record, or despite the destruction of all record of them and their views. The pseudonymy hypothesis has the same consequences and in addition must account for two anomalies: first, a peculiar literary convention in which a writer attributes his or her work to a virtually unknown author as a way of giving that work a ring of authority; and, second, that a writer dissents from the views of the school with which he/she is associated by writing on topics that no one in that school ever wrote on, failing totally to disagree with any view for which that school is known.

The ludicrous consequences of the forgery and pseudonymy hypotheses make the case for eponymy more attractive while leaving open questions about the exact dates the fragments were written, and the consanguinity of two of their authors to famous Greek men. There are strong arguments in favor of, and little against, giving an approximate dating for the fragments by Phintys, Perictione I and Aesara of Lucania. Idiosyncracies of style, the appearance of archaisms, and of Doric expressions in an Ionic text make it impossible at present to date these works more precisely than *circa* 4th-3rd centuries, B.C. However, the very nature of these idiosyncracies may argue in favor of eponymy. Indeed, the hypothesis that the ideas contained in these texts, if not the inscripted texts themselves, represent the ideas of the women philosophers who are named as their authors, avoids the pitfalls of both the forgery and pseudonymy hypotheses.

NOTES

1. Taylor, Thomas, *Political Fragments of Stobaeus*, Chiswick, England: privately published (1822).
2. Thesleff, Holger, "An Introduction to the Pythagorean Writings of the Hellenistic Period," *Acta Academiae Aboensis, Humaniora*: XXIV:3: (1961).
3. Thesleff, *op. cit.*, p. 71-73. (Excepting the letter Theano to Rhodope.)
4. Zeller, Eduard, *Philosophie der Griechen*, Volume 3.2. 4th edition, 1902, p. 97ff.
5. *Ibid.*, 114, 122-126.
6. Gruppe, O.F., *Über die Fragmente des Archytas und der alteren Pythagoreer*, Berlin: Eine Preisschrift, 1840.
7. Thesleff, *op. cit.*, p. 72.
8. Taylor, A.E., *Plato: The Man and His Work*, London: Methuen, 1978 reprint of 1926 edition, p. 8.

9. *Op. cit.*, p. 76.
10. *Ibid.*
11. Iamblichus, Protr. IV, 16, 18, 20, 32, 22, *Ps.-Archytae Fragmenta*, ed. J. Nolle. Tübingen: Diss. Monast. (1914) 7-8.
12. Philostratus, *ibid.*, p. 53.
13. Thesleff, *op. cit.*, p. 80.
14. Thesleff, *op. cit.*, p. 80.
15. Thesleff, *op. cit.*, p. 82.
16. Excerpted from presentations made by Vicki Lynn Harper, Ph.D. in November, 1983, to the Minnesota Philosophical Society, Minneapolis, and in December, 1984, to the American Philosophical Association, Eastern Division Meetings, New York.
17. *Lives*, 528.
18. Fohalle, René, "La Langue d'un Texte 'Dorien' ...," *Étrennes de linguistique offèrtes par quelques amis a Emile Benveniste*, Paris: Geuthner (1928).

5. Aspasia of Miletus

MARY ELLEN WAITHE

I. BACKGROUND

Aspasia, who died *circa* 401 B.C., is known as a rhetorician and a member of the Periclean philosophic circle. Her reputation as a philosopher has been memorialized by Plato, who makes her *Epitaphia* the subject of Socrates' conversation in the *Menexenus*. She is also memorialized in a fresco over the portal of the University of Athens in Greece, shown in the company of Socrates, Phidias, the sculptor (with chisel in hand) whose gold and ivory statue of Athena was dedicated on the Acropolis in 438, B.C.,[1] Sophocles, the playwrite, Pericles, the general of the Peloponnesian Wars (and Aspasia's spouse), Plato, as a young man (who was born after Pericles died), Antisthenes, (who lived 444-365 B.C.), Anaxagoras, (who lived 500-428 B.C.), a youthful Alcibiades, (450-404 B.C.), Ictinus, the architect of the Parthenon, (completed 438 B.C.),[2] Polygnotus, and Archimedes (who lived 287-212 B.C.). Clearly, some of the figures represented in the fresco could not have been present simultaneously, and some, notably, Archimedes, could not ever have been part of Aspasia's famous *salon*. Despite, or perhaps because of her public participation in Greek intellectual life, she was tried for impiety and acquitted after Pericles came to her public defense.

II. THE *MENEXENUS* AND PERICLES' FUNERAL ORATION

There are certain historical events mentioned in Aspasia's speech in the *Menexenus* as well as in Pericles' Funeral Oration reported

A History of Women Philosophers / Volume 1, ed. by Mary Ellen Waithe
©*Martinus Nijhoff Publishers, Dordrecht – Printed in the Netherlands*

in Thucydides. For example, at 241c5 she mentions the Battle of Tanagra, the Athenian victory at Oenophyta, which is also mentioned in Thucydides.[3] This battle took place in the summer of 457 B.C.[4] Aspasia's mention at 243c2 that the Athenian ships blockaded at Mytilene were aided by 60 civilian ships is a reference to an event which occured in 406 B.C.,[5] the summer following the 3rd year of war is likewise mentioned by Thucydides.[6] Aspasia's mention of the peace followed by "civil war" that was "mild in form" against the tyrants in Eleusis, is a reference to an event in 403 B.C.,[7] also mentioned by Thucydides.[8] She also mentions Pericles first funeral oration, following the battle of Samos, which took place in 439 B.C. but is not quoted by Thucydides. It is Pericles' second Funeral Oration,[9] given around March of 431 B.C., (assuming that March is "winter's end") that is most similar to Aspasia's *Epitaphia*. Aspasia's speech differs most from Pericles' in that hers, as reported by Plato, includes the description of the Mytilene Battle, which occurred after Pericles delivered the Funeral Oration.

III. TWO ARGUMENTS ABOUT THE *MENEXENUS*

There are two views of the *Menexenus*. First, there is that body of literature which dismisses the *Menexenus* as being of no particular philosophic interest. Those who hold this view, admit themselves to be at a loss to explain that, in spite of its apparently non-philosophic character, it was written by Plato and is his only non-philosophical work! The second view is that, although Plato wrote the *Menexenus,* the view which he ascribes to Aspasia is very much Aspasia's, and that he wrote it because he recognized Aspasia's reputation as a philosopher/rhetorician, but disapproved of the influence that philosophers like her had on Greece. Furthermore, the very style and content of the dialogue were intended by him to make his disapproval clear.

According to Pamela M. Huby,[10] those who identify the *Menexenus* as just a piece of satirical writing must account for those ancients who took Aspasia's speech "at least perfectly seriously." She says:[11]

This unanimity on the part of the ancients has been a considerable stumbling-block to those moderns who have taken notice of it.

She rebukes Meridier:[12]

> We are invited to regard Dionysius of Halicarnassus and Hermogenes as fools, to take the heroic course of rejecting a perfectly good sentence of Cicero as an idiotic interpolation, and finally, to admit that Plato's satire was so subtle that it was interwoven with many passages that are not satirical at all.

The "perfectly good sentence of Cicero"[13] mentions that the Athenians in his day devoted a solemn day annually to the public recitation of the dialogue. Huby remarks that most writers regarded Cicero's comment as nonsense and hence have treated the sentence as an interpolation by a copyist. Huby credits Taylor,[14] with making the point that the satire was so subtle that it was interwoven with many non-satirical passages.

Clearly the dialogue is much more than a simple satire. Taylor's comment that many passages are not satirical at all is well taken. But does every passage have to be satirical for the piece as a whole to be taken as satire? I believe that Bloedow's analysis about Plato's intentions hit closer to the mark. And in doing so, tells us much about Aspasia's influence and reputation as a philosopher. Bloedow, criticizing Pohlenz' claim that Plato was concerned to correct a critical view of Aspasia presented by Aischines queries whether:[15]

> Aspasia was not merely a literary creation but, to the contrary, had enjoyed a reputation of considerable substance? And if this be the case, would it not be more likely that what Plato had in mind is not a literary but a real Aspasia?

But who is the "real Aspasia?" Bloedow[16] suggests:

> ... what Plato had in mind is not the literary, but the historical Aspasia, not, however, as the consort of Perikles, but

as a leading member of the Periklean circle, and thus, with others, a co-architect of the Sophistic movement. As such she will have contributed significantly to the development of oratory, the 'handmaid of the New Thought', which in Plato's view had such negative consequences for Athens.

IV. ASPASIA AND SOPHISTIC RHETORIC

What were the alleged negative consequences of Sophistic rhetoric in Plato's view? Friedlander[17] asks:

> When Plato was writing the *Menexenus*, was he not yet aware of the critique of democracy that he would expound later in the *Republic*? There, in Book VIII, it is excessive freedom which is the misfortune of a democratic government; and in the *Laws* (III 698a et seq.) it is said expressly, *as if to contradict the popular thesis of the Menexenus* that it was not complete freedom from any kind of authority ... which brought victory to the Athenians. On the contrary, reverence ruled and the people were servants of the laws (*Laws* III 698b, 699c). This produced "friendship" ... within and power without. Only later were the people introduced to "complete freedom", to the detriment of the state as a whole.

And what are we to make of the report that Aspasia was Socrates' teacher in rhetoric? It is Plato, as much as Socrates, who has learned much about rhetoric from Aspasia. What Plato has learned is the potential harmfulness of rhetoric as a branch of philosophy. Philosophy, the discipline that is supposed to enlighten and disclose the truth, also has the power to persuade those, who unlike Plato and Socrates, are insufficiently astute to recognize its potential for obscuring the truth. If Plato wanted to exempt Socrates from responsibility for the authorship of the dialogue, he had means of doing so other than alleging that Socrates was merely quoting someone who was his teacher in rhetoric. But Aspasia *was* his teacher in rhetoric, and Plato's too. What she, as a central figure of the Sophistic rhetoric had to teach, was what

Plato and Socrates learned as a result of Pericles' *Epitaphia*, namely, the power of public speaking to influence the public by making the public believe that its history was other than it really was. Bloedow[18] remarks:

> ... if we take into account the combination of the attribution to Aspasia with the intense irony in, not the 'distortion of history' but the self-portrait of Athens in 386, we are no longer required to take this alleged distortion of history as turning out 'for the greater glory of the Athenian demo-cracy'; rather, the Athenians are condemned out of their own mouths (no less than the democracy is condemned in the *Gorgias*). But the primary object of condemnation is one of the principal sources of the rhetoric in question – Aspasia, the 'enlightened' Ionian, the only female member of the Periklean circle.

What happens if we take seriously the idea that Plato was writing a piece of incredible satire? Could Bloedow be correct in suggesting that the entire piece is an attempt to show precisely what the Sophistic rhetoricians were doing by blatantly satirizing their style? Such a satirization would require that the dialogue be inter-spersed with "perfectly serious" parts, and with sufficient ex-amples of historical accuracy to "confuse the reader with the facts," just as the Sophistic rhetoricians did. And because the dialogue *is* interspersed with perfectly serious parts containing historically accurate information, we can take Plato's claim seriously, viz., that Aspasia is the author of the *Epitaphia*. Taking Plato seriously does not require that we take him to be providing a historically accurate recording of every line in that original speech, for everyone who would have been Plato's audience would know that it is Thucydides' version that was the accurate one. Taking Plato seriously in his satirization of Aspasia requires that we take seriously the fact that she and Pericles collaborated on his speech writing. Known as a great general and great public orator, would Pericles have sought the collaboration of his wife in the composi-tion of this important speech? There appears to be no reason not to conclude that this is what happened. After all, Aspasia was at the center of the philosophic circle of sophists; a circle devoted to the analysis and creation of rhetoric. Pericles was selected to deliver the *Epitaphia*; this great honor would have made it imperative that he prepare well, and follow the advice of his colleagues, including Aspasia, on points of style and substance.

CONCLUSIONS

What conclusions may we draw about Aspasia? She was clearly an influential intellectual with a keen mind for the political potential of public rhetoric. She was active in the inner circles of ancient political and intellectual life. She was perceived as a threat by Aischines and Plato, not personally, but politically and intellectually. Plato, at least, seemed to consider her to represent the abuses of philosophy: the use of wisdom and the truth in the form of her mastery of rhetoric, to control and deceive the public about the history of Greece. And in this sense, she taught rhetoric to him and to Socrates. Her public trial on charges of impiety shows that others perceived her as a threat also. And, commemoration of her in the fresco over the Library entrance at the university showed that her contribution to Athenian leadership of the Greek states was also valued.

NOTES

1. Edinger, H.G., transl. *Thucydides, The Speeches of Pericles*, New York: Ungar (1979), p. VII.
2. Edinger, *op. cit.*, XVIII.
3. Thucydides, *The Peloponnesian War*, Thomas Hobbes translation, edited by David Grene, Ann Arbor: The University of Michigan Press, (1959), p. 61.
4. Bury, Richard, *History of Greece*, p. 356.
5. Bury, *op. cit.*, pp. 500-501
6. Thucydides, *op. cit.*, pp. 161-165.
7. Bury, *op. cit.*, p. 500.
8. Thucydides, *op. cit.*, p. 64.
9. Thucydides, *op. cit.*, pp. 108-115.
10. Huby, Pamela M. "The Menexenus Reconsidered", *Phronesis* 2(157), 104.
11. *Ibid.*

12. Meridier, L., *Plato*. Paris: Société d'édition "Les Belles Lettres," (1920), p. 76.
13. Cicero, *De Oratore*, XLIV, 151.
14. Taylor, A.E., *Plato, The Man and his Work*, London: Methuen (1978), pp. 43-44.
15. Bloedow, Edmund F., "Aspasia And The 'Mystery' Of The Menexenos," *Wiener Studien* (Zeitschrift für Klassiche Philologie und Patristic) Wien, Bohlau N.F. 9(75) 46.
16. *Op. cit.*
17. Friedlander, Paul, *Plato*, V. 2, Hans Meyerhoff trans., Princeton: Bollingen (1964), Chapter 16, pp. 216 ff.
18. *Op. cit.*, pp. 47-48.

6. Diotima of Mantinea

MARY ELLEN WAITHE

Diotima and Aspasia are the only two women who are characterized as philosophers in the Socratic dialogues of Plato although
other women, notably Axiothea of Philesia and Lasthenia of
Mantinea, are known to have been students of Plato. Both Diotima
and Aspasia are widely regarded as non-philosophers: the former
because she is assumed to be the only fictitious person created by
Plato, the latter because her role as author of the *Epitaphia*, which
comprises most of the *Menexenus*, is viewed as an example of
Platonic cynicism. In Section I of this chapter, I discuss various
aspects of Diotima's philosophy and distinguish it from that of
Plato and of Socrates. In Section II I present the evidence others
have given to the effect that Diotima was not a historical person
but rather was a fictitious character created by Plato. In Section
III I examine the evidence in favor of the historicity of Diotima
and in Section IV offer textual support for that claim.

Plato's *Symposium* is Apollodorus' report of Aristodemus'
report of a dinner party at which the guests make a speech about
the nature of love. When it is Socrates' turn to speak, he repeats a
conversation which he claims to have had many years ago with
Diotima, a priestess from Mantinea. While the evidence cannot
incontrovertibly prove that Diotima was a real person who in fact
had the conversation with Socrates reported in the *Symposium*, I
can show that the recent philosophic tradition which portrays
Diotima as Plato's only fictitious character rests on unsubstanti-
ated assumptions and inconclusive interpretations of Plato's text.
It is therefore important to examine the question of Diotima's
historicity.

A History of Women Philosophers / Volume 1, ed. by Mary Ellen Waithe
© *Martinus Nijhoff Publishers, Dordrecht – Printed in the Netherlands*

I. DISTINGUISHING DIOTIMA FROM PLATO AND SOCRATES

1. *Diotima's Concept of Beauty*

In what may be an attempt to platonize Diotima's philosophy, many authorities including Grote, Taylor, Zeller, and Rosen identify Diotima's concept of beauty with the Platonic forms or ideas. As Grote[1] notices in the *Republic, Phaedrus, Phaedo*, and elsewhere, Plato recognized many distinct Forms or Ideas including the Ideas of Good and of Beauty. Zeller[2] and Taylor[3] claim that the absolute Beauty mentioned by Diotima is identical with the Form of the Good expressed by Plato in other dialogues. Stanley Rosen[4] claims that:

> The Eros of Diotima's teaching, as the striving for complete- ness or immortality, is not a simple, unilinear phenomenon. It leads us both toward the gods and the Ideas....

In a note to this passage Rosen elaborates:

> The Ideas are not mentioned in the *Symposium*; ... [s]till, there can be no doubt that, according to Diotima, Eros points us toward the Ideas.

Ann R. Cacoullos in "The Doctrine of Eros in Plato"[5] apparently agrees with Rosen:

> ... the lover of wisdom comes in the end to be completely indifferent to particular physical instances of beauty; his "love" is directed to the Form of Beauty and the expressions of this love is wholly other than the usual expressions of love.

Harry Neumann[6] takes a different position from that of Rosen and Cacoullos and notes that Diotima's speech "reveals a crucial difference between the good and the beautiful." Love's real goal is not the Beautiful but the Good: immortality acquired by gener- ating an offspring of the soul. "Men seek the beautiful to obtain the good and not vice-versa."[7] Diotima's concept of absolute Beauty only resembles Plato's Idea of the Good:[8]

... it is not only the ultimate object of knowledge, it is also, and primarily, the final goal of love.

On the other hand, Diotima's concept of the Good does not function as a Platonic Idea. It is not a universal; it is not a means but an end in itself since it is identical with the particular happiness of an individual. The end of Diotima's eros is not contemplation of the Idea of the Good, or even of the Idea of the Beautiful, but reproduction of one's soul in others through the Idea of the Beautiful. Diotima (205A1-206A13)[9] clearly means that the object of love is happiness created by being in possession of the Good forever. But for Diotima the Good is a selfish good; one's own good is the acquisition of immortality by reproducing oneself through the idea of the Beautiful.

Kelson[10] claims that Diotima presupposes the Good and the Beautiful to be identical. He may be oversimplifying, but he is on the right track in realizing that if Diotima's *eros* leads to Platonic Ideas, it leads to a perversion of what we know to be the concept of Platonic Ideas. Of course, this may conflate what should perhaps remain two distinct questions: whether Diotima's "Absolute Beauty" is a Platonic Idea *at all*, and whether it is specifically identical with the Form of the Good as described in the *Republic* 472-478. Moreover, Diotima's language in describing Beauty is enormously Parmenidean in details and in tone.[11] Neumann would agree with Kelson, and Rosen appears to move towards the view that if Diotima's *eros* leads to the Platonic Ideas, it leads to a somewhat unfamiliar concept of the Ideas. First, Neumann:[12]

> Although, or perhaps because, Diotima's sophistical *eros* feels no need for union, even with the idea of beauty itself, it does not involve a rejection of the independent existence of the ideas. The idea of the beautiful has an existence separate from that of the lover who needs it as a means. To him absolute beauty is no more than a tool, if a most valuable one. In this sense, he values his mortal self and its fame over the loftiest objects of knowledge. Diotima's mortality is not as sad for her, as some have supposed. This would, of course, not be true, if Diotima regarded the good as an idea transcending her individual self. In that case, happiness would

mean union with the universal good, if the possession of this absolute is happiness. Since one is most oneself when happy, a man would become what he truly is by subordinating himself to the absolute good. This idealistic train of thought arises from the concept of the good as an ideal, *a notion alien to what one has rightly described as Diotima's "Ruhmbergierde."*

Rosen appears to change his opinion as to whether Diotima's concept of *eros* leads to the Platonic Ideas:[13]

Diotima's description of beauty does not presuppose the theory of Ideas, but may be understood as part of the preparation for its *subsequent development* by Socrates. ... [There is nothing in Diotima's] description of beauty in itself which renders it in a realm altogether separate from its appearances to man. Its separateness is rather as a unique form, visible not in something else, but by virtue of those instances which dwell within it.... Even if it is true that Plato was in possession of [the theory of ideas at the time he wrote the *Symposium,*] it is certainly excluded from the *Symposium.*

For Diotima, then, not only isn't the Good and Idea, but her concept of Beauty is an idea at the level of appearances, not at the level of Platonic Ideas or Forms.

2. *Diotima's Concept of Immortality*

According to Grote:[14]

... in the *Symposium*, the soul can only reach immortality in a metaphysical sense by its prolific operation ... by leaving a name and a reputation to survive it....

But how does one do this? If one is to leave more than just a name and a reputation, if one is to give birth to ideas, to virtue in others, one must first know one's own soul and give birth, so to speak, to oneself. What kind of concept of self-identity does Diotima adopt?

a) *Immortality and Personal Identity*

In his "Love, Self and Plato's *Symposium*," Martin Warner takes up D.W. Hamlyn's argument that "it is possible to be loved full-stop," i.e., without there being anything that the love is for, or on account of. Warner notes that it would be impossible for Diotima to agree with Hamlyn:[15]

> Diotima is made to integrate into her account of love an analysis of what it is for a human being to persist through time, according to which there is no more to a person that his qualities.... Diotima holds that the continued existence of an organism is constituted by the replacement of what is worn out by something which resembles it; hence we may be said to be immortal in our children and other offspring.

The issue is familiar to those who have considered the basic theories of personal identity. If we have a concept of personal identity such as that which Plato offers[16] in the *Phaedo* (115c-d), the *Theatetus* (154b-157c) and in *Alcibiades I* (129b-130c), namely that there is something essentially "me" that underlies all the potentially changeable qualities and attributes that I have, we can explain that I am now the same person I was when I was a child. The fact that every quality or attribute I can identify with my younger self has changed does not mean that I am a different person from my young self in the same way that I am a different person from my younger sister. I may, of course, have a different personality than I had as a child, but that is not the same thing as being two different people.

If we identify "being the same person" with "some being's remaining alive," we might be begging the question when we ask, as Diotima would, whether "I" can become complete by becoming immortal even if this were to require "my" death. Diotima would answer "yes" to this question, although she might clarify that we should distinguish between becoming immortal and having proof of immortality. According to Diotima, I become immortal, not because some part of me (such as my soul, my psyche or my body) is immortal, but because I generate an offspring of my soul. My immortality is proven when my soul lives on after the death of

my body through the regeneration of its qualities in my beloved.
Warner notes:[17]

> But if this is so, then in talking of the human person we are
> not picking out an underlying substance, but a set of over-
> lapping similarities and continuities through time; the chang-
> ing mental and physical qualities of which Diotima speaks.
> And this raises the question of why we should pick out some
> such likenesses and continuities rather than others to consti-
> tute a pivotal concept like 'person'.... Diotima, then, needs
> to be taken seriously in her account of the identity of the
> person; on her account there is no underlying metaphysical
> "self," but rather a collection of qualities. This at once
> legitimizes her extensions of the notion of "immortality,"
> and her notion of love's being properly of qualities.
> ...
> If there is no more to the person than his qualities, then in
> loving a person we are loving (some at least of) his qualities.
> But if this is so, it immediately becomes appropriate to ask
> questions about the worth of those qualities.... Thus it
> becomes legitimate to claim that our love should be propor-
> tioned to the worth of the qualities loved, and that we should
> love those properties that are worthy of love wherever they
> are instantiated; thus the move to the more "impersonal"
> stages of Diotima's account of love is difficult to block.
>   Further, if the highest kind of concern we can have for
> others is of this sort, then the love in question is liable to be
> either linked with desire for the worthy qualities ... or else
> purely contemplative (as it comes close to being at the final
> stage of Diotima's spiritual journey)....

b) *Immortality and the Doctrine of Recollection*

Plato connects the theory of the immortality of the soul with his
doctrine of the recollection of ideas. The most famous example of
this is Socrates' coaching the slave boy in the *Meno* to recollect
laws of geometry that his soul learned in a previous existence.[18]
The connection between the theory of the immortality of the soul
and the doctrine of the recollection of ideas is also established in

the *Phaedo*,[19] and the *Phaedrus*.[20] Not only is Diotima's psyche incapable of recollection of the sort developed by Plato's doctrine (it does, however, "forget") it is not immortal at all. For Diotima, a person can achieve immortality of a very un-Platonic kind; the soul, however, does not achieve immortality at all. Diotima's "immortality" is metaphorical, not metaphysical.

c) *Immortality and the Transmigration of Souls*

Although Diotima holds that the desire for immortality leads a person to strive to generate an offspring of the psyche, this offspring is always human, never animal. Hence, the soul of a person who lacks the virtue to generate an offspring of the soul does not follow the path of Plato's unvirtuous man and become reincarnated as a woman or as an animal.[21] Moreover, Diotima is noncommittal on the origins of the human psyche, but her portrayal of it indicates that individuals develop certain qualities in their souls which become features of them as a person. A person can become immortal by reconstituting in someone else (the beloved) the complex qualities that have come to constitute that person's soul. Diotima's soul is regenerated; it is not, as is Plato's soul, reincarnated. The Platonic soul is eternal and transmigratory. Diotima's soul is markedly non-Platonic: it is not eternal – if you fail to generate an offspring of your soul, it presumably ceases to exist when your body dies and you fail to achieve immortality. Diotima's soul is also not transmigratory. It can be metaphysically unique to the lover (if not to the beloved) who develops the specific cluster of *qualities* which are then reproduced in the beloved. There is no evidence that Diotima would share Plato's view that a person's soul can have transmigrated from some other, deceased person or animal. For this reason Diotima's concept of the soul may have feminist implications: the soul of a woman cannot be construed either as the transmigrated or as the reproduced soul of a man of inferior virtue. And while she does not consider reproduction of the (male) lover's qualities in the soul of a (female) beloved, there is nothing in her theory of immortality which precludes this. She does, however, assume that male-female reproduction is limited to physical reproduction, while not considering whether female-female reproduction of the soul is possible.

3. *The Independence of Eros from Reason*

In the *Republic* Plato represents Socrates as someone who is
convinced that *eros* is not directed toward the good unless reason
and spiritedness (*thumos*) somehow direct *eros* that way. According to Socrates the nature of *eros* is a compulsive craving for the
lover[22] akin to the thirsty man's parched craving for water; it is
a craving for drink *simpliciter* and not for that which is good to
drink. In the *Phaedrus* we find Socrates portraying *eros* as he
portrayed it in the *Republic*: as a "flood of passion" which gives
the lover a vivid recollection of the Form of Beauty which cannot
be attained unless the "higher elements of the mind" guide the
lover "into the ordered rule of the philosophical life."[23]

But in the *Symposium*, where Socrates repeats what he identifies as Diotima's concept of *eros*, we find reason subordinated to
the instinct of *eros*. According to Diotima the instinct for *eros* (for
immortality and for reproduction) exists independently of reason.
For Diotima, reason only serves the ends of *eros*: reason aids the
lover in living the erotic life. Diotima's position can be distinguished from the Socratic position in the *Republic* where *eros* aids
the lover in living the philosophical life so that the lover may
experience a recollection of the Form of Beauty.[24] Diotima claims
instead that the end of *eros* is given by an innate, natural pur-
posiveness, an instinct. *Eros* aims at immortality naturally; it
doesn't require reason to identify or to select its goal. *Eros* can use
reason to achieve immortality, but unlike the Platonic *eros*,
Diotima's *eros* does not use reason for the sake of perfecting
reason, attaining wisdom, knowing truth, or knowing the Form of
Beauty. Rather, Diotima's *eros* uses reason for a goal that is not
reason's own: generating an offspring of the soul.

4. *Summary*

In this part I have discussed several aspects of Diotima's philosophy that are markedly different from and in some cases inconsistent with several famous Platonic and/or Socratic positions. Her
concept of the good appears not to function as a Platonic Idea.
Moreover, her concept of the good is of a selfish good: one's good
is identified as the acquisition of immortality by reproducing

oneself through the idea of the Beautiful. But even the idea of the Beautiful is not a Platonic Idea; it is an idea at the level of appearances not at the level of Platonic Forms.

Diotima's concept of immortality differs vastly from that offered by Plato through Socrates. The soul or psyche is not itself immortal, yet an individual can achieve the closest thing to the real kind of immortality described in the *Meno, Phaedrus, Phaedo, Timeaus* (and elsewhere) by generating an offspring of the soul. This position commits Diotima to a very non-Platonic concept of personal identity. Whereas Plato's *Phaedo, Theatetus*, and *Alcibiades I* develop Plato's theory that there is something that is essentially "me" that is more than just the sum of all my qualities and attributes, Diotima has a theory of personal identity that in some ways resembles that developed in recent decades by Derek Parfit. For Diotima there is no more to a person than his or her qualities. I can therefore be immortal and continue to "exist" so long as my qualities survive. And my qualities survive only if I generate an offspring of *my* psyche. Since the Diotiman soul is not immortal, her position is inconsistent with Plato's positions on recollection and transmigration. This makes hers a more feminist conception of the soul: it is unique to each lover, consequently the soul of a woman cannot be construed in Plato's sense as the transmigrated soul of a man of inferior virtue. A woman's soul is not a degenerated soul halfway to becoming the soul of a beast.

Diotima's *eros* also differs from Plato's *eros* with respect to its relation to reason. Diotima subordinates reason to the instinct of *eros*: *eros* neither needs reason to identify or select its goal, nor does it need reason for the sake of reason itself. Diotima differs from Plato with respect to many of his key concepts and doctrines: the concept of the good, the concept of immortality, the theory of personal identity, the doctrine of ideas, the doctrine of transmigration of souls, and the role of reason. Plato scholars can usually find inconsistencies in Plato's thought on an issue from one dialogue to another. But where is it the case that many marked inconsistencies respecting important central concepts can be found between one dialogue and all or most of the rest of his dialogues? Yet Diotima differs from Plato on many issues. This raises a serious problem for the tradition that claims that Diotima was a fictitious creation of Plato's and not a historical person. I turn now to an examination of the truth of that traditional claim.

II. THE TRADITION OF DIOTIMA AS A FICTITIOUS CHARACTER

The question of Diotima's historicity cannot be adequately examined outside the context of her speech in the *Symposium*. I have already examined some of her ideas and contrasted them to the positions maintained by Plato in his other dialogues. In this section I want to examine some of the claims that have been made to the effect that Diotima is not a historical person. While the historicity of Diotima cannot be proved beyond a shadow of a doubt, we can examine the arguments on both sides of that issue and determine which argument is more plausible.

The major arguments in favor of considering Diotima not to be a historical person who held the views Socrates attributes to her are:

A. It is out of character for Plato to cast a woman in so central a role as Diotima is cast, Aspasia's role in the *Menexenus* notwithstanding. Plato is just "feminizing" philosophy.

B. Socrates cannot seriously be considered to have learned anything from a woman. Socrates is being sarcastic. The Diotima position belongs to the historical Socrates.

C. The *Symposium* should be viewed as an example of Plato's literary talents as a novelist; the Diotiman position is a Platonic position in disguise. It belongs to the historical Plato or to the Platonic character "Socrates."

D. No other mention of Diotima is to be found in any ancient sources except in reference to the *Symposium* itself.

1. *The "Plato is Feminizing Philosophy" Argument*

Certainly it is unusual and unexpected to find a woman cast by Plato as a philosopher. With the exceptions of Diotima and Aspasia, women have not appeared as philosophers in the Platonic dialogues, although Lasthenia of Mantinea and Axiothea of Philesia are known to have been Plato's students. According to this argument, Diotima represents Plato's feminization of philosophy. This argument involves several claims, including the claim that Diotima (and Aspasia) represent the "womanish aspects of philosophy."[25] Rosen characterizes Diotima and Aspasia as representing:[26]

... the domain of the political-religious [which] is essentially that of peace, associated with the womanly arts of child-rearing, housekeeping, weaving and the like.

Rosen treats Diotima and Aspasia as masculine women. The suggestion is that Plato gave them masculine characteristics to let his reader know that his characterization of them as philosophers was intentionally misleading.[27] Diotima's *bona fides* are further challenged; she is compared to someone whose homosexuality is not the product of a philosophic search for beauty, but whose sexual orientation is itself ambiguous because her philosophic prowess and spiritual authority is downright un-ladylike:[28]

Instead of a womanly man [Agathon], we are presented with a masculine woman, who dominates Socrates, prefers children of the psyche to those of the body, and herself aspires to synoptic vision....

2. The "Socratic Wit" Argument

This argument suggests that if Diotima cannot successfully be considered a fictitious creation of Plato, perhaps she is a fictitious creation of Socrates. According to this argument we must understand the appearance of Diotima as another example of the famous Socratic wit. Socrates' characterization of Diotima as a priestess, and his mention of her in connection with forestalling the plague at Athens by ten years, must be understood as an attempt to establish her *bona fides* in much the same way he attempts to establish Aspasia's credentials in the *Menexenus*. The "Socratic Wit" argument holds that the very need to establish Diotima's credentials should serve as a clue that she is not at all what those credentials represent her to be. Instead, she has been woven *cum dossier* out of Socratic whole cloth. According to this argument, Socrates here is the supreme ironist, representing through Diotima the views on love that Socrates held as a young man. He portrays her as a priestess, giving a ring of authority to the views of the young Socrates. This permits the mature Socrates to change his views on the nature of erotic love while preserving his customary modesty and humility about the authoritativeness of his earlier views because he attributes those earlier views to someone else.

If we take the "Socratic Wit" argument seriously, then we have to account for the views attributed to Diotima. If they do not represent Diotima's views, whose views are they? The most likely responses — that they are either the views of Plato/ "Socrates" or the views of the historical Socrates (and Plato's dialogues do portray the historical Socrates) — are both susceptible to the Thesis A/Thesis B controversy discussed below. And to resolve the controversy we must examine the dramatic and compositional chronology of the various dialogues in which Plato or Socrates takes a position on an issue inconsistent with that taken by Diotima in the *Symposium*.

3. *The "Plato as Novelist" Argument*

According to this argument, the *Symposium* should be viewed as an example of Plato's literary, as well as philosophic talents. M.M. Bakhtin[29] suggests that the *Symposium* is Plato's attempt to beat Aristophanes at his genre, literature, and to beat Pausanias and Phaedrus in their genre, rhetoric. According to Bakhtin, the *Symposium* is a kind of proto-novel, an opinion shared by Gold[30] and to a lesser extent by Erde.[31] The *Symposium* demonstrates that philosophy can be all that rhetoric and literature are: comedy, satire, after-dinner speeches, historical reconstruction, literary criticism, as well as prose, poetry, song, and rhyme. On the other hand, the *Symposium* can also be seen as Plato's use of his own literary convention — philosophic, or, rather Socratic, dialogue — in a way that took revenge on Aristophanes' merciless treatment of philosophers in general and Socrates in particular in the *Clouds*.

In his *Plato*, Paul Friedlander states:[32]

> There is little doubt that the essential features of Diotima are a creation of the platonic Socrates — the highest embodiment, as it were, of the more or less vague "somebody" whom he frequently posits playfully in conversation or debate as another person in order to conceal himself ironically.

We also have it on the authority of John P. Anton:[33]

> ... [that] the experience and the doctrines for which [Dio-tima] stands belong to the Platonic Socrates, is too obvious a point to require further discussion.

While Friedlander cites irony as the reason for his opinion that Diotima was not a historical person and Anton invokes a claim so "obvious" as not to require argument, Bury hypothesizes that good manners may have required Socrates to invent a person to whom his own views could be attributed:[34]

> Socrates begins by exposing the ignorance of Agathon; next he makes the amend honorable by explaining that he had formerly shared that ignorance until instructed by Diotima.

Bury,[35] Levinson,[36] Rosen,[37] and Anton[38] all suggest that Plato wrote the *Symposium* in such a way that Socrates' and Diotima's concept of *eros* are identical. Rosen characterizes Diotima as Plato's personification of an earlier erotic stage of development of his character, "Socrates."[39] According to Rosen, we are to view Plato as an author plotting out a great many dialogues and intending to make his beloved teacher Socrates the main character in each. Like any good serialist Plato knows that it is not enough that the dialogues each constitute an individual philosophic treatise. Each must show the development not only of Plato's thought, but of Socrates'. To accomplish this, Plato inserts a number of historical "clues" into the texts of his dialogues. Among other things, these clues show Socrates at his pre-Diotiman, Diotiman, and post-Diotiman stages of erotic development. And, what is more, these "clues" show not only aspects of Socrates' own development as a philosopher, but also aspects of his development as a personality created by Plato. That is to say, Plato uses the dialogues as a vehicle for exhibiting his own development as a Socratic philosopher, and as a vehicle for exhibiting the development of the character "Socrates" as both a philosopher and an individual.

Referring not only to the "mythical" Diotima but to the "mythical" Socrates, John Anton notes:[40]

It is a safe assumption to make here that Socrates not only agreed with what he heard but also that he made the soul-shaking decision to conduct his life accordingly.

Anton denies that Diotima is the author of the speech Plato attributes to her. In his view Diotima is nothing more than Plato's clever literary device. Anton[41] appears to accept the opinion of Sykoutris that there were "erotic mysteries" into which Socrates was "initiated." But he resists the conclusion that it was Diotima who initiated Socrates and suggests that the initiation may have taken the form of Socrates' self-revelation. Anton then argues that Socrates learned erotic philosophy from Diotima, who, perhaps, had prophetic reservations about whether Socrates could successfully implement her teachings.

According to Anton, Socrates tried for nearly 25 years, from 440-415/6, to implement Diotima's teachings and failed not only in becoming the beloved of Alcibiades (whom he knew by 433 when Alcibiades was at the age of puberty),[42] but failed also in making a philosopher out of that rhetorician. Socrates' physical attraction for Alcibiades prevented him from seeking a more suitable lover, i.e., one whom (like Plato?) he could transform into a philosopher. Socrates' failure to overcome and transcend his sexual desires for Alcibiades represented his failure to be able to live up to Diotima's teachings. Anton conjectures that Plato (and I daresay, other followers of Socrates) knew all of this and, therefore, structured the dramatic rendering of the story of Agathon's symposium in an ambiguous manner so that Socreates' interpretation of Diotima's philosophy could be preserved for history without tarnishing Socrates' image. Anton says:[43]

> Diotima succeeded in teaching Socrates the art of erotics by putting him on the right path of eros, but when his turn came to do the same for Alcibiades he produced no similar results, despite all their meetings, exchanges and apparent mutuality of concern. Did Socrates know he was going to lose?
> ... What kept him going for so long a period? There can be only one answer to all these questions. Socrates must have felt a deeply strong attraction to think he could win Alcibiades over to philosophy. Socrates' struggle to change his role

from lover to beloved must have been at once agonising and tormenting. He must have suspected the dangers lying behind every turn of the adventure and yet he kept on trying....

[T]he secret of the *Symposium* is no other than *a masterfully covert* effort to explain Socrates' failure without comprising the erotic wisdom put in his charge.

Anton assumes that what Plato represents as "Diotima's" philosophy really is Socrates' philosophy of *eros*, but since Socrates' failure with Alcibiades is well known, Plato could preserve his mentor's image by fictionalizing the existence of Diotima. Socrates would thereby be saved from having his failure to live his own philosophy known to all posterity.

It has been suggested[44] that the various speeches given by the symposiasts should be understood as Plato's attempt to set out a variety of conceptions of the nature of *eros*. Each conception of *eros* elaborated in the *Symposium* ought to be understood as representative of one way in which people really do conceive of *eros*. No one of these various perspectives are "right" or "wrong" from an objective standpoint (presumably Plato's), yet there is something appropriate about each of the concepts. *Eros* is not one or the other conception (and hence not Diotima's), but is some combination of these conceptions (and hence somewhat Diotima's, somewhat Alcibiades', etc.). What the "right" conception is varies from person to person.

Under this view it is wrong to consider Diotima's position as Plato's because his own position is never stated. Plato simply leaves us to cogitate about this enigmatic dialogue and to come to the conclusion that what *eros* consists in varies from person to person and might, for any particular individual, consist in some combination of the positions offered by the symposiasts. The "Variety-Pack" argument leaves open the question whether Diotima is the originator of the Diotiman concept of *eros* or whether the character "Diotima" functions as historian of a popular concept. Given Plato's claim at the beginning of the *Symposium* that what he has written is Apollodorus' report of Aristodemus' account of Socrates' recollection of a conversation held 25 or so years earlier, it is clear that we may not assume that (a historical) Diotima's arguments would have been perfectly transcribed. For this reason, even if Plato were functioning merely as Diotima's historian, we should expect the Diotiman speech to have been heavily seasoned by him, and perhaps by Socrates, Apollodorus, and Aristodemus. If Plato presented a popular view of *eros* as Diotima's own view, then it is equally plausible to attribute that view to a historical Diotima, or to some other source. Therefore the "Variety-Pack" argument is inconclusive respecting the historicity issue.

4. *The "No Ancient Evidence" Argument*

According to this argument, if Diotima were a real person she would not be completely unknown to contemporaries and to students of Plato. She is nowhere mentioned in the Platonic-era writings except in the *Symposium*. There is no evidence that she existed or that anyone other than Plato (if we assume him not to be fictionalizing her) knew of her. Again, it might be claimed that a priestess known by Socrates to have been responsible for delaying a plague ten years would be famous on that account alone! Yet mentions of the plague include no record of her priestly intercession. This argument asks whether the god-fearing, hero-worshipping Athenians could have failed to commemorate such intercession. Why doesn't Thucydides, who was 20 in 440 B.C., mention her in his *History of the Peloponnesian Wars*? Why is she not mentioned in Xenophon's *Symposium*, or in any of Aristophanes' works?

5. *Objections to Arguments*

In this section I have examined several of the traditional arguments in support of the position that Diotima was not an historic person. We saw that there were many variations on the traditional argument that Diotima's views should not be ascribed to a historical woman, but rather to Socrates or to Plato. One feature of the traditional argument that Diotima is a fictitious character is the claim that Diotima is Plato's way of exemplifying the "feminine" qualities of philosophy. In a female character, these qualities include passivity, beauty, a non-philosophic lesbianism and/or sexual ambiguity. Diotima is at once earth-mother, priestly mediator between men and gods, and Socrates' dominatrix. One version of this argument is that Diotima stands for the character "Socrates" who, by Plato's authorial invention conceals himself in the guise of a priestess for ironic effect or because good manners require it.

The "Socratic Wit" version of the traditional argument is also not without its merits. Socrates was famous for his sarcasm and irony. Nevertheless, his references to Diotima are rather specific. She is identified as a priestess, as a Mantinean, and as the person responsible for postponing a deadly plague – one that counted among its victims the famous Pericles (who died) and the almost equally famous historian Thucydides (who recovered). But the "Socratic Wit" argument fails to account for the total absence of audience reaction to this piece of allegedly superb irony. No one present catches on. No one laughs. No one doubts him. Indeed, the reaction is precisely what would be expected to a report that everyone recognizes and accepts as completely factual: polite attentiveness.

A.E. Taylor claims[45] that Plato's dialogues give a careful reader access to a biography of his beloved mentor, the historical Socrates. According to Taylor, Plato would never falsify any important detail about Socrates. If Rosen is correct, and if "the teaching of Diotima is not the final stage of Socrates' teaching as presented in the corpus of Platonic dialogues," then we should be able to arrange the dialogues chronologically according to Socrates' age in each and trace the steady development of his views on the nature of erotic love. Specifically, we should see him progress beyond the Diotiman stage.

Anton's clever deduction of the nature of the "secret" of the *Symposium* suggests two theses concerning the historicity of Diotima. Thesis A claims that Diotima's theory is either Socrates' or Plato's own theory. Thesis B claims that the views that Socrates attributes to Diotima are representative of her own views. Proponents of Thesis A characterize the Socratic dialogues either as a chronicle of the life of the historic Socrates, or as a chronicle of the development of Plato's own thought, or as some combination of the two. In the first case, proponents of Thesis A should be able to look at other biographical Socratic dialogues (*Phaedo, Apology, Crito*), determine Socrates' age at the dramatic date of the dialogues and order them chronologically according to Socrates' age in each. The chronology will enable proponents of Thesis A to compare the positions taken by Socrates on some of the central concepts and theories discussed by Diotima to the positions that Plato represents the historical Socrates to have taken. Proponents of Thesis A should be wary if the chronological arrangement of the dialogues shows Socrates to have vacillated wildly on the issues at hand:

— whether Diotima's concept of absolute Beauty is an idea on the level of Platonic Forms or an idea on the level of appearances
— whether Diotima's concept of immortality is that of an immortal soul which transmigrates and which is based on a Platonic concept of personal identity
— whether Diotima's *eros* bears the same relationship to reason as does Plato's concept of *eros*.

Alternatively, if proponents of Thesis A want to claim that Diotima represents Plato's views (i.e. the views of the Platonic character "Socrates"), they should be able to do so without needing also to claim either, (1) that Plato would attribute to "Socrates" views that are inconsistent with views the historical Socrates is known to have held; or (2) that Plato held inconsistent views on the issues mentioned above. If either claim is essential for Thesis A to be sustained, then Thesis A is tantamount to a claim that many of Socrates' and/or Plato's most important philosophical doctrines were held inconsistently by them. In this case, Thesis B would offer a less controversial answer to the question whether Diotima is a thinly-veiled Socrates or "Socrates"/Plato.

Thesis B claims that the views Socrates attributes to Diotima are in fact representative of Diotima's own views and are not the views of either the historical Socrates or of the Platonic character "Socrates." Thesis B is less plausible than Thesis A if its proponents are not able to show that there are irreconcilable differences between Diotiman and Platonic/Socratic philosophy — differences that cannot be reconciled by alleging that Plato's/Socrates' position on the relevant issues changed over time from the "Diotiman" to what we now know as the "Platonic" or "Socratic." Proponents of Thesis B must be able to show either, (a) that Socrates, both before and after the dramatic dates of the *Symposium*, expounded positions that are incompatible with those presented as Diotiman; or (b) that the dialogues in which Plato maintains theories that are incompatible with the Diotiman theories were composed so close to the composition date of the *Symposium* as to involve Plato in serious doctrinal inconsistencies if the Diotiman positions are presumed to be Platonic.

Even if proponents of Thesis B can demonstrate the appropriate inconsistencies between the relevant Diotiman and Platonic/ Socratic theories, the "lack of ancient evidence" argument merits consideration. A critic of this argument might ask whether we would think much of Socrates as a philosopher if the *Clouds* were the only surviving contemporaneous record of information about him. Clearly, we must recognize a historiographic fact: that the form the available evidence takes and how extensive or how profuse it is, has in part determined what it has been taken to be evidence of. Who knows what accidents may have caused the destruction of other evidence? That the *Symposium* provides the sole surviving evidence of Diotima's existence does not at all support the claim that the *Symposium* is a historical novel whose central character is a fictitious person. I now turn to an examination of the evidence in support of the claim that Diotima was a historical person.

III. THE HISTORICAL DIOTIMA

In this section, I will (1) introduce evidence from Platonic dialogues other than the *Symposium* that support the plausibility of a Socrates-Diotima encounter; (2) review the archeological evidence in support of the historicity of Diotima; (3) present some of the oldest textual support for that claim; and (4) present some modern opinions on the historicity of Diotima.

1. *Evidence from Plato*

Would Socrates seek the advice of a woman who was a priestess and a philosopher? If Plato can be taken to be a reasonably reliable source of information about the historical Socrates, we know that Socrates was a deeply religious person with a long history of listening to his personal "daemon" and consulting with priestesses.[46] In *Apology* 21a Socrates relates Chaerephon's inquiry of the priestess at Delphi whether anyone was wiser than Socrates. Taylor[47] dates this event to "before the beginning of the Peloponnesian war, i.e., when Socrates was under 40." Since Socrates introduces the story of Chaerephon's question to the Delphic priestess as evidence at his trial, we can safely assume that Socrates had no reservations about consulting priestesses and even had faith in their teachings. Further, Chaerephon's consultation of the priestess of Delphi took place within ten years of the Socrates-Diotima encounter.

Socrates' habit of consulting priestesses is described by him in the *Meno* where he reports himself as having:[48]

> ... heard from men and women who understand the truths of religion ... priests and priestesses of the sort who make it their business to account for the functions which they perform.

Since it is clear that Socrates was a very religious person, a person who listened to his daemon and who consulted religious authorities, there is nothing unlikely about his having consulted with Diotima, a priestess from Mantinea. However, it should be noted that in two respects his conversation with Diotima is distinctly different from those reported with other religious authorities: Diotima's speech is "spoken like a sophist,"[49] and is much longer than those of other priests.[50] These differences are insufficient to prove that Diotima's speech is either a Socratic or a Platonic fabrication, for certainly Socrates' own reports of consulting with religious advisors show that there is nothing unlikely about his having had the conversation reported in the *Symposium*.

2. The Archeological Evidence

The ancient roll of Plato's *Symposium* is housed in the Oxford University Collection.[51] It is one of the oldest roll papyri surviving. In the Museo Nazionale di Napoli there is a small bronze relief which, according to classical archeologist Paolino Mingazzini, is an overlay for the wooden cover of the cassette or container that originally housed the roll of the *Symposium*.[52]

Otto Jahn, the noted classical numismat, describes the bas-relief:[53]

We see, in a simple scene, furnished only by a stool, a woman seated, dressed in a long tunic over which is thrown a cape that covers a portion of the lower body. The crown of her head is covered by a kind of headpiece that reveals only the front of her hairdo. The entire pose clearly shows that this woman is busy talking and that she is paying close attention to the object of her talk: she looks ahead, the head and the entire body leaning forward as she speaks: the right leg crossing the left, and on the right thigh leans the elbow of the right arm which is itself extended forward from the elbow; the hand ... making a gesture undoubtedly commensurate with the intensity of the discourse. We know that for the ancients, crossing the legs while seated is considered an indecent posture, especially in women; but when this pose is found on monuments of art they indicate a state of mind which, totally engrossed in what it is doing, forgets public manners. ... Such a gesture expresses the condition of a person who is totally self-absorbed either in sorrow ... in meditation ... or in the purely intellectual activity of getting one's thoughts in order. ... Thus, with no fear of error we can acknowledge that, in an animated discourse the object of which absorbs the entire attention of her mind, the woman in our bas-relief is addressing herself to the man in front of her.

He is standing, dressed in a simple cloak that is draped over his arms in such a way that one of his arms hangs down alongside his body while one end of his cloak is rolled around his left arm; the chest, shoulders and right arm are completely bare. ... His body leans heavily to the right, the weight placed mostly on the right leg which is slightly forwardly extended. His head is tilted to the right, [he is] bald headed, flat nosed, with eyes buried under a protuberant brow, thick lipped and has a long beard.

After contrasting the bronze with other bronzes and statuary of the Platonic era, and after describing the figure of Eros that appears between the female and male figures, Jahn concludes:[54]

> I believe in effect, that what we have here is Socrates, whose eyes and attention are fixed on the words of Diotima, who, in an animated discourse, teaches him the *nature of love* or, as she herself says, initiates him to the *mysteries of Eros*. And as they are engrossed in this "holy meditation," the god himself approaches them with the priestess' headcovering [a ceremonial garment used for religious rites] and the little ornamented box, symbols of initiation.

Paolino Mingazzini reports that a comparison of the male figure of the relief reveals that it is identical to two 4th century B.C. statues of Socrates, both of which were, Jahn suggests, modelled after the bronze statue of Socrates the Athenians commissioned Lysippus to create. While Eros is clearly depicted as a mythological creature with angel-like wings, in contrast, the portrayals of Socrates and Diotima are, Mingazzini and Jahn agree, lifelike. Although Mingazzini acknowledges that we do not know (independently of this evidence) whether there ever actually existed any such person as Diotima, or what her connection to Socrates may have been, he says that:[55]

> ... for those who have read the *Symposium*, she is undoubtedly a real person, resembling that portrayed in the bas-relief.

Moreover, he claims, the realistic portrayal of Socrates and Diotima on the bronze overlay to the cassette containing the *Symposium* must be considered in conjunction with the two surviving bas-relief bronzes that covered the sides of the box. These bronzes contain funerary imagery. The bronzes are archeologically dated to 340-330 B.C., so it is likely that the roll of the *Symposium* which was contained in the cassette was issued as a kind of commemorative edition, perhaps the centenary of the Diotima-Socrates meeting of 440 B.C. Since this commemorative edition would have appeared only 7-17 years after Plato's own death, at the time when Plato's nephew, Speusippus was head of the Academy, it is unlikely that the depiction of Diotima as a real, non-fictitious, non-mythological person would have been in error. Certainly Plato knew whether Diotima existed or not. And if Plato knew, how could his own students, who undoubtedly discussed her speech in the *Symposium* and helped prepare this and other editions of it, be mistaken as to Diotima's historicity?

With the discovery of the bronze, then, we have strong ancient evidence (albeit, not testimony) supporting the existence of the historical Diotima. With this evidence, Plato's own dialogue can provide further evidence of Diotima's existence. Indeed, as I show below, the question whether Diotima was a real or fictitious person was first raised at the end of the 15th century. The conclusion that she was a product of Plato's imagination has had the status of received doctrine ever since.

3. *The Written Testimony*

For half a millenium, there is no mention of Diotima in any of the popular literature and plays, nor in the scholarly histories, encyclopedias, or philosophical writings. Her teachings, her erotic philosophy, indeed all mention of her existence survive only in the recensions of Plato's *Symposium*. It is in the 2nd century A.D. before she is again mentioned — together with Thargelia and Aspasia — in Lucian's *The Eunuch*. While *The Eunuch* quickly builds into a comedy (perhaps even a farce), it opens with the matter-of-fact mention of Diotima, Thargelia, and Aspasia as evidence that even women were philosophers. They are mentioned in connection with a eunuch's appeal to Diocles to be permitted to have an "official" career as a philosophy teacher. The eunuch is considered an effeminate, unmanly man, who identifies with the women as he pleads with Diocles. He argues that since these women were known to be practicing (i.e., teaching) philosophers and not merely students of philosophy, he, the eunuch, the "womanly man," ought likewise to receive an official "seal of approval" as a philosophy teacher and be permitted to have students "committed" to him. Were it the case that Aspasia, Diotima, and Thargelia were jokingly referred to as philosophers, one would expect a satirist to capitalize on the joke and to suggest that women, and those like the eunuch, who were perceived to be womanly, were not capable of teaching philosophy. But this is not what happens. Instead the focus of the argument concerns whether a eunuch is an appropriate educator of pubescent young boys. There is no suggestion that Diotima, Thargelia, and Aspasia were anything but practicing philosophers. Indeed, Lucian in *The Portraits* names Diotima among the famous women whose "portraits" or biographical sketches are added to the collection of influential ancients. There is no suggestion that Diotima is known to be anything other than a long-deceased philosopher-priestess.

Other second century writers have given similarly straightforward accounts of Diotima without any suggestion that she is not a historical person. Aristides mentions her in his *Orations,*[56] as does the scholiast to Aristides.[57] Maximus of Tyre (Maximus Tyrius), *circa* 125-185 A.D., mentions Diotima three times.[58] Clement of Alexandria, who lived *circa* 150-213, also mentions her.[59] In the last half of the 4th century, Themistius (*circa* 317-388) mentions Diotima as the teacher of Socrates.[60] Indeed, as late as the 5th century we find Proclus (*circa* 410-485) referring three times to Diotima with no suggestion that he believed her to be anything other than a historical person.[61]

For almost nineteen hundred years, from the time Plato wrote the *Symposium* (perhaps as early as 388 B.C. – only the roughest estimates can be made of the dates Plato wrote his dialogues) to 1485 when Marsilio Ficino published his *Oratio Septima II*, nowhere is the suggestion found that Diotima was anything but a real person who had the conversation with Socrates that is recorded by Plato. For nearly nineteen centuries Diotima was, as the archeological evidence supports, considered a historical person. Ficino's remark on the absurdity of thinking a woman a philosopher achieved and retained the status of received doctrine for the next 500 years. Indeed, had some artisan not created what classical archeologists and numismats agree is a realistic portrayal of Diotima on the 4th century, B.C. equivalent of a book-jacket, Diotima might still be considered a fictitious creation of Plato. Although the archeological evidence does not *prove* that Diotima really existed, it shows why the burden of proof should rest on those who, almost two milennia later, and on the basis of no evidence whatsoever, *assumed* that she did not.

2. *Two Modern Opinions on the Historicity of Diotima*

In this section I consider the views of A.E. Taylor, the historian of philosophy, and Walther Kranz, the eminent classical philologist.

a) *A.E. Taylor on Diotima.* Taylor[62] says:

> ... I cannot agree with many modern scholars in regarding Diotima of Mantinea as a fictitious personage; still less in looking for fanciful reasons for giving the particular names Plato does to the prophetess and her place of origin. The introduction of purely fictitious named personages into a discourse seems to be a literary device unknown to Plato, ... and I do not believe that if he had invented Diotima he would have gone on to put into the mouth of Socrates the definite statement that she had delayed the pestilence of the early years of the Archidamian war for ten years by "offering sacrifice" at Athens. ... [T]he purpose of the reference to the presence of Diotima at Athens about 440 is manifestly not merely to account for Socrates' acquaintance with her, but to make the point that the mystical doctrine of the contemplative "ascent" of the soul, now to be set forth, was one which the philosopher's mind had been brooding over since his thirtieth year.

It should be noted that while Taylor considers Diotima to be a historical figure, he does not claim that the speech with which she is identified was literally a speech of the historical Diotima. In any event, Plato's *Symposium* is only alleged to be a fourth-hand report of her views reconstructed 25 years *post hoc*. However, Taylor does claim that the early Socratic dialogues contain Plato's substantially accurate biography of Socrates and the history of Socratic teachings. It is Taylor's view that "the information which he supplies about him is intended to be taken as historical fact."[63]

b) *Walther Kranz on Diotima.*[64] Kranz touches briefly on the question of Diotima's historicity in two articles: "Diotima"[65] and "Diotima von Mantinea."[66] In both articles he claims that there was, indeed, an historical person, Diotima. In "Diotima" he draws a parallel between Holderlin's character "Diotima" (from the Hyperion works) who was inspired by the real woman, and Plato's "Diotima" and her real-life model. Kranz offers several reasons for his view that there really was such a person.

First, Kranz notes that the masculine version of "Diotima" was a popular name then, so a real person may very well have been called "Diotima." The use of a real-sounding name makes her seem just as real as other characters named in the *Symposium*, all of whom are real people who would have valued being accurately portrayed. Second, Kranz reminds us that according to Plato, Diotima was a priestess from the Peleponnesos who received a government invitation to assist Athens in combatting the periodic outbreaks of plague that persisted for a decade preceeding the Peleponnesian War. Thucydides confirms that oracles spoke of the threat of war and disaster. In such circumstances a city-state might well have brought in a priestess from elsewhere. It is reasonable to suppose that a Mantinean priestess would be in Athens during the period. Socrates would have been a young man then.

Kranz' third argument is that Aischines, Xenophon, and Plato all say that Aspasia was a teacher of Socrates. Xenophon also describes Socrates speaking with the hetaera Theodote about the value of her life. It would have been perfectly natural for Socrates to have visited with Diotima during her stay in Athens. It should be noted, however, that Kranz believes that because so much time would have elapsed between the actual Diotima-Socrates encounter and the writing of the *Symposium*, the conversations recorded by Plato were entirely created by him.

IV. IN SUPPORT OF THESIS B

In Section I of this chapter I distinguished Diotima's philosophy from those of Socrates and Plato. I showed that it is debatable whether Diotima's concept of absolute Beauty functions as a Platonic Idea and suggested that her concept of Beauty may better be understood as an idea at the level of appearances instead of at the level of Forms. In addition we saw that her concept of immortality is not that of an immortal soul which transmigrates. Rather, her concept of immortality is that one becomes immortal through the process of generating one's own qualities in the beloved. One becomes immortal because one's qualities survive in the person of the beloved, and not because one's soul continues to live. Diotima's concept of personal identity is also different than Plato's concept of personal identity. We saw that Diotima's *eros,* although a rational and intellectual *eros,* does not bear the same relation to reason as does Plato's concept of *eros.* Diotima's *eros* uses reason instrumentally, for its own end, namely, the peculiar kind of immortality she outlines.

In Section II, I examined the Thesis A/Thesis B controversy. Thesis A claims that the philosophic positions attributed to Diotima ought to be understood as belonging either to (1) the Platonic character "Socrates," or (2) the historical Socrates. Thesis A is implausible unless it overcomes two related objections: first, that Socrates, both before and after the dramatic dates of the *Symposium*, expounded theories inconsistent with those presented as Diotima's; and second, that it is unlikely that Plato, when writing the dialogues, would attribute to Socrates positions inconsistent with those Socrates was known to have actually held. This second objection is relevant whether we consider the Socrates of the *Symposium* to have been the historical Socrates, or the Platonic character "Socrates." In the latter case this second objection is particularly compelling if the dialogues containing competing positions were written during the same period, because this would involve Plato in several serious and simultaneous doctrinal inconsistencies. Fortunately, the claim that Diotima stands for the historical Socrates or for the Platonic "Socrates" requires comparison with only one other dialogue, the *Phaedo*; however, it will be useful to consult additional dialogues.

1. *Immortality, Transmigration, and Personal Identity*

Because, according to Diotima's conception, the soul is not immortal, the question whether it transmigrates never arises. Diotima's lover wants only to leave behind (after death) a beloved who is an offspring of the lover's soul in the sense that the beloved develops the same qualities or virtues that the lover exemplifies. Not so with the historical Socrates. In the *Phaedo,*[67] Socrates maintains that the soul is immortal and transmigrates.[68] Perhaps

Socrates changed his mind on immortality and transmigration between the time of Agathon's symposium (418/15 B.C.) and the time of the *Phaedo* (399 B.C.)?

Taylor has controversially suggested that many of the other dialogues, including the *Timeaus, Meno*, and *Phaedrus*, contain more or less factual accounts of parts of Socrates' life. If Taylor is correct in assigning the *Timeaus'* dramatic date to 421 B.C., then Plato represents Socrates as having held the immortality and transmigration positions consistently from 421 B.C.[69] until the date of Agathon's symposium (418/15) when Socrates, disguising himself as the character "Diotima," abandons that position. However, he resumes it by 411/04, (Taylor's estimate of) the dramatic date of the *Phaedrus* (248 sq.) and maintains it through 404/2, the dramatic date of the *Meno* (81b-85b), and until his death in 399 as reported in the *Phaedo*. If Thesis A correctly claims that Diotima stands for the historic Socrates, then for most of his life Socrates held a view of the soul that was incompatible with the Diotiman view. Indeed, the Diotiman view represents a serious, temporary vacillation from the view of the soul as immortal and transmigrating; a view otherwise held by Socrates throughout his life.

We should note that it may well be unreasonable to treat each of the mentioned dialogues as wholly accurate biographies of Socrates. However, there is little doubt that the *Phaedo, Apology*, and *Crito* are biographical. Although there is much disagreement among Plato scholars about precisely when Plato wrote each of the dialogues, most authorities agree that the *Meno, Phaedo,* and *Symposium* were composed during the same period.[70] Since the Diotiman concept of the soul is incompatible with that of Socrates and of Plato (represented by the character "Socrates" in the *Meno*), proponents of Thesis A must account for Plato having *concurrently* attributed to Socrates and/or to himself incompatible positions on the nature of the soul. Clearly, the simpler, less controversial approach is to attribute the Diotiman position to the historical Diotima and the Socratic position to the historical Socrates or the Platonic character "Socrates."

The Socratic/Platonic concept of the soul involves a view of the person as an underlying "something" in which adheres the qualities that the person has. The Diotiman concept of personal identity is that a person is the sum of his or her qualities: that there is no essential "me" underlying my attributes. In the Diotiman view, the person is identical with the moral and intellectual qualities that he or she exemplifies. Consequently, according to Diotima the person achieves immortality by reproducing those qualities or "giving birth to an offspring of the soul." Since to my knowledge no scholar has suggested that Plato's theory of personal identity is attributed to Socrates, I will not examine whether the historic Socrates could have consistently held both the Diotiman and the Platonic concepts of personal identity. Rather, we should inquire whether the Diotiman concept can plausibly be accounted for by suggesting either that Plato abandoned his theory of personal identity before writing the *Symposium* or that he abandoned the Diotiman theory (assuming, as do proponents of Thesis A, that it is his own) after composing the *Symposium*.

The Platonic theory of personal identity is developed in the *Phaedo* (115 c-d), *Theatetus* (154b-157c), and elsewhere. Taylor, Ryle, and Brandwood agree (as do other Plato scholars) that the *Phaedo* and *Symposium* were composed at about the same time and that the *Theatetus* was composed at a later period. If the *Phaedo* and *Symposium* are of concurrent composition, it could not be the case that Plato abandoned his theory of personal identity before writing the *Symposium* or that misfit theory would not have been contemporaneously introduced in the *Phaedo*. Similarly, since the *Theatetus* is later than the *Symposium*, it could not be claimed that Plato maintained the Diotiman theory of personal identity after composing the *Symposium*. Proponents of Thesis A can either attribute a marked inconsistency to Plato concerning his theory of personal identity, or they can accept the simpler hypothesis (Thesis B) that the misfit theory is in fact Diotima's.

2. *Eros and Reason*

In Section I.3, I noted that in both the *Republic* (437e-439d) and the *Phaedrus* (254b-256b) Plato portrays *eros* as unable to achieve its goal unless directed by reason.[71] Similarly, in the *Phaedo* Socrates has a conversation with Simmias (68b-c) in which the former distinguishes lovers of wisdom from lovers of reputation and claims that true philosophers look forward to death as a vehicle for attaining true wisdom which exists only in the afterlife. Socrates contrasts "true philosophers" with those who, distressed at the prospect of dying, want to leave a reputation behind. Unlike the Platonic *eros*, Diotima's *eros* does not need reason to identify immortality as its goal because it naturally, instinctively aims at that goal. Diotima differs from both the "true philosophers" and the "lovers of reputation" described in the *Phaedo* in several additional ways. First, the goal of Diotima's lover is to leave behind a reputation of sorts: an offspring of the soul. The goal is *not* to attain wisdom. She also differs from the lover of reputation described in the *Phaedo* because her lover does not fear death since through death her lover *proves* that he has achieved her peculiar kind of immortality: an immortality of one's qualities, not of one's soul. Finally, since Diotima is not a lover of wisdom but a lover of immortality, she uses reason instrumentally for *eros'* own end.

Because this relationship of *eros* to reason has ramifications for Plato's theory of Ideas, we must consider the possibility that the Diotiman position is the position of Plato himself. Once again we can examine estimates of composition dates for the relevant dialogues and question the possibility that Plato merely changed his mind about the relationship of *eros* to reason. I have already noted a concensus that the *Phaedo* and *Symposium* were composed during the same period. If Thesis A is correct then Plato held both the Diotiman and the Platonic positions simultaneously: a significant doctrinal inconsistency. When Thesis A is viewed in the light of Ryle's claim[72] that the early books of the *Republic* were composed at about the same time as the *Symposium*, although under the title *Ideal State*, the criticism of doctrinal inconsistency is strengthened. Brandwood[73] holds that the *Republic* I-X *was* composed first in a group immediately following the *Phaedo/Symposium* group. His dating would fortify my criticism of doctrinal inconsistency. This claim is further strengthened when we consider that according to Ryle[74] the *Phaedrus* was composed about six years after the *Symposium* and *Phaedo* and that according to Brandwood (who estimates not dates but order of composition) the *Phaedrus* was the last work of a group which consisted of *Republic* I-X, *Parmenides*, *Theatetus*, and *Phaedrus*. If proponents of Thesis A are to be taken seriously, Plato held his view of the relationship of *eros* to reason throughout the early and middle periods of his writing career:[75] the misfit Diotiman position is merely an abberation of an otherwise consistent position. Clearly, the simpler hypothesis is: reject Thesis A and identify the "misfit" view as Diotima's.

3. *The Idea of Beauty*

In Section I.1, I noted that there was some controversy over whether Diotima's concept of Beauty functioned as a Platonic Idea on the level of Forms or as an Idea at the level of appearances. While many scholars assumed that Diotima's absolute beauty was a Platonic Form — an assumption which may account for the willingness of historians to consider Diotima to be Plato in disguise — on closer examination of her speech, nothing indicates a conception of beauty as anything separate from specific instances of it. This is consistent with her theory of personal identity: just as there is nothing essentially "me" underlying my qualities, there is no absolute "beauty" underlying specific instances of it. There are, of course, more perfectly beautiful *things*, but no absolute Beauty existing independently of those objects. This does not *preclude* her having a theory of Forms (and thus being Plato in disguise); rather we can only note the absence of such a theory. Nothing that Diotima says is inconsistent with the theory of Forms; nevertheless, such a theory is not in her speech.

Plato's general theory of Ideas was developed close to the composition date of the *Symposium* (*Phaedo, Republic*) or even earlier (*Protagoras* 360c),[76] but Plato is not involved in any inconsistency by failing to include his theory in Diotima's speech in the *Symposium*. Note how his theory of Ideas relies on his Doctrine of Recollection, and in turn on the Doctrine of the Immortality of Souls and the Doctrine of Transmigration. Note also the relationship of these doctrines to Plato's theory of personal identity. We see that Diotima *could not consistently hold* a Platonic theory of Ideas given her (incompatible) views on the immortality of the soul, transmigration, and personal identity. For these reasons, proponents of Thesis A could not consistently claim that Diotima is really Plato in disguise.

4. *Summary*

In this Section I have examined whether the Thesis A/Thesis B controversy could conceivably be resolved in favor of Thesis A by claiming that with respect to the issues, (a) immortality of the soul, (b) transmigration of the soul, (c) concept of personal identity, (d) relationship of *eros* to reason, and (e) beauty as an idea on the level of Platonic Forms, the Diotiman position represented that of either the historical or the Platonic Socrates. We saw that it was not possible to ascribe the Diotiman position to either Socrates or Plato without involving either or both in serious doctrinal inconsistencies. Moreover, it was shown that the inconsistencies could not be accounted for by claiming that either Socrates or Plato changed their views on these issues over time. When we also take the archeological and other ancient evidence into account, we realize the flimsiness of received opinion about Diotima.

NOTES

1. Grote, George, *Plato and the Other Companions of Socrates*, London: Murray (1867), p. 223.
2. Zeller, Eduard, *Plato and the Older Academy*, London (1888), p. 507.
3. Taylor, A.E., *Plato, the Man and his Work*, London: Methuen (1978 reprint), p. 231-232.
4. Rosen, Stanley, *Plato's Symposium*, New Haven: Yale University Press (1968), p. 199.
5. Cacoullos, Ann R., "The Doctrine of Eros in Plato," *Diotima* (Athens): 1(1973):84.
6. Neumann, Harry, "Diotima's Concept of Love," *American Journal of Philology*: 86: (1965):38.
7. *Ibid.*, 42.
8. *Ibid.*
9. All references to the *Symposium* are to the Michael Joyce translation, reprinted in Edith Hamilton and Huntington Cairns, eds., *Plato: Collected Dialogues*, Princeton: Princeton University Press, (1961).
10. Kelson, Hans, "Platonic Love," *American Imago*: April, 1942: 75, n.1.
11. I owe these observations to Professor Edward N. Lee.
12. *Op. cit.*, 47-48. Italics mine.
13. *Op. cit.*, 271-272.
14. *Op. cit.*, V. 3, p. 17-18.

15. Warner, Martin, "Love, Self and Plato's *Symposium*," *Philosophical Quarterly*, 29: (1979): 335-6.
16. All references to Platonic dialogues are to the Hamilton and Cairns edition, *op. cit.*
17. *Ibid.*, 337-339.
18. *Meno* 82b-85b.
19. 72e ff.
20. 248a ff.
21. *Timeaus*, 42c.
22. *Republic*, 437c-439d.
23. *Phaedrus*, 254-b-256b.
24. *Republic, loc. cit.*
25. Rosen, *op. cit.*, 224.
26. *Loc. cit.*
27. *Loc. cit.*
28. *Op. cit.*, 203.
29. Bakhtin, M.M., "Discourse in the Novel," *The Dialogic Imagination*, J.M. Holquist and C. Emerson, translators. Austin: University of Texas Press, (1980).
30. Gold, Barbara K., "A Question of Genre: Plato's *Symposium* as Novel," *MLN*: 95 (1980): 1353.
31. Erde, Edmund L., "Comedy and Tragedy and Philosophy in the *Symposium*: An Ethical Vision," *Southwestern Journal of Philosophy*: 7(1976): 161.
32. Friedlander, Paul, *Plato*, Vol. I, New York: Pantheon (1958): 148.
33. Anton, John P., "The Secret of Plato's *Symposium*," *Southern Journal of Philosophy*: XII: 3(1974): 278.
34. Bury, Robert, *The Symposium of Plato*, 2nd edition, Cambridge (1932), p. xxxix.
35. *Op. cit.*
36. Levinson, R.B., *In Defense of Plato*, Cambridge: Mass. (1953), p. 32.
37. *Op. cit.*
38. *Op. cit.*
39. Rosen, *op. cit.*, 221.
40. *Op. cit.*, 280.
41. *Op. cit.*, 281.
42. *Protagoras*, 309b.
43. Anton, *op. cit.*
44. This argument was suggested to me in part by Professor Edward N. Lee of the University of California, San Diego, in his paper "Eros and Integration: The Riddle of the *Symposium*," presented by him on October 21, 1983 at the University of Minnesota, and by personal communication with him.
45. Taylor, A.E., *Socrates*, Westport, CT: Greenwood Press (1975) reprint of 1951 edition.
46. *Apology*, 31d, 33c-d.

47. Taylor, A.E., *Plato's Biography of Socrates, op. cit.*, 26.
48. *Meno*, 81a-b.
49. 208c.
50. I wish to thank Professor Edward N. Lee for this observation.
51. As: P. Oxy 843.
52. Mingazzini, Paolino, "Su Duo Oggetti in Terracotta Raffiguranti Socrate," *La Parole del Passato: Rivista di Studi Antichi*, XXV: (1970): 351-358.
53. Jahn, Otto, "Socrate et Diôtime, Bas-Relief de Bronze," *Annales de l'Institut Archéologique*, XIII: (1841): 3-4.
54. *Op. cit.*, p. 9, italics in the original, translation and square brackets mine.
55. *Op. cit.*, 356, translation mine.
56. Aristides, *Orations*, Volume II, oration 46, p. 127 in Jahn, Otto, *Platonis Symposium*. Bonnae, 1875.
57. *Ibid.*, Volume III, p. 468.
58. Maximus Tyrius, *Dissertation*, XXIV.4; XXIV.7, and XXVII.4.
59. Clement of Alexandria, *Stromates*, VI, p. 755.
60. Themistius, *Orationes*, G. Downey, ed., Vol. I, p. 237, (165d).
61. Proclus, *Commentary on Plato's Timeaus*, p. 325; *Commentary on Plato's Republic*, p. 420, p. 421.
62. Taylor, A.E., *Plato, the Man and his Work, op. cit.*, 224.
63. Taylor, A.E., *Socrates, loc. cit.*
64. I wish to thank Linda L. McAlister, Ph.D. for translating the Kranz articles and preparing a report on them. This section is entirely based on that report. Professor McAlister is a member of the Project on the History of Women in Philosophy and author of two chapters of Volume IV of this series.
65. Kranz, Walther, "Diotima," *Die Antike* II, 313ff.
66. Kranz, Walther, "Diotima von Mantinea," *Hermes*, No. 61, p. 437ff.
67. 72ff.
68. 70c sq.
69. *Timeaus*, 41e sq., 90e sq.
70. See, for example, Taylor, *Plato, the Man and his Work, op. cit.*, Leonard Brandwood, *A Word Index to Plato*, Leeds: W.S. Maney & Son, Ltd. (1976), Gilbert Ryle, *Plato's Progress*. Cambridge: Cambridge University Press (1966).
71. In the *Republic Eros* is directed toward the Good, while in the *Phaedrus*, it is directed toward a recollection of the Form of Beauty.
72. *Op. cit.*
73. *Op. cit.*
74. *Op. cit.*
75. To my knowledge, this issue does not arise in the later writings.
76. Taylor, *op. cit.*, Brandwood, *op. cit.*

7. Julia Domna

BEATRICE H. ZEDLER

"The philosopher Julia," as she is called by a 3rd century historian, lived during the period which followed Marcus Aurelius the
Stoic and preceded Plotinus the Neoplatonist.[1] Though, so far as
we know, she did not write any philosophical works, she devoted
herself to the study of philosophy when her busy life as an empress permitted. Among those who have been called philosophers
she is, with the possible exception of Marcus Aurelius, unique in
having her name on more than three hundred and fifty different
varieties of coins and on more than one hundred and eighty public
buildings or statues and in being officially declared a divinity.[2]

We shall first look at the life-story of this eminent woman and
then consider why she was called a philosopher.

I. JULIA DOMNA'S BIOGRAPHY

Julia Domna was born in 170 A.D. in Emesa, a town on the river
Orontes in Syria, near the site of the modern city of Homs. Her
personal name, *Domna*, which might seem to suggest the Latin
word *domina*, meaning "lady," is not derived from the Latin, but
may be an Aramaic name for *Martha*. Though we shall use the
name, *Julia*, to refer to her, *Julia* was her surname. Her father,
Julius Bassianus, was the high priest of the temple of Elagabal, the
sun-god, in Emesa, an ancient religious center.[3]

There is no record of Julia's early education, but it is probable
that she may have met some of the most eminent and cultivated
pilgrims as guests in her father's house and learned from their
conversations. It is likely that Septimius Severus made her ac-

A History of Women Philosophers / Volume 1, ed. by Mary Ellen Waithe
© *Martinus Nijhoff Publishers, Dordrecht – Printed in the Netherlands*

quaintance when he was stationed in Syria as the commander of a Roman legion.[4] She was only about nine or ten years old at the time, but several years later, after the death of his first wife, he married Julia.

Lucius Septimius Severus had been born in 145 or 146 A.D. in Leptis Magna (which today is Lebda) on the north coast of Africa. After learning Greek and Latin at school he went to Rome to study law. Under the Emperor Marcus Aurelius he was appointed to a succession of posts in Spain, Sardinia, Africa, and Syria. In 186, in the reign of Commodus, he was governor of Gallia Lugdunensis (central France).[5]

It was at this time that he sought Julia Domna as his wife. When he thought of marrying for a second time, he may, from his tour of duty in Syria, have remembered meeting or hearing of the young daughter of the high priest of Emesa. His choice of the Syrian girl as his wife has been attributed to his belief in astrology. According to a 4th century writer, Severus had made inquiries about the horoscopes of marriageable women, and "when he learned that there was a woman in Syria whose horoscope predicted that she would wed a king (that is, Julia), he sought her for his wife."[6]

Julia and Septimius Severus were married in 187 A.D. when she was seventeen and he was forty-one or forty-two. Their first child, a son, was born in Lugdunum (Lyons) on April 4, 188. He was named Bassianus after Julia's father. A second son, Geta, named after Severus' father and brother, was born in Rome the following year.[7]

In 191 Severus went to Pannonia as governor. Here, while he was in command of three legions with his headquarters at Carnuntum on the Danube, he learned of the murder of the Emperor Commodus, of the murder of his successor, Pertinax, three months later, and of the selling of the throne to the highest bidder, Julianus. Severus himself was then acclaimed emperor by his troops. As he and his soldiers swiftly marched on Rome, the senators voted to take the throne from Julianus, who was killed soon after, and they proclaimed Severus as emperor. In the year 193, the date of Severus' triumphal entry into Rome, not only did his own name appear on coins but also the name of IULIA DOMNA, and during this year the imperial name, *Augusta*, was given to Julia.[8] Thus within six years of her marriage to Severus the prophecy of her horoscope was fulfilled; she was now married to a king.

But two other generals also aspired to the throne: Niger in the East and Albinus in Britain. On hearing that Niger's soldiers had proclaimed their leader as emperor, Severus marched to the East and defeated Niger's troops. Niger was killed in 194 and his wife and children were put to death. Severus continued to campaign in the East against those who had supported Niger's cause. In 196 Julia, who had accompanied her husband to the East, was given the title, *Mater Castrorum*, Mother of the Camp, in recognition of her presence in her husband's campaign.[9]

Next Severus turned his attention to Albinus, whom some of the senators wanted as emperor. Marching against Albinus who had crossed from Britain to the mainland of Gaul, he defeated his army near Lugdunum (Lyons) in 197 A.D. Not only was Albinus killed, but also his wife and children, his friends, and at least twenty-nine senators who were believed to have been his supporters.[10]

The fact that Severus chose to crush his two rivals, Niger and Albinus, instead of merely naming them as his successors, was said to have been partly due to Julia's ambition.[11] But doubtless Severus himself also wanted his sons to inherit the throne. To give the appearance of legitimacy to his rule Severus adopted Marcus Aurelius Antoninus, who had died in 180 A.D., as his father and claimed Aurelius' deceased son, Commodus, as his brother. In addition, Severus gave his son Bassianus the name, Marcus Aurelius Antoninus, but this son is known in history by his nickname, Caracalla.[12]

A few months after Severus' victory at Lugdunum Julia accompanied her husband on another journey to the East and in 203 to Africa. In 204 the *Ludi Saeculares*, the Secular Games, were held in Rome to mark the beginning of a new age. Unlike any previous empress, Julia had a conspicuous role in the ceremonies.[13] But despite the honor that she received in Rome and throughout the empire, the first few years of the 3rd century were not pleasant for Julia because she had an enemy at court.

Plautianus, who like Severus was a native of north Africa, enjoyed the confidence of the emperor. He had risen to the rank of prefect of the praetorian guard, achieved great wealth and power, had statues erected to him throughout the Roman world, and arranged in 202 A.D. to have his daughter, Plautilla, marry Bassianus (now called Antoninus or Caracalla), the older son of Severus and Julia, although neither Julia nor the bridegroom were in favor of the marriage. Julia resented Plautianus' influence over her husband, and Plautianus, says Dio the historian:

> often treated Julia Augusta in an outrageous manner; for he cordially detested her and was always abusing her violently to Severus. He used to conduct investigations into her conduct as well as gather evidence against her by torturing women of the nobility.[14]

Fortunately, Severus' brother, Geta, as he lay on his deathbed in the year 204, told Severus that Plautianus was not to be trusted. Shortly thereafter, Plautianus was accused of plotting to murder the emperor and was himself put to death in 205 A.D.[15] Dio reports that someone plucked a few hairs from Plautianus' beard, carried them to Plautilla and Julia, who had known nothing of the affair, and exclaimed, "Behold your Plautianus!" thus "causing grief to the one and joy to the other."[16]

Julia also had another problem. Her sons spent too much time in the pursuit of pleasure, and moreover, they hated each other. Severus tried in vain to bring his sons under control and to get them to live in harmony with each other. In 208 when Severus, Julia, and their sons went to Britain on a campaign, Severus hoped that his sons would benefit from being away from Rome and settling into the discipline of military life. He wanted them to learn to be good co-emperors. Geta was left in charge of the province under Roman control, while Severus and Caracalla marched against the barbarians. When a serious illness confined Severus to his quarters, Caracalla attempted to gain control of the army, made slanderous attacks on his brother, and tried to persuade the physicians to hasten his father's death.[17] Severus' last advice to his sons was to pay the soldiers well and live in peace with each other. He died at Eboracum (York) on February 4, 211, after having ruled for almost eighteen years. His body was cremated, and Julia and his sons took his ashes to Rome and placed them in the mausoleum of the emperors.[18]

As a leader Severus had been quick to grasp a problem and to take effective, though sometimes ruthless, action. He had brought about many military reforms and administrative changes. He had also undertaken vast public works. He had replaced fallen bridges, repaired roads throughout the empire, put up new structures including the Arch of Severus, and restored many old buildings.[19] In this last task Julia had helped by restoring a meeting-hall for women in the Forum of Trajan and by rebuilding the Temple of Vesta.[20] Her numerous journeys with her husband and the evidence of coins and inscriptions suggest that Severus had valued her work as his empress. But now she was left alone to cope with the problem of the dissension of her two sons who were heirs to the throne.

The advisers appointed by their father recommended, in the presence of Julia, that the empire be divided, with Caracalla to have all Europe and Geta to have Asia; but Julia objected, saying: "Earth and sea, my children, you have found a way to divide.... But your mother, how could you divide her?"[21] The idea was abandoned, but the hatred between the two brothers continued, with each trying to thwart what the other attempted to do. Finally, maddened by a desire for sole power, as the historian Herodian says, Caracalla resorted to a desperate scheme.[22]

In 212 he persuaded his mother, Julia, to invite them both to her apartment to achieve a reconciliation. When Geta entered the room, some soldiers, acting on Caracalla's orders, rushed to attack him. Geta ran to his mother for protection, but they killed him in her arms, wounding the hand with which she tried to protect him. Caracalla then ran through the palace, shouting that he had escaped grave danger and had barely managed to save his life. Not satisfied with having tricked his mother, he forbade her to mourn for Geta and ordered her to rejoice as though at some great good fortune. Geta's friends and supporters were killed. His name was erased from inscriptions, his portraits were mutilated, and any mention of him was regarded as treason.[23]

As emperor, Caracalla spent much of his time on campaigns, travelling to the German provinces, the Balkans, and into Asia Minor and Egypt. Julia accompanied her son to the East, living for a time at Nicomedia on the Sea of Marmara and later at Antioch. When her son was with the army, all petitions and letters came to her and so, in fact, she conducted much of the business of the Empire. She also held public receptions for prominent men.[24] The Emperor entrusted so much responsibility to his mother that contemporary gossips accused him of incest.[25] She had her own praetorian guard and her own royal retinue.[26]

Carcalla spent the winter of 216 in Edessa. On April 8, 217 he was murdered, at the order of one of his generals, Macrinus. When news of the murder reached Julia in Antioch, Dio says, "She mourned now that he was dead, the very man whom she had hated while he lived; yet it was not because she wished that he were alive, but because she was vexed at having to return to private life."[27]

When Macrinus at first made no change in her circumstances and sent her a kind message, her spirits revived. But her hopes for the future were dashed when Macrinus ordered her to leave Antioch. Moreover, by this time, Dio says, she "was already in a dying condition by reason of cancer of the breast that she had had for a very long time."[28] She chose to starve herself to death and died at Antioch in May or June of the year 217 at the age of forty-seven. Her ashes were carried to Rome. Some years later her sister, Julia Maesa, had the urn placed in "the shrine of Antoninus," probably the same mausoleum that contained the ashes of her husband, Severus.[29]

Under Emperor Severus Alexander, Julia Domna's grand-nephew and the last of the Severi, Julia was deified. Coins issued in honor of her deification bear the words, DIVA IULIA AUGUSTA.[30]

II. "THE PHILOSOPHER JULIA"

As empress, Julia was busy fulfilling her official duties, but she also pursued her own intellectual interests. The main historical evidence for this comes from two of her contemporaries, Philostratus and Dio Cassius. Philostratus speaks of her as "the philosopher Julia," mentions "Julia's circle of mathematicians and philosophers," and says that he belonged to that circle.[31] Dio, after describing Plautianus' hostile behavior towards Julia, says, "For this reason she began to study philosophy and passed her days with the sophists."[32] Then, referring to the time when Julia handled official correspondence for her son and held public receptions for prominent men (in Nicomedia and Antioch in Asia Minor about 215 to 217) Dio said of Julia that "she devoted herself more and more to the study of philosophy with these men."[33]

These comments of Julia's contemporaries suggest the following questions:

A. Who were the members of Julia's circle and what were their interests?
B. Who were the sophists of her time?
C. What philosophy did she study?
D. What philosophy did she herself seem to favor?

Though the questions are not mutually exclusive, they can provide a framework for our study. Our effort to answer them may give us a glimpse into Julia's intellectual and philosophical life.

A. *Who were the Members of Julia's Circle?*

Philostratus speaks of "Julia's circle of mathematicians and philosophers." The term *mathematicians*, we are told, means *astrologers* here.[34] Julia is believed to have retained her interest in astrology from the Syrian religion of her childhood, an interest that was shared by her husband. Though we lack the names of the astrologer-mathematicians in Julia's circle, many names of other possible members have been suggested.

What some scholars have done is to work out a list of some of the most prominent intellectuals of Julia's time and conclude that almost all of them must have belonged to Julia's circle. In addition to Julia's sister, Julia Maesa, and her nieces, Julia Soaemias and Julia Mamaea, the lists have included the following names:

1. The lawyer Papinian, possibly Julia's cousin, who served as praetorian prefect under Septimius Severus and initiated important legal reforms.[35]
2. Ulpian, pupil of Papinian, who served as a member of the council of Septimius Severus.[36]
3. Oppian the poet, who dedicated a work on hunting to the Emperor Caracalla, saying "the great Domna had given him to the great Severus."[37]

4. Athenaeus of Naucratis, author of *Deipnosophistae* (*The Sophists at Dinner*), an account of a banquet which contains a storehouse of miscellaneous information.[38]

5. Alexander of Aphrodisias, commentator on Aristotle, who may have owed his position as head of the Aristotelian school at Athens to the patronage of Severus and Caracalla.[39]

6. Serenus Sammonicus, learned author of *Rerum Reconditarum Libri* who was killed, on the order of Caracalla, after the death of Geta.[40]

7. Galen, Greek physician and author of medical and philosophical works, who served as court physician in Rome from the time of Commodus through the first few years of the reign of Septimius Severus, until his death in 199 A.D.[41]

8. Marius Maximus, who wrote a *Life of Septimius Severus* which was used as a source for the *Augustan History*.[42]

9. Dio Cassius, author of *Roman History*, who also wrote a little book on dreams and portents, foretelling Severus' future greatness, a work for which Severus praised him.[43]

10. Gordian, proconsul of Africa to whom Philostratus dedicated *Lives of the Sophists*. He became emperor in 238 and is said to have "passed his days with Plato and Aristotle, Cicero and Vergil."[44]

11. Several sophists whom we shall mention in the next section (B).

Julia may have known many if not all of the men named in the above list. She very likely knew Papinian, Ulpian, Galen, Dio, and Gordian, but we lack the evidence for asserting with confidence that any of the ten men actually belonged to her circle.

Recalling Dio's statement that Julia "passed her days with the sophists," we may turn to the second question and ask:

B. *Who were the Sophists?*

To the student of ancient philosophy the term *sophist* might recall Protagoras' "Man is the measure of all things," or Gorgias' work, *On Not-Being or on Nature*.[45] It might also recall Plato's and Aristotle's view of a sophist as one who has only apparent knowledge, but not true wisdom.[46] But in Julia's time *sophist* was not a pejorative term, nor did it designate a philosophical position. It was in effect a title or honorary term, applied to the orators and teachers of rhetoric who had reached the peak of rhetorical skill. The sophists of the 2nd and 3rd centuries A.D. were among the most popular and highly esteemed intellectuals of their time. They were honored by emperors, entrusted with prestigious government posts, and they became so wealthy that they were able to give magnificent gifts like public buildings to their communities.[47] They showed in their lives how the art of persuasive speaking could be a means to success in public life. One of our main sources of information about them is Philostratus, who was a member of Julia's circle.

In his *Lives of the Sophists* Philostratus distinguishes between "ancient sophistic," founded by Gorgias of Leontini in the 5th century B.C. and "the second sophistic," founded, he says, by Aeschines. The ancient sophistic art was a philosophical rhetoric since those who used it took positions on themes that philosophers treat of, like courage, justice, and how the universe has been fashioned to its present shape.[48] In the second sophistic (Philostratus prefers the word "second" to the word "new"), "the followers of Aeschines handled their themes with a view to elaborating the methods of their art."[49] That is, their topics, drawn from the history and literature of ancient Greece, were merely occasions for them to display their rhetorical skill.

Philostratus presents in his book those to whom the term *sophist* has been applied. Though a sophist, in his view, is not a philosopher, he begins by listing eight philosophers who seemed to be sophists because they expounded their theories with ease and fluency.[50] After that he discusses the real sophists, nine representing the ancient sophistic (Gorgias, Protagoras, Hippias, and Prodicus are included in this group) and more than forty-three representing the second sophistic. Though this work was probably not written until after Julia's death, it is reasonable to assume that as a member of Julia's circle who was an expert on the history of sophism, Philostratus might have shared his knowledge with her.

That he did so is evident in a letter that he is believed to have written to "Julia Augusta." In this letter he tells her that Plato was not envious of the sophists but admired and adopted the literary form used by Gorgias, Hippias, and Protagoras. He then mentions other examples of people who have thought that the sophists should be emulated, including Aspasia the Milesian who "is said to have whetted the tongue of Pericles to imitate Gorgias." He adds: "And Aeschines, too, the Socratic, whom you [i.e., Julia] recently discussed as writing his dialogues in a notably severe style, did not hesitate to write like Gorgias in his discourse about Thargelia."[51]

Philostratus concludes his letter by saying:

> Then do you too, O Queen, please urge Plutarch, boldest of the Greeks, not to take offense at the sophists and not to fall foul of Gorgias. If you do not succeed in persuading him, at least you know, such is your wisdom and cleverness, what name to apply to a man of that sort. I could tell you, but I can't.[52]

Because Plutarch had died half a century before Julia was born, the authenticity of the letter has been questioned, but in asking Julia to speak to a dead man, Philostratus may have been deliberately using an ancient literary artifice.[53] In any case, it is likely that Julia heard about Gorgias and other ancient sophists from Philostratus.

In addition to suggesting what Julia may have known of the history of sophism, Philostratus' *Lives of the Sophists* can help us identify those sophists of the 2nd and 3rd centuries A.D. whom Julia could have known.

Among the sophists who were known to Septimius Severus (and so perhaps also to Julia) were the following: Apollonius of Athens who, while on an embassy to Emperor Severus at Rome in 196 or 197 A.D. entered and won a declamation contest;[54] Heracleides of Lycia, high priest of Lycia, who, though notable as a sophist, broke down in the midst of an extemporaneous speech in the presence of Emperor Severus;[55] Aelian, a Roman who lived during the reign of Severus, spoke Greek perfectly and wrote works on history and on the nature of animals.[56]

A sophist who was well known to both Severus and Julia was Antipater of Hierapolis. He tutored their sons, served as Imperial Secretary to Severus and later as governor of Bithynia, a post which he lost because he was too harsh. He wrote a lament for the death of Geta which displeased Caracalla and died at the age of sixty-eight of "voluntary fasting."[57]

Philostratus says that Hemocrates of Phocis was "a member of the sophistic circle" and that Heliodorus "must not be deemed unworthy of the sophistic circle."[58] In neither case does Philostratus explicitly identify the "circle" as Julia's circle, but that meaning is possible.

Of Philiscus the Thessalian, Philostratus says that at Rome "he attached himself closely to Julia's circle of mathematicians and philosophers, and obtained from her, with the Emperor's consent, the chair of rhetoric at Athens."[59] He held the chair of rhetoric at Athens for seven years but was deprived of the immunity from public service that holders of such chairs were often granted. When he tried to plead his case before Emperor Caracalla, he made such a bad impression that the Emperor kept interrupting him and making critical comments about his hair and his voice, but eventually Philiscus did receive an exemption from public service as a reward for a declamation he gave.

We know that Philostratus himself belonged to the circle. After mentioning Julia by name, he says, in another work: "I belonged to the circle of the empress, for she was a devoted admirer of all rhetorical exercises."[60] Towards the end of *Lives of the Sophists* he lists himself as a sophist, but modestly limits his remarks to one sentence:

> But of Philostratus of Lemnos and his ability in the law courts, in political harangues, in writing treatises, in declamation, and lastly of his talent for speaking extempore, it is not for me to write.[61]

A modern writer who has critically examined the alleged membership of Julia's circle reaches these limited but certain conclusions: that there *was* a circle of sophists and philosophers; that Julia herself enjoyed participating in discussion; and that Philostratus the biographer and Philiscus the sophist were — at least for a time — members of this circle.[62]

C. *What Philosophy did Julia Study?*

The texts of Julia's contemporaries do not give us a direct answer to this question. In *Lives of the Sophists* Philostratus stresses the rhetorical style of the men he presents. There are, however, passing references to some sophists' interest in Plato and the Academy.[63] We also know from Philostratus that it had been the custom in the time of Marcus Aurelius for the emperor to appoint not only the heads of the chairs of rhetoric for Athens and Rome, but also, directly or through a delegate, professors of Platonism, Aristotelianism, Stoicism, and Epicureanism. This custom may still have been in effect in Julia's time.[64] In any case, it points to the basic types of philosophy that a 2nd or 3rd century student might desire to know. But perhaps Julia's main philosophical interest can be found in a work that was written at her command.

D. *What Philosophy did Julia herself seem to Favor?*

Julia had commanded Philostratus to write the biography of Apollonius of Tyana. Her attention had been called to some memoirs of Apollonius written by Damis, one of his disciples, and she wanted Philostratus to edit these memoirs and present them in a good style.[65] In obeying this command, Philostratus also made use of other sources. He says that he hopes that his work will honor the memory of Apollonius and "be of use to those who love learning."[66]

Who was Apollonius and why should Julia and others "who love learning" be interested in him? The answer to both of these questions are implicitly contained in Philostratus' book.

Apollonius had been regarded by some as just a magician or wizard and Philostratus' story includes examples of seemingly magical power. Even in the report of his more ordinary activities it is hard to distinguish fact from fiction.[67] But in reality Apollonius was a Neopythagorean philosopher who lived in the 1st century A.D. He was born in Tyana in Cappadocia (Turkey). As a young student he encountered the philosophy of Plato, the Peripatetics, the Stoic Chrysippus, Epicurus, and Pythagoras. At the age of sixteen he adopted the life of a Pythagorean ascetic.[68] He gave up meat and wine, condemned the sacrifice of animals to the gods, wore only garments of linen, had long hair and a long beard, lived a life of poverty and chastity, and spent five years in complete silence. He travelled to Babylon where he interviewed the Magi, to India where he conversed with the Brahmans, to Egypt and the upper Nile where he met the Gymnosophists or naked philosophers, to Greece, Italy, and Spain. He was falsely accused of treason by the emperors Nero and Domitian but escaped punishment. He died during the reign of Nerva (that is, between 96 and 98 A.D.).

Pythagoras, whom Apollonius regarded as his spiritual ancestor, had founded in the 6th century B.C. a religious society which cultivated learning, especially mathematics, and prescribed a strict rule of life as a means of purifying the immortal soul.[69] Neopythagoreanism was a revival of traditional Pythagorean teachings, mingled with some Platonic and mystical elements. Moderatus of Gades and Apollonius of Tyana were its main representatives in the 1st century A.D.

Some have regarded *The Life of Apollonius* by Philostratus as a novel or as an imaginative embellishment of a legend. But regardless of the extent to which the book is or is not historically accurate, it is of interest to us "as a record of the principles by which Julia was animated," as a writer of our time has said.[70] In the absence of any writings by Julia herself, we shall look to this work that Julia commissioned in an effort to discover the ideas that interested her: ideas that she may have held and wished to promote. Embedded in the narrative of a remarkable life, they touch on a variety of topics, among them: God, man, immortality, personal ethics, and political philosophy.

Apollonius clearly expressed his preference for the philosophy of Pythagoras. He says: "... my own system of wisdom is that of Pythagoras, a man of Samos."[71] From Pythagoras he learned the rule of life that he follows and from him he learned to worship the gods, "to be aware of them whether they are seen or not seen."[72] He recognized God as a creator who brought all things into being because He is good.[73]

His mode of worship was one that Julia, as daughter of the high priest of Elagabalus, understood since each day he prayed to the sun, which he saw as the governor of the seasons and source of light and of fire.[74] He also, like Julia, allowed statues of the gods in temples. He thought such statues, whether of Apollo, Zeus, or Athena, represented the effort of the human mind to conceive ideal reality, but he sharply criticized as irreverent the Egyptian custom of representing the gods in the form of animals.[75] In the view of Apollonius:

there is between man and God a certain kinship which enables him alone of the animal creation to recognize the Gods, and to speculate both about his own nature and the manner in which it participates in the divine substance. ... good men have in their composition something of God.[76]

He held that each person has an immortal soul; the source of the existence of this soul is "in the unbegotten."[77] Like Plato he thought of the soul as "being bound and fettered in a perishable body;" he compared life to a prison and death to an escape.[78] He was aware that there are differences of opinion about the soul, but Philostratus thinks that if we are convinced of Apollonius' teaching on the soul, then "cheerfully and with due knowledge of our own true nature, we may pursue our way to the goal appointed by the Fates."[79]

What that way should be is clear in many texts in Apollonius' biography. Though no formal treatise on ethics is presented, there is repeated stress on the need for acquiring the virtues of wisdom, courage, temperance, and justice. Apollonius thought that the man who loves wisdom is greater than the famous Colossus of Rhodes.[80] With regard to courage he stresses that it is not enough to possess that virtue as a quality; one must also practise it.[81]

Apollonius both exemplified and taught the virtue of temperance. In the use of material goods he limited himself to basic necessities. One of the worst vices, he thought, was the vice of greed.[82] He also criticized gluttony and drunkenness. He thought that to keep one's mind clear and composed it is better to be a "reveller in sobriety," that is, to drink water.[83] He did not, however, demand complete abstinence from wine, of his companions or of kings. He said:

> ... in the case of a king a philosophy that is at once moderate and indulgent makes a good mixture ...; an excess of rigor and severity ... might be construed as due to pride.[84]

The topic of chastity is discussed when Damis, Apollonius' disciple, wonders whether eunuchs possess that virtue. Apollonius thinks not, since their sexual abstinence may not be due to choice. He says in effect that true chastity like any true temperance does not consist in the inability to be intemperate in one's acts or desires, but in the free decision to keep one's acts and desires under control.[85]

In his discussion of justice he also stresses the positive meaning of virtue. The question arises: Does the mere abstention from injustice constitute justice? From the Brahmans of India Apollonius learned that justice is something more than not being unjust. It requires one to positively do what is just and to influence others not to be unjust.[86]

Apollonius was interested not only in the ethics of the individual but also in the ethics of society, especially in how harmony can be achieved in society and how philosophy can aid the work of the ruler. Realistically he acknowledged the existence of rivalries among the people of a city, but thought that such rivalry should be directed towards seeing who can best discharge his duties on behalf of the common good. Echoing Plato's *Republic*, he says: "... to me it seems best that each man should do what he understands best and what he best can do."[87]

Apollonius regards monarchy as a good form of government if the human flock is governed by a just shepherd.[88] He himself had lived under many emperors, two of whom he mentions as being opposed to philosophy and philosophers. Nero had issued a proclamation that no one should teach philosophy in Rome.[89] Domitian made wisdom a penal offense and issued an edict against philosophers.[90] But the Roman emperors Vespasian and Titus had asked Apollonius for help. In reply to Vespasian Apollonius said that kingship cannot be taught, but he did give some general guidelines: exercise your power with moderation; let the law govern you as well as your people; reverence the gods; be a good sovereign.[91] What may have interested the Empress Julia in this part of the narrative was the thought that philosophy can give guidance not only in one's personal life, but also in the exercise of political power.[92]

Though the *Life of Apollonius* was not finished before Julia's death, its content was known to her; it was written at her command and with her encouragement. As one writer says, it affords "glimpses available nowhere else into the mind of a woman who played a dominant part in a crucial period of Roman history."[93] It suggests that she herself favored a philosophy which acknowledges the existence of God (or gods), the closeness of man to the divine, the immortality of the soul, the need of acquiring the intellectual and moral virtues, and, the guidance that philosophy can give to those who exercise political power.

Though Neopythagoreanism was to be superseded by Neoplatonism, at least some of the themes that Julia could have found and admired in Apollonius' thought are familiar teachings of classic philosophy.

III. CONCLUSION

Why, then, was Julia called a philosopher? In summary, we can say: She studied and discussed philosophy and ordered the writing of a work about a Neopythagorean thinker whose ideas she thought should be better known. She was knowledgeable about the ancient sophists and about the rhetoricians of the "second sophistic" of her time. Through her "circle" she herself learned and she encouraged others to learn. The fact that she was an empress was especially significant. Some earlier rulers, such as Nero and Domitian, had banished philosophy and persecuted philosophers, but Julia Domna used her imperial power to protect philosophy and help philosophers flourish. This was no small achievement.

NOTES

1. Philostratus, *The Lives of the Sophists*, tr. by W.C. Wright (London: William Heinemann; New York: G.P. Putnam's Sons, 1922), pp. 300-301.
2. Gerard J. Murphy, *The Reign of the Emperor L. Septimius Severus from the Evidence of the Inscriptions* (Jersey City, N.J.: St. Peters College Press, 1945), pp. 103-104; Mary Gilmore Williams, "Studies in the Lives of Roman Empresses: Julia Domna," *American Journal of Archaeology* vol. 6 (1902), p. 304 & p. 297; Maurice Platnauer, *The Life and Reign of the Emperor Lucius Septimius Severus* (Westport, Connecticut: Greenwood Press, 1970 reprint of 1918 edition), p. 144.
3. Godfrey Turton, *The Syrian Princesses: The Women Who Ruled Rome A.D. 193-235* (London: Cassell & Co., 1974), pp. 3-13; Platnauer, *op. cit.*, p. 46.
   On Julia's name, see Anthony Birley, *Septimius Severus: The African*

Emperor (London: Eyre & Spottiswoode, 1971), pp. 118, 297; Platnauer, p. 143, note 5, thinks her name might have had some association with Proserpine, daughter of the goddess Demeter.

On the sun-god Elagabalus, see Herodian of Antioch, *History of the Roman Empire from the Death of Marcus Aurelius to the Accession of Gordian III*, tr. by Edward C. Echols (Berkeley & Los Angeles: University of California Press, 1961), Bk 5, chap. 3, p. 139.

4. Turton, *op. cit.*, pp. 4, 13.
5. Aelius Spartianus, "Severus," II-IV in *Scriptores Historiae Augustae*, tr. by David Magie (London: William Heinemann; New York: G.P. Putnam's Sons, 1921), vol. 1, pp. 371-377. This work, known as *Augustan History* is a collection of biographies of Roman emperors seemingly by six authors: Spartianus, Capitolinus, Gallicanus, Lampridius, Pollio, Vopiscus. The real authorship of the work has been a subject of controversy, but information given in the work is drawn from Greek and Latin writings of the 3rd century. – On Severus' early career, see also Platnauer, pp. 38-44.
6. Spartianus, "Severus," III, 9 in *op. cit.*, vol. 1, p. 377. Spartianus repeats this story in his account of Antoninus Geta III, 1 in *Augustan History*, vol. 2, p. 37.
7. Turton, *op. cit.*, pp. 4, 13-14. A question has been raised as to whether Bassianus was the son of Severus' first wife or of Julia. Platnauer sets forth the texts on this question on pp. 48-53. It seems clear that Bassianus (later known as Caracalla) was Julia's son, not her stepson.
8. Platnauer, pp. 60-69; Spartianus, "Severus," V-VII in *Augustan History*, vol. 1, pp. 381-387; Herodian, *History*, Bk. 2, chapters 10-12, pp. 64-70; *Dio's Roman History*, tr. by E. Cary, Bk. 74, section 15 & 17; Bk. 75, sec. 1 (London: William Heinemann; New York: G.P. Putnam's Sons, 1927), vol. 9, pp. 153, 159, 163. Cassius Dio Cocceianus (usually referred to simply as Dio) is one of the main sources for the history of the Severan dynasty. He lived during the reign of Septimius Severus, Caracalla, and the three following emperors. In giving references to this work I am using the traditional book numbers from the Greek text of Boissevain, given on the left-hand page in the Loeb Classical Library edition.

    For reference to names on coins, see Murphy, *op. cit.*, p. 2 and Williams, *art. cit.*, p. 261.
9. Dio, *Roman History*, Bk. 75, pp. 173-201; Spartianus, "Severus." VIII-IX in *Aug. Hist.* vol. 1, pp. 389-393; Spartianus, "Pescennius Niger," in *Aug. Hist.*, vol. 1, pp. 430-459; Birley, *op. cit.*, chapter on "War against Niger," pp. 172-188; Platnauer, pp. 74-98; Williams, *art. cit.*, pp. 261-263; Murphy, *op. cit.*, p. 103.
10. Herodian, Bk. 3, chapters 5-8, pp. 85-93; Spartianus, "Severus," X-XIII, pp. 395-401; Capitolinus on "Clodius Albinus," in *Augustan History*, vol. 1, pp. 460-493; Dio, Bk. 75, pp. 203-217; Birley, chapter on "War against Albinus," pp. 189-200; Platnauer, pp. 99-113.

11. Turton, *op. cit.*, p. 51; Capitolinus, "Clodius Albinus," IV in *Augustan History*, l. 1, pp. 465-467.
12. Spartianus, "Severus," X in *Aug. Hist.*, p. 395; Spartianus, "Geta," I in *Augustan History*, vol. 2, pp. 32-33; Dio, Bk. 75, 7, p. 213; Bk. 76, 9, p. 257; Murphy, p. 102.

   The name *Caracalla* came from a Celtic or German word for a hooded cloak that Bassianus (M. Aurelius Antoninus) often wore. See Dio, Bk. 78, 3, p. 345.

13. The Secular Games were thought to have been held at intervals of 110 years, a *saeculum*, that is, the longest span of human life. See Herodian, Bk. 3, chap. 8, p. 93; Birley, pp. 227-230; Murphy, p. 35; Williams, p. 273; Dio, Bk. 75, 5-13, pp. 216-225.
14. Dio, Bk. 75, 15, p. 233; Herodian, Bk. 3, chapters 10-12, pp. 97-102. In Williams' interpretation, p. 268, Plautianus persuaded Severus to bring Julia to trial for adultery, an offense which in a woman of the imperial family would be equivalent to treason, but the empress was acquitted.
15. Dio, Bk. 76, 2-5, pp. 242-247; Herodian, Bk. 3, chapters 11-12, pp. 98-102; Platnauer, pp. 130-133, esp. note on p. 133.
16. Dio, Bk. 76, 4, pp. 246-247. Plautilla was banished and several years later she was put to death at the command of her former husband, Caracalla. See Birley, pp. 233, 294; Williams, pp. 273-274.
17. Herodian, Bk. 3, chapters 14-15, pp. 104-107; Dio, Bk. 76, 14, p. 269.
18. Dio, Bk. 76, 15, pp. 271-273; Herodian, Bk. 3, chap. 15, pp. 107-108.
19. Herodian, Bk. 3, chap. 6, p. 86; Dio, Bk. 76, 1, pp. 238-241; Murphy, pp. 29, 43-80; Platnauer, pp. 158-188; H.M.D. Parker & B.H. Warmington, *A History of the Roman World from A.D. 138 to 337* (New York: Macmillan, 1958), pp. 80-88.
20. Williams, p. 275; Joseph McCabe, *The Empresses of Rome* (New York: Henry Holt & Co., 1911), p. 202.
21. Herodian, Bk. 4, chap. 3, pp. 113-114.
22. *Ibid.*, chap. 4, p. 114.
23. *Ibid.*, chapters 4-6, pp. 114-118; Dio, Bk. 77, 2, pp. 280-283; 77, 12, pp. 306-309; Spartianus, "Antoninus Caracalla," II-IV in *Augustan History*, vol. 2, pp. 7-11; Williams, p. 281.
24. Herodian, Bk. 4, chapters 7-11, pp. 119-127; Spartianus, "Caracalla," V-VI in *Aug. Hist.*, vol. 2, pp. 13-17; Parker & Warmington, *op. cit.*, pp. 92-96; Dio, 77, 7 to 78, 3, pp. 293-343.
25. Herodian, Bk. 4, chap. 11, p. 123 notes that the people of Alexandria in jest called Julia *Jocasta*, the name of the woman who was both mother and wife to Oedipus. Spartianus, "Severus," XXI, vol. 1, p. 421 had referred to Caracalla as: a man "who took his own stepmother to wife — stepmother did I say? — nay rather the mother on whose bosom he had slain Geta, her son." Spartianus repeats the story in more detail in "Caracalla," X, vol. 2, (of *Augustan History*), p. 27.

   The question of whether Julia was Caracalla's stepmother or mother has already been mentioned (see note #7). The evidence points to the fact that Julia was Caracalla's mother.

The charge of incest would seem to be an invention of gossips and enemies. Julia surely could not forget that Caracalla had tried to murder his father, that he had tricked her into inviting his younger brother Geta to her apartment where he had him killed in her arms, and then had ordered her to rejoice in Geta's death. — Moreover, we are told that Caracalla became impotent. See Dio, 77, 16, p. 319; Turton, pp. 106, 118.

26. Dio, 78, 23, p. 391.
27. *Ibid.* For details of Caracalla's murder, see Dio, 4-8, pp. 347-355; Herodian, Bk. 4, chapters 12-13, pp. 127-130; Spartianus, "Caracalla," VII, *Aug. Hist.* vol. 2, p. 19; Parker & Warmington, p. 96; Turton, pp. 128-130.
28. Dio, 78, 23, pp. 391-395; Turton, pp. 130-131.
29. Williams, p. 296. The Severan dynasty which appeared to end with the death of Julia was in fact to continue for 17 more years. Julia's sister, Julia Maesa, who had lived in Rome during Severus' reign and was now a widow, was determined that her family would retain control of the empire. She had two daughters, Julia Soaemias and Julia Mamaea. Both were now widows, but each had a son. Through Julia Maesa's influence Soaemias' son became Emperor Elagabalus in 218, and after he and his mother were killed in 222, Julia Mamaea's son became Emperor Severus Alexander. When Severus Alexander and his mother were murdered in 235, the Severan dynasty came to an end. See Turton, Chapters 8-12; Parker & Warmington, pp. 102-114.
30. Williams, p. 297.
31. Philostratus, *The Lives of the Sophists*, p. 301; *The Life of Apollonius of Tyana*, tr. by F.C. Conybeare (London: William Heinemann; New York: Macmillan, 1912), vol. 1, Bk. 1, chap. 3, p. 11.
32. Dio, 75, 17, p. 233.
33. *Ibid.*, 77, 18, p. 327.
34. See editor's note in Loeb edition of Philostratus, *Lives of the Sophists*, p. 301; Turton, p. 10.
35. Under the influence of Papinian, from Severus' reign date the first laws against abortion, laws protecting minors, laws ensuring a wife's claim on the money she brings to her husband at the time of her marriage, and laws clarifying the status of slaves. See Platnauer, pp. 181-182; Turton, p. 62. After the death of Geta, Papinian was put to death at Caracalla's order. See Spartianus, "Caracalla," IV in *Augustan History*, vol. 2, p. 11.
36. Ulpian's writings, together with those of Papinian and the jurist Paul, comprise over half of Justinian's *Digest* (533 A.D.), a codification and collection of Roman law.
37. See his *Cynegetica*, tr. by A.W. Mair (London: William Heinemann; New York: Putnam, 1928), bk. 1, p. 3. See critical comment of G.W. Bowersock, *Greek Sophists in the Roman Empire* (Oxford: Clarendon Press, 1969), p. 108.
38. See English translation by Charles B. Gulick (Cambridge: Harvard University Press; London: William Heinemann, 1951).

39. Alexander dedicated one of his works, *De fato*, to Severus and Caracalla in gratitude for his appointment. See Platnauer, p. 145.

40. See Spartianus, "Caracalla," IV in *Aug. Hist.*, vol. 2, pp. 10-11; Bowersock, *op. cit.*, p. 107.

41. See Turton, p. 61; Bowersock, pp. 58-75, esp. 63-64.

42. Neither his work nor Septimius Severus' autobiography which was also used as a source by the writers of the *Augustan History*, is extant. See Spartianus, "Severus," XV in vol. 1, p. 407; Spartianus, "Geta," II in vol. 2, p. 35; Lampridius, "Severus Alexander," in vol. 2, p. 187.

43. See Platnauer, pp. 3-4; Dio, Bk. 72, 23, p. 119. Dio claims to have been an eye-witness of the events he describes in his *Roman History* (See Bk. 72, p. 109). But we have no evidence for asserting that he was a member of Julia's circle. (In describing some of Caracalla's undesirable qualities, Dio says: "He possessed the craftiness of his mother and the Syrians, to which race she belonged." See Bk. 77, 10, p. 299.)

44. Capitolinus, "The Three Gordians," in vol. 2, *Augustan History*, pp. 392-393; Bowersock, pp. 6-8, 106. — For scholarly guesses about the membership of Julia's circle, see Platnauer, pp. 144-145; McCabe, *op. cit.*, pp. 200-202; Parker & Warmington, *op. cit.*, p. 132; J. Bidez in *Cambridge Ancient History* (Cambridge: Cambridge University Press, 1939), pp. 613-614. Bowersock (p. 103) thinks the source of the lists is Victor Duruy's *Histoire de Rome*, vol. 6 (1879).

45. Joseph Owens, *A History of Ancient Western Philosophy* (New York: Appleton-Century-Crofts, 1959), pp. 157-165; Kathleen Freeman, *Ancilla to the Pre-Socratic Philosophers* (Oxford: Basil Blackwell, 1948), pp. 125-129.

46. Plato, *Sophist*, 233; Aristotle, *Metaphysics* IV, 2, 1004b 17-26.

47. James M. Campbell, *The Influence of the Second Sophistic on the Style of the Sermons of St. Basil the Great* (Washington, D.C.: Catholic University of America, 1922), pp. 14-19; W.R. Wright, Introduction to his translation of Philostratus, *Lives of the Sophists*, pp. xv-xix.

48. Philostratus, *Lives of the Sophists*, Bk. 1, p. 7; also p. 57, #18.

49. *Ibid.*, Bk. 1, p. 7. Philostratus mentions the following examples of topics of the sophists' declamations: "Isocrates tries to wean the Athenians from their empire of the sea" (p. 221); "Callias tries to dissuade the Athenians from burning the dead" (p. 257); "Demosthenes, after breaking down before Philip, defends himself from the charge of cowardice" (p. 309).

50. Philostratus, *Lives of the Sophists*, Bk. 1, p. 13.

51. Philostratus, Letter 73: "To Julia Augusta," in *Letters of Alciphron, Aelian, and Philostratus*, tr. by A.R. Benner & Francis H. Fobes (Cambridge: Harvard University Press; London: William Heinemann, 1949), pp. 541-545.

52. *Ibid.*, p. 545. Plutarch had attacked the sophists in a work which is now lost. The "name to be applied" was probably some uncomplimentary term.

53. See Bowersock, *op. cit.*, pp. 104-105 and Graham Anderson, "Putting Pressure on Plutarch: Philostratus' Epistle 73," *Classical Philology* vol. 72 (Jan. 1977), pp. 43-45. Anderson (p. 44) thinks that "the anachronism is deliberate and purposeful and ... no obstacle to Philostratus' authorship of the letter."

54. Philostratus, *Lives of the Sophists*, Bk. 2, #20, pp. 255-259.

55. *Ibid.*, #26, pp. 279-285.

56. *Ibid.*, #31, pp. 305-307. His books are entitled *Variae Historiae* and *De natura animalium* (curious stories of animal life).

57. *Ibid.*, #24, pp. 269-271.

58. *Ibid.*, #25, pp. 271-279; #32, pp. 307-311.

59. *Ibid.*, #30, pp. 301-305.

60. Philostratus, *Life of Apollonius*, Bk. 1, chap. 3, p. 11. This Philostratus, who was born on the island of Lemnos about 172 and had studied rhetoric at Athens and Rome, should not be confused with two (or three) other men of the same name. See Bowersock, pp. 2-5.

61. Philostratus, *Lives of the Sophists*, Bk. 2, pp. 313-315.

62. Bowersock, pp. 103-104.

63. Philostratus, *Lives of the Sophists*, pp. 13-15, 21, 61, 179.

64. *Ibid.*, Bk. 2, #2, p. 183. As mentioned in Note #39, Alexander of Aphrodisias evidently owed his appointment to Severus and Caracalla. Sometimes, however, according to Lucian, the head of a philosophical school was selected by the vote of the leading Athenian citizens. See M.L. Clarke, *Higher Education in the Ancient World* (Albuquerque, New Mexico: University of New Mexico Press, 1971), pp. 8-9, 78-79.

65. Philostratus, *Life of Apollonius*, Bk. 1, chap. 3, p. 11. Some modern writers have wondered whether Damis ever existed or was fabricated by Philostratus to give an air of authority to his work. See introduction to vol. 1 of Loeb edition of this work, pp. vii-viii; also introduction to abridged version of Philostratus' *Life of Apollonius*, tr. by C.P. Jones, introduced by G.W. Bowersock (Middlesex, England: Penguin Boooks, 1970), pp. 17-19. — If Damis were a fictitious invention, it would leave unanswered the question of what documents prompted Julia to issue her command to Philostratus.

66. Philostratus, *Life of Apollonius*, Bk. 1, chap. 3, p. 11. Philostratus also used a book by Maximum of Aegae, other treatises by Apollonius that are no longer extant, and letters of Apollonius, some of which had been preserved by the Emperor Hadrian. He also travelled to places where the sage was remembered and honored.

67. B.F. Harris, "Apollonius of Tyana: Fact and Fiction," *The Journal of Religious History*, vol. 5 (1969), pp. 189-199.

68. Philostratus, *Life of Apollonius*, Bk. 1, chap. 7, pp. 17-19.

69. Owens, *op. cit.*, pp. 30-33; Iamblichus, *Life of Pythagoras*, tr. by Thomas Taylor (London: John M. Watkins, 1965, reprint of 1818 ed.).

70. Turton, p. 57.

71. Philostratus, *Life of Apollonius*, Bk. 1, chap. 32, p. 91.

72. *Ibid.*

73. *Ibid.*, Bk. 8, chap. 7, p. 315 (in vol. 2).

74. *Ibid.*, in vol. 1, Bk. 2, chap. 38, p. 217; Bk. 3, chap. 15, pp. 257-259; in vol. 2, Bk. 6, chap. 4, p. 17; chap. 10, p. 29; Bk. 7, chap. 31, p. 235.

75. *Ibid.*, in vol. 2, Bk. 6, chap. 19, pp. 77-81.

76. *Ibid.*, Bk. 8, chap. 7, pp. 313-315.

77. *Ibid.*, Bk. 6, chap. 11, p. 43.

78. *Ibid.*, in vol. 2, Bk. 7, chap. 26, p. 223. — But like Pythagoras he accepted a doctrine of reincarnation; he recalled his own earlier incarnation as the pilot of a ship. See vol. 1, Bk. 3, chap. 19, p. 271 and chapters 23-24, pp. 277-283. For his argument on the soul, see vol. 2, Bk. 8, chap. 31, p. 405.

79. *Ibid.*, Bk. 8, chap. 31, p. 405.

80. *Ibid.*, in vol. 1, Bk. 5, chap. 21, p. 509.

81. *Ibid.*, Bk. 1, chap. 28, p. 81; Bk. 4, chap. 31, p. 421.

82. *Ibid.*, Bk. 1, chap. 34, p. 99; in vol. 2, Bk. 6, chap. 2, p. 7.

83. *Ibid.*, in vol. 1, Bk. 2, chap. 36, p. 213; chap. 37, p. 217.

84. *Ibid.*, p. 217.

85. *Ibid.*, Bk. 1, chap. 33, pp. 93-97; chap. 36, pp. 105-107.

86. *Ibid.*, in vol. 1, Bk. 3, chap. 25, pp. 283-284; in vol. 2, Bk. 6, chap. 21, pp. 91, 97.

87. *Ibid.*, in vol. 1, Bk. 4, chap. 8, p. 361.

88. *Ibid.*, Bk. 5, chap. 35, pp. 547-549. He seems to think that such a monarchy is equivalent to a democracy; that the government of one man, if it provides for the welfare of the community is, in fact, a democracy (p. 549).

89. *Ibid.*, Bk. 4, chap. 47, p. 463. On Nero and the philosophers, see Bk. 4, chapters 35-47, pp. 431-463.

90. *Ibid.*, in vol. 2, Bk. 7, chap. 11, pp. 167-169. On Domitian and the philosophers, see much of Books 7 and 8.

91. *Ibid.*, in vol. 1, Bk. 5, chap. 27, p. 523 to chap. 29, p. 531; chap. 36, pp. 553-555; chap. 38, p. 561; in vol. 2, Bk. 6, chap. 31, p. 117.

92. Philostratus' *Life of Apollonius* was to become a subject of dispute between pagans and Christians. In 305 Hierocles in *The Lover of Truth* drew a parallel between Apollonius and Christ and concluded that Apollonius was superior. To this Eusebius of Caesarea replied in *Contra Hieroclem*. For an account of the further history of the polemic see G.R.S. Mead, *Apollonius of Tyana: The Philosopher-Reformer of the First Century A.D.* (London and Benares: Theosophical Publishing Co., 1901), pp. 28-52. This polemical use of Philostratus' work was neither the intention of its author nor of his royal sponsor.

93. Turton, p. 58.

8. Makrina

CORNELIA W. WOLFSKEEL

I. BIOGRAPHY

Makrina, whose life is transmitted to us by her brother Gregory,[1] bishop of Nyssa from 371-376, was born in Neocaesarea, in the old town Kabeira which had become the metropole of the Roman province Pontus Polemoniacus in the second century. Makrina was from an aristocratic family. Basilius and Emmelia, her parents, belonged to those aristocrats who owned a big estate (latifundium) in the area of the Pontus. They survived seven years (304-311) of persecution of Christians under the government of Galerius and Maximilius Daja by hiding themselves with their whole household and servants in the wilderness. Their property was confiscated, but probably returned when Constantine, the Great, came to power. Makrina's paternal grandmother, the famous Makrina, the Older, was a pupil of Gregory Thaumaturgos, who preached the gospel in the area of the Pontus and was a man well educated in Christian religion and Greek philosophy as well. Gregory of Nyssa tells us how his sister Makrina lived an ascetic life on the family estate Annesi, northwest from Neocaesarea, together with her mother Emmelia, former slave women, and other aristocratic lady-companions. The choice for the ascetic life was also made by Makrina's brothers Basil and Petrus. The latter stayed in the convent when Basil thought it his duty to return to the life of active church politics. Makrina was honoured and admired by her third brother Gregory, who praised her highly in his *Vita Macrinae*. Gregory mentions the fact that he had a philosophical discussion on the topic of the soul and the resurrection with his sister on her death bed (*P.G.* 46, 959 sq.).[2] This discussion was written down

A History of Women Philosophers / Volume 1, ed. by Mary Ellen Waithe
© *Martinus Nijhoff Publishers, Dordrecht – Printed in the Netherlands*

by Gregory in the dialogue *De anima et resurrectione*, almost immediately after Makrina's death. It becomes clear from this dialogue, as we shall elucidate below, that Makrina was well educated and familiar with Greek philosophy. Makrina was educated by her mother, Emmelia. She did not receive any formal training like her brothers, who were educated at Athens. She proves to have a sharp mind and a remarkable knowledge of the topics discussed in Greek philosophy since Plato's time. According to Van der Meer and Bartelink[3] *De anima et resurrectione*[4] is in many ways a counterpart of Plato's *Phaedo*.

II. MAKRINA AND THE SPIRITUAL TRADITION

1. *The Unity and Immortality of the Soul*

In the dialogue *On the soul and resurrection*, Makrina defends the soul's immortality, whereas Gregory plays the part of the adversary in order to make the truth of the thesis more obvious. The existence of the soul is taken for granted in this dialogue, as it was in the whole ancient world. Makrina describes the nature of the soul as follows:

> The soul is a created substance, living and intellectual, infusing through itself the power to live and to grasp objects of sense into an organic body, gifted with senses, as long as the nature receiving those powers holds together (*P.G.* 46, 29b).

The description of the faculties of the soul reminds us of Plato's *Phaedo*, except that Makrina calls the soul a created substance. In the *Phaedo*, Plato puts the soul on a level between the visible world and the intelligible world of the Ideas (69d). In the *Timaeus*, he says that the soul is created by the Demiurgos as far as its higher, rational part is concerned.[5] According to Makrina, the soul is the principle of life and movement, because the remnants of a dead body fall into pieces and disappear at death. The concept that the soul is the principle of life is found in Plato's *Phaedo* (105c9-d12), as is the concept that the faculty of thinking and perceiving cannot be something material. However, Makrina's argument to prove the soul's immortality is not exactly the same as that in Plato's *Phaedo*. According to Makrina, there must be an intellectual and spiritual power which can coordinate and interpret the results of every act of sense-perception. This spiritual power is the soul, which is one. It is because of this *one-ness* that the soul will stay on after the death of the body, for the un-composite will not perish when the composite[6] perishes. This means that the soul, which is the principle of life, is immortal. This argument appears in chapter 7. Gregory opposes her because she has also said the soul would stay with the elements into which the dead body has returned. Makrina, however, keeps her thesis extant. For in her opinion, the soul is an indestructible spiritual one-ness which cannot be divided into parts, wherever it is. The soul will not, as Gregory suggested, be with one element and leave the others alone, in her opinion. The one-ness and indivisibility of the soul are the guarantee that it is indestructible.

Since Makrina's asceticism can best be comprehended against a background of several centuries of Christian and Pagan asceticism, it seems desirable to describe briefly the general intellectual and spiritual climate of the fourth century before discussing Makrina's philosophy in more detail. It also seems necessary to say a few words about some important preliminary questions. The development of the position of women in early Christianity, and its relationship to asceticism, which became one of the main characteristics in Christianity and Paganism as well in the fourth century, should at least be superficially examined.

2. *Asceticism*

E.R. Dodds[7] notes that a strong tendency towards asceticism and a preference for the hereafter were general features of fourth century Paganism and Christianity. This tendency already existed in the first century before Christ. The early Neoplatonists considered life on earth inferior to a life free from the body and its surroundings in the material world. According to the later Platonists, man's soul actually is an intermediary[8] between the intelligible world and the visible world, to which his body belongs; therefore, man does not feel at home on earth and he wants to transcend this life on earth. An essential feature of man's soul is, however, trying to get in touch with the intelligible world. Man's destiny, during his life on earth, is to reach the heaven of the world of the Ideas by leading a pure and chaste life on earth. Man has to live mentally-directed towards the intelligible world in order to protect his soul from a new incarnation after death. This has to be the main purpose of man's life on earth, but he has to take care of visible things as well. Generally speaking, in Platonism, man's soul has a twofold task during man's life on earth. This twofold task could give rise to an antithesis in the soul because it is between the intelligible world and the visible world. For Plotinus and Porphyry, the intermediary position of the soul could give rise to asceticism as a consequence of an exaggerated transcendentalism. But the combination of the emotional longing to transcend life on earth, and asceticism, the latter sometimes combined with a depreciation of all material things, is a general characteristic of Neoplatonism,[9] not limited to Plotinus and Porphyry. In Neoplatonism, moral virtue and ascetic life are considered to be a necessary task of the human soul's efforts to free itself from the boundaries of embodied life, and hence no virtuous life is possible without at least a certain degree of asceticism. An ascetic life is necessary in order to reach the world of Ideas, which Neoplatonists identified with the divine Mind (Nous) and which they also regarded as the true example of virtue.

The purification of ascetic life underlies the intellectual functioning of the human mind,[10] this is, as Porphyry writes to his wife Marcella[11] the only way to reach God. Man and woman are considered equal, as far as their souls are concerned in Neoplatonism — this holds for all Platonic thinkers. Both man and woman in principle are able to lead the ascetic life and to follow the intellectual training by means of which they can reach the real aim of life, the "homoiosis theooi", or, unification with God.

The combination of moral virtue and asceticism is also present in other Neoplatonic writers and is even older than Neoplatonism. There are traces of asceticism even in the later Stoa, as a moral condition to liberate the mind from the need to be occupied with the concerns of daily life in order to enable the mind to concentrate on God, which is the true aim of the wise man's life.[12]

3. *Gnosticism*

We find ascetic features in Gnosticism, which held the visible world in contempt and viewed the visible world as evil itself. Matter was considered as an independent principle and the source of evil[13] in the system of Basilides and in the Neopythagorean Numenius.[14] The visible world is not created by the supreme God, in the system of Valentinus, but by some unintelligent and inferior demiurge. This world is consequently evil.[15] Hyle (matter) is evil itself, according to the doctrine of Mani.[16] The common opinion of all gnostic systems is that man must be saved from this world.[17] The contempt of this world in gnostic systems, from Simon, the Magus (*Acts* VII, 9-10) on, leads to a certain similarity of Gnosticism to asceticism and encratism,[18] which were already rooted in primitive Christianity. However, this similarity is not based on any fundamental link between Gnosticism and Christianity.

4. *Gnosticism, Christianity, and the Inferiority of Women*

Unlike Christianity in its original form, Gnosticism in its many variations holds that the original evilness of this world is a given fact. Gnosticism explained the original evilness of this world as either due to the creation of the world by lower divinities, or by a creator who made it from evil matter. Christianity, on the other hand, maintains the goodness of the Creator and the original goodness of this world as His creation extant. The world became evil through human disobedience to the will of God. There is a certain tension between a world-accepting and a world-rejecting temper in early Christianity, as well as in Neoplatonism and preceding Platonic systems. This visible cosmos has to be accepted as something good, because it is dependent upon God, its Creator, who is the cause of its existence, but, because it is in fact evil, it must be rejected.

Total renewal of this cosmos by divine power from above was expected in a very short time in the early Christianity[19] of the first century. This might have mitigated the tendency toward a total world rejection among Christians, while inducing ascetic tendencies. These tendencies seem to have been present among first century Christians because both St. Paul, and the author of the so-called *Revelations of St. John*, consider virginity[20] better than the state of married life for men and women.

Quispel, in *Gnosis als Weltreligion*[21] points to the fact that in late antiquity man suffered from feelings of insecurity, due to the continual changing of his world. Man tried to find an escape from these horrible feelings by seeking rescue either in some kind of "Gnosis" or in erotic orgies, according to Quispel. This "Gnosis" is what Quispel calls "eine mythische Projektion der Selbsterfahrung" ... an interiorization and losing oneself in the unknown areas of one's own soul, and a hatred of this world. Woman is depreciated as inferior to man in all gnostic systems. This may be the consequence of the "mythische Projektion der Selbsterfahrung". It is psychologically possible that woman was considered dangerous to men, and represented the personification of those feelings from which they tried to escape by leading an ascetic life. In the *Gospel of Thomas*, 114,[22] women are considered unworthy of life; even Mary has to be transformed into a male.

Although the differences between Christianity on the one hand and Gnosticism and Platonism on the other, may have been quite fundamental, they did not always keep people from trying to conciliate them in many respects. Clemens Alexandrinus considered real "Gnosis" as a kind of progress in Christian life (*Strom.* VI, ch. 12, 101), but he keeps the original goodness of this visible world and of God, its Creator extant (*Strom.* VI, ch. 16, 137). However, he seems to be influenced by Gnosticism in subordinating woman to man. This, however, did not change the traditional position of women in the ancient world. It seems, though, to have given a doctrinal "justification" for already existing prejudices with regard to the subordination of woman to man.

III. MAKRINA AND WOMAN'S SOUL

1. *Makrina on the Soul and the* πάϑη (Pathe)[23]

In *De anima et resurrectione*, Gregory recounts the definition of the soul given by Makrina (*P.G.* 46, 29a). In his opinion, this definition does not explain all the faculties of the soul. He thinks that the soul has more faculties than those of thinking, giving life and sense-perception. There are also desire and anger, which we can recognize as the motives of many of our actions. They obviously are uncorporeal, and therefore must belong to our soul (rather than to our body) or there have to be other souls in us as well. Both possibilities are out of the question. Since the essence of the soul is the faculty of thinking, "pathe" cannot essentially belong to it, nor could there be other souls in us.

Makrina answers that Gregory has made his point. There are undeniably πάθη (pathe) like desire and anger inside us. Whether these pathe belong to our soul or are added to it later, has to be investigated. Makrina remarks that they, when speaking about the soul, have to take the Holy Scripture into consideration. The soul is made "in God's image", so it is like God, and cannot have "pathe". She wants to keep the former definition of soul extant (*P.G.* 46, 53c). Gregory again asks what to think of pathe like desire and anger. Makrina answers that those inner movements do not belong to the soul's essence and that they are merely "incrustations" of the soul, for we are all able to fight our pathe, an ability which sometimes is of great use to us (*P.G.* 46, 56a).

In the above mentioned discussion between Makrina and Gregory, (the main features of which we described only briefly), Makrina shows her knowledge of ancient Greek philosophy, including Plato's *Phaedo* and Aristotle's doctrine of the soul.[24] Their discussion about the soul and the pathe continues (*P.G.* 46, 59a sq.) with Makrina's comment that all pathe can be reduced to desire and anger. The pathe could never belong to the soul's essence, which is its faculty for thinking. Gregory points to the fact that in the Holy Scripture,[25] pathe are not always bad. Therefore, they are not always to be considered as bad. Makrina agrees with this, but she maintains that even the pathe of which we can make a good or a bad use do not belong to the soul's essence. Makrina stresses the unity of the soul, which is indestructible and immortal because of this one-ness. The immortal human soul stays after the death of the body until its reunion with its own body, which is restored into a spiritual body from the constituents of the original mortal body at the day of resurrection (see below). Soul and body certainly belong together in Makrina's view. However, she does not follow Aristotle in this matter. In

Makrina's opinion, during man's life on earth, soul and body are linked together-in a way which surpasses our understanding (*De an. et ress.* ch. VII, 2). They are not mixed up with each other. Aristotle, however, thinks the soul to be the "entelecheia" (entelechy) of the body (*De Anima* II, 1, 412a3-b9). In his opinion, the soul is the essence of a natural body and is not separable from the body. Consequently, the soul dies with the body. This holds for the souls of plants and animals and for the human soul as well. However, the human soul also possesses the faculty of thinking or Nous (*De Anima* 413b24-27). It comes from outside and is indestructible (*De generatione animalium* II, 3, 736b22 sq.). Makrina notes that the phenomena of the soul are the power of giving life, that of thinking and the capacity of being creative in matter (VII, 2, VIII, 3), and that although Aristotle investigated all phenomena of the soul, he nevertheless taught that the soul was mortal (*De anima et resurrectione* VII, 2). She obviously reproaches Aristotle with the fact that he did not conclude from these phenomena that the soul was a unity and consequently immortal. (See also ch. III, 2.) Makrina's concept of the unity of the soul underlies her criticism of Plato's view of the pathe in his *Phaedrus*, where in his famous metaphor of the charioteer he says the two lower parts of the soul to be responsible for the "pathe". The human soul which is one and "God-like" is essentially "apathes" in her opinion.

Nothing is directly known of Makrina's views on the question of the equality of the souls of men and women. However, from her discussion of the nature of the soul and of human creation, it becomes apparent that Makrina found no essential difference between the souls of men and those of women. According to Makrina, the essence of the soul is its capacity for rational thought. The pathe are not essential parts of the soul. Unlike Clemens of Alexandria, Makrina does not blame women for all the evil pathe or vices. According to her, the pathe are not parts of the essence of the soul and consequently, even if women did partake more of the evil pathe or vices than did men, this would be due to choice, made by individual women, and not due to the essential nature of a woman's soul. On Makrina's account of the nature of the soul, women and men are made in the "image and likeness of God". In this respect the views of Makrina and her brothers are compatible.

Basil, the Great, (Makrina's elder brother), commenting on *Genesis* I, 26[26] explicitly says.

> Also woman possesses the characteristic of being created in the image of God, in the same way as man possesses this characteristic. Their natures are equal in honour, equal are their virtues, equal their profits and similar their condemnation.

Basil considers the souls, i.e., the rational minds, of both man and woman made in the image of God. The great Cappadocian is of the opinion that man and woman are equally capable of realizing the likeness of God by their virtue. This likeness of God is only fully realized by Christ Himself,[27] who was perfect in every way. Basil considers woman fully equal to man as far as her mental and spiritual capacities are concerned: "for she is made in God's image and consequently has a rational mind and by this the power of dominating all other creatures and her own lower desires."

Makrina's brother Gregory, bishop of Nyssa, also thinks woman to be made in God's image. In *On the creation of man*, (ch. 16, *P.G.* 44, 192a, sq., a passage which illustrates the fact that the exegesis of *Gen.* I, 26-28 had become a great problem in Christian circles of the fourth century), Gregory introduces his own explanation of the words "He made them male and female", requesting his readers not to get angry, when he deals with this subject more thoroughly. This proves that during Makrina's lifetime, the image-doctrine was still an issue. Gregory's exegesis of *Gen.* I, 26-28 is in favour of the spiritual equality of man and woman. Woman is as fully a human being as man is. God's image, which can only be understood spiritually, has nothing to do with gender. Those categories are merely applicable to the corporality of a human being.

2. *The Traditional Views of Women's Souls*

Makrina and her brothers, Basil and Gregory, who were Fathers of the Church, had a more liberal opinion on women than that which had generally been held by theologians, (including some philosophers), since St. Paul.

a) *Clemens of Alexandria.* Clemens takes a Platonic position when he stresses the equality of man and woman with regard to their souls in *Strom.* IV, ch. 8,[28] but in the same chapter he goes on to defend the subordination of women to men on grounds of their physical differences.[29] Clemens tries to defend his theory about women in the context of this passage by quoting St. Paul's well-known words in I *Cor.* II, stressing the point of woman's subordination to man on the so-called "natural order of creation". Clemens certainly does not take a gnostic position, when, again quoting St. Paul, (this time in *Ephesians*) he stresses the point that life in a body is not evil in its own right. However, he does not seem to be altogether free from gnostic sympathies where the position of women is concerned; when in *Strom.* III, ch. 10, 63, he quotes from a gnostic writing, the so-called *Gospel of the Egyptians*, where the Lord says that He had come to finish "the works of woman"![30] The Gnostics understood the works of woman to be the whole natural order of birth and death which, in their view, was evil in its own right and caused by Eve. Clemens does not think of creation as bad and evil in its own right. He nevertheless accepts the Gospel as genuine, and interprets "the works of woman" to mean sins like avarice, contentiousness, love of fame, madness, love for women, love for boys, fancy living and prodigality. Clemens considers Eve the cause of all this evil. He takes for granted that "woman" or "the female" stands as a symbol of all evil, this, in spite of his (abovementioned) Platonic conception of the equality of man and woman *qua* soul. Here Clemens seems to be very near Gnosticism.

b) *The Pauline and Later Jewish traditions.* The combination of ascetic (especially encratistic) tendencies and the conception of woman as a being inferior to man, is also found in later Jewish tradition. It exists in all kinds of gnostic systems and also in the tradition formed by those Christians who mainly based their conception of woman on Paul's negative statements in this matter,[31] which they isolated from their context and his other more positive statements with regard to women.

Since the appearance of Gerhard Delling's *"Paulus' Stellung zu Frau und Ehe"*, (Stuttgart 1931), it has become accepted that Paul's opinion regarding women was strongly influenced by the

Jewish rabbinical tradition. According to at least some representations of that tradition, woman was to be considered inferior to man. Even the religious teaching of the Torah was considered superfluous for girls in some Jewish circles.[32] On the other hand, St. Paul also seems to be affected by the contemporary ascetic influences in the Jewish tradition in his subordination of the state of marriage to that of virginity with regard to both man and woman. Those ascetic tendencies in late Jewish tradition are found in Philo Alexandrinus.[33]

Many of St. Paul's so-called negative statements with regard to women may be derived from the Jewish tradition. However, in *Eph.* 5, Paul orders husbands to love their wives just as Jesus Christ loved the Church. In *Rom.* 16, 10-17 Paul recognizes women's work in the Lord, indicating that in spite of his background, his attitude towards woman is not always negative. *Gal.* 3, 28 holds the same more positive attitude. However, later interpretors (including many Fathers of the Church) have overlooked this fact. Many of St. Paul's negative statements regarding women are in contradiction to the attitude of Jesus Christ towards women in the *Gospel of St. John*.[34] Jesus Christ talked to women. This was rather revolutionary in his time. It was considered illegal, by lawful Jews, to speak much to women.[35] A man could bring evil upon himself and make himself inherit the Gehenna even by speaking to his own wife ... and much more by speaking to other women according to *Aboth* 5.

It is remarkable that Christian writers, especially many of the so-called Church Fathers, did not base their views towards women on the *Gospel of St. John*, but on some isolated statements of St. Paul, even though the *Gospel of St. John* was already well-known in the first centuries after Christ. It seems highly probable that many Christian writers already had their prejudices in this matter, prejudices which were very common in late antiquity.

The tendency to stress woman's submission seems to have grown stronger and stronger in Christian tradition as time continues. The so-called *Acts of Thecla*[36] were eventually recognized as not belonging to the canonic writings, for it seemed impossible that Paul could have commanded women to teach the gospel. The Synod of Gangra[37] speaks of the natural submissive state of women. That an official Synod could make such statements is evidence that the submissive state of women was generally accepted in clerical circles in the fourth century.[38] Also, the fourth century commentaries on *Genesis* show that the statement that women are made "in the image and likeness of God" was still very much an issue at the time of Makrina's discussion with Gregory. And while Makrina does not explicitly discuss the "image" issue, it is clear from her discussions of the nature of the (genderless) soul as created "in God's image," that her view was in marked contrast to the view of many Christian writers of the early Church. It is highly improbable that Makrina considered women more inclined to make an evil choice than men, since she was accustomed to very pious and virtuous women. Her mother Emmelia joined her in a pious life as did several other women. Moreover, her paternal grandmother, Makrina the Old, a pupil of Gregory Thaumaturgos[39] and so indirectly of Origen, was honoured in the family for her Christian faith and virtue. In Makrina's opinion, every human soul that turns away from God and yields completely to the pathe, loses its natural intellectual and moral powers, being blinded by its strong desire and attachment to the pathe (*De anima et resurrectione, P.G.* 46, 101).[40]

c) *Origen, Tertullian, Cyprian and Chrysostom on the Image Question.* Origen, like all members of the Alexandrian School, explains "in our image and likeness" (*Gen.* I, 26) in a spiritual way.[41] He refers to the creation of the spiritual man: the creation of mind (= nous) and soul; the former is male, the latter is female in every human being, man or woman. There is a soul, gifted with mind (= nous) present in every human being in Origen's opinion. It is in the capacity of his mind (= nous) that a human being is made in God's image. The image of God is the Logos;[42] therefore the human mind (= nous) participates in the divine Reason,[43] as the divine Reason, the real "eikoon" of God, participates in God, the Father. Origen's favoured explanation of man's creation in God's image does not exclude man or woman. Nevertheless, Origen takes refuge in some isolated passages in *St. Paul's Letters* in order to stress women's submissive state.[44] Also, the writings of the Jew, Philo of Alexandria, may have influenced Origen and other Christian writers in their attitude towards women. Philo had great influence on Patristic thought. He considered actual woman inferior to man, this in spite of the fact that in his opinion, woman was created in God's image.

The Alexandrians explained "in the image" spiritually,[45] and had the dogmatic basis for the spiritual equality of man and woman. In spite of this they took refuge in the *Letters of St. Paul* and held that women are inferior to men. Didymus, the Blind, another Alexandrian writer, takes a position similar to Origen's. He thinks that the souls of man and woman are both made "in the image of God".[46] In his opinion, it is right to make the same moral commands to men and women, because both are made "in God's image". However, with regard to marriage, Didymus follows St. Paul in I *Cor.* 11, 3, in thinking it right that a husband is the master of his wife and has command over her.[47] Didymus allows women to prophesize, but they may not explain or write down anything the Holy Spirit tells them, for that would be teaching and against the prescriptions of St. Paul.[48]

Tertullian and Cyprian, the Africans, take their own unique positions on the image question. Tertullian considered both man and woman to be made in God's image in his writing *Adversus Praxean* (*P.L.* 2, 162).[49] Here, he thought of spiritual being in a material sense, assuming that both man and woman reflect the Trinitarian image in soul and in body. Cyprian held that man and woman are made "in God's image" *qua* soul and body.[50] He thinks that whatever God says in the Scriptures to the male, is also said to the female,[51] and finds no scriptural argument for a general suppression of women. In contrast, Tertullian bases his opinion that women are inferior to men on St. Paul's negative statements. The most striking evidence can be found in his writing *De virginibus velandis* ch. 8 and 9 (*P.L.* II, 950 sq.), where he says that women are not allowed to speak in a gathering of the Church, nor to teach or baptize, according to I *Cor.* 14, 34 and I *Tim.* II, 12. Tertullian explicitly says in *De virg. vel.* ch. 4 that all women must wear their hair long and hide it under a veil, in order to prevent the desire of the angels (cf. St. Paul in I *Cor.* XI, 8, 10).[52]

The tendencies to consider woman as submissive and subordinated to man by nature seem — we have stressed this point before — to have become stronger and more obvious in the fourth century. The Antiochenes, especially in contrast to the Alexandrians, had great difficulties with the image question.[53] The

Antiochene School generally kept extant the doctrine that only the male human being was created "in God's image". According to this school, being created in God's image and likeness meant that the male could dominate the world. The Antiochene writer John Chrysostom explicitly says in his commentary on *Genesis* I, 26[54] that woman is not made in God's image because she does not have the power of domination. He finds "Paulinean" arguments to stress woman's inferiority in other writings, such as *On Marriage.*[55] Woman is not allowed to earn a living outside the house or to make profits as a business woman. Chrysostom says that minding public affairs is the natural task of the male and is forbidden to women. It is woman's glory to be subordinated to man. She is created in this way, which means that she lacks intellectual power. In his view, woman should never compete with man. We find similar ideas regarding woman in the writings of other members of the Antiochene School including Diodoros of Tarsus[56] and Theodoretus of Cyrus.[57] The ideas of the Antiochene School are rather alarming — even if we take into consideration that, in late antiquity, the position of woman in everyday life was not emanipated in our sense of the word.

Woman is officially considered inferior to man in the West, in the fourth century. Ambrosius, bishop of Milan, explcitly says[58] that in the order of nature woman is subordinated to man. He basis himself in this respect on St. Paul's negative utterances with regard to woman. She is the cause of the fall, in his view, although he thinks it more important that by God's providence she also is the cause of mankind.[59] God wanted more people than the guiltless Adam alone to be saved, therefore, He made Eve from Adam as a helper for him. The latter means that she is not equal to Adam.[60] Ambrosius thinks man to be made in the image of God in the capacity of his soul, whereas he excludes woman to be made in this way.[61] What is true for most post-Pauline traditions, however, is not true for all theologians, especially not for some fourth century theologians in Cappadocia, the homeland of Makrina. We saw that Gregory of Nazianz (Gregory Nazianzus) and Gregory and Basil, Makrina's brothers, treated the image issue in favour of woman.

3. *Mary, the Mother of Christ in Patristic Literature*

Most Church Fathers speak respectfully of Mary,[62] whatever they thought about woman. Since the origin of Patristic Literature, Mary has been considered the new Eve.[63] This concept was already present in the *Proto-Gospel of James*, which dates from the second century.[64] Mary obediently listened to God's message as Eve listened to the devil. Mary let herself become an instrument for God's salvation of mankind. This development is linked with the development of theology, especially of Christology.[65] The more the focus of theology is on the incarnation of the Logos, the more it is on Mary, Christ's mother. There is a discussion among the Fathers, in particular those of the fourth century, about Mary's position in God's plan of the salvation of mankind. This discussion leads up to the Council of Ephesus in 431 which recognized Mary as "theotokos" (deipara), God-bearer, or the Mother of God. As such, Mary had to be a forever sinless virgin.[66] The members of the Council explicitly stress Mary's virginity *ante et post partum*. Theodoretus of Ancyra says:

> If Christ was born in the way we are born, He would have been a man.[67] He would have been recognized as God by those, who had insight, however, if he saved his mother's virginity, when he was born".[68]

Mary's virginity was originally praised on more or less ascetic grounds. Her virginity is part of her ethics. The new Eve had to be a woman of high morality. Since virginity was considered a better state of life than married life, Mary's virginity is highly praised.[69] This virginity provides her with spiritual gifts. Origen (*In Joh. Ev., P.G.* 14, 1, 3) praises her spiritual motherhood, seeing her as a virgin who lived an ascetic life. This same view is found later in Jerome (*Ep.* 22, ch. 37 and 38), who says that no woman would be able to lead an ascetic life, were it not for Mary.[70] Jerome, like Ambrosius, Pope Damasius and (n.b.) Tertullian, greatly admires Mary's spiritual motherhood. Jerome and Sulpicius Severus[71] take Mary as a model for all women. In Origen's opinion, Mary received the blessing of becoming the virgin Mother of God because of her spiritual efforts to concentrate on the heavenly life.

In the fourth century Mary had already become the pure and sinless instrument for God's salvation of mankind. Mary's obedience to God is highly praised among the Church Fathers[72] who stress the passivity of her obedience.[73] Epiphanius speaks of Mary as an "officina" (ergasterion) for God's salvation of mankind (*Ancoratus, P.G.* 43, 159). Cyrillus of Alexandria calls Mary the temple of God, because the Divine Logos made her His temple (*Adv. Nest.* I, 9; *P.G.* 76, 660). Fourth century theology demanded a forever sinless virgin to be Christ's mother. However, the picture of this virgin seems to be loaded with the projections of the Fathers. The holy virgin of fourth century Christology is more passive than the virgin of the Gospel. She is a woman whose whole life is dependent on her obedience to God. This necessarily makes her a very passive woman in the view of the Fathers, who seem to project their own ideal woman on Mary.

When the fourth century Church Fathers used Mary as an example for all other women, they did not even think of taking the very special circumstances of her life into consideration. The great honour which they paid to the "deipara" did not become a factor for the liberation of women. On the contrary, women had to be humble and obedient in every respect. The fourth century Church Fathers summoned women to adopt what they thought to be Mary's attitude and behaviour in life as the right way of life for all women. In spite of the unrealistic picture of Mary which most of the Fathers[74] of the fourth century had, they all honoured her as the new Eve. Where Eve is connected with the fall, Mary is connected with salvation. Where Eve is connected with death and punishment, Mary is connected with life and grace. The passive Mary-picture[75] of the fourth century accords with the increasing tendencies to stress the submissive state of women. Since Mary became the example for the "virgines Christi" (who were greatly honoured in the Old Church, almost in the same way as the martyrs) in the fourth century,[76] this passivity[77] greatly influenced their lives.

4. *Woman and Anthropomorphic Thinking about God*

The anthropomorphic conception of God was another factor which might have induced the tendencies to consider woman inferior to man. This conception existed in certain Christian circles in the fourth century. Some evidence of anthropomorphism can be found in Basil's *De structura hominis* (*L'origine de l'homme* ch. I, 5, 13, éd. Sources Chrétiennes, nr. 160, p. 276) where Basil calls God incomprehensible by His greatness. Many people have absurd ideas about God; they thought that He had the same corporeal form as a human being had. Basil calls this "the Jewish way of thinking about God" on the ground that the Old Testament spoke about God as "having hands, feet, etc.".

Evagrius, archdeacon of Constantinople and later a monk in the Egyptian desert, mentions in his letters that some people thought about God anthropomorphically and warns against this.[78] Arnobius (*Adv. Gentes* III, 8) explicitly says that God is not a man, although His name is masculine. The tendency to speak of God in metaphors, mainly of the male gender, existed from the origin of Christianity.[79] In late antiquity people sometimes confused sexual and grammatical genus, although use of the masculine article does not restrict reference to the male.[80] Ancient prejudices with regard to women influenced Church Fathers' views of women as indicated by their preference for the negative statements of St. Paul. These prejudices survived and increased through the willingness of the uneducated to accept man's superiority based on their misunderstanding of the Holy Scripture. Even the Church Fathers' view of Mary, the new Eve, is loaded with the projections of what they thought an ideal woman should be, namely, obedient and passive.

In the Old Church, the women martyrs,[81] including the "virgines Christi", were honoured for their active virtue, for standing up for the Lord, and their faith in Him in the face of death. However, when martyrdom disappeared, the old prejudices against women which had not died, flourished more and more. It was these prejudices, that determined the picture of woman for many centuries to come. Makrina's philosophy and that of her brothers stand in contrast to this tradition.

IV. MAKRINA ON CREATION, REINCARNATION, AND RESURRECTION

A description of man's creation follows Makrina's discussion of the pathe. According to the Holy Scripture, man is the crown of creation. Plants and animals preceded man in the order of the creation of the visible world (*P.G.* 46, 60B). Makrina says that a vegetative soul is present in plants, while a soul with vegetative functions and the faculties of sense-perception is present in animals. The essence of the human soul is the power of thinking, but the soul is also connected with animal nature. Makrina is convinced that the soul is immortal and that it is the guardian of the elements into which the body returns after death. According to Makrina, the body will be rewoven from its old components into a body with a much finer structure. This new spiritual body will have a likeness to the former body, so that the soul may recognize its own.

Makrina leaves the argument for the Christian doctrine of resurrection as it is until the end of the dialogue, and returns to the discussion of the pathe in ch. 12. According to Makrina, misuse of the pathe leads to evil, good use to virtue. It is all a question of individual choice. The soul becomes free of all pathe after the death of the body. Gregory makes an objection here. He wants to know what we must think of the soul's highest desire,[82] its longing for God. His sister answers that the soul has no need for any pathos after death, for it is drawn to God (= the Good and Beautiful itself) by God Himself.

1. *Makrina and the Plotinian Tradition*

Makrina's identification of God with the Good and the Beautiful seems to be of Neoplatonic origin, to wit *Enn.* I, 6 of Plotinus. Plotinus, who emphasizes the twofold task of the human soul in *Enn.* IV, 3, 4 (éd. Bréhier), calls the beauty of the visible world an exhortation for the soul to seek the beauty of the intelligible world, of which the visible world is an eikoon or an agalma, a resemblance (*Enn.* I, 6 *"On the Beautiful"*; *Enn.* II, 3, 18, 1, 8-22). However, Plotinus asks why have the souls left God, their Father? (*Enn.* V, 1, 1). Plotinus has souls, incorporated in a body, in mind here.[83] So we must assume that he stresses the point that man's soul in a body should be directed towards the intelligible world and to God. His monistic perspective required him to assume no substantial cause of evil.[84] There is no evil in the intelligible world (*Enn.* I, 8, 2, 1. 25-31; Ch. 3, 1. 1-12), of which the visible world is an eikoon (image). The visible world also partakes of goodness (*Enn.* IV, 8, ch. 6, 1. 1-28); however, the dark element of the "*hylè*" (μὴ ὄν)[85] also belongs to it. Therefore Plotinus could approve of the beauty and perfection of the visible world, but he had to prefer the intelligible world to the visible world, since the former is on a higher level than the latter.[86] Plotinus explicitly says that the visible world did not come into existence by a fall of the soul (*Enn.* II, 9, 4). For Plotinus, the human soul in a body has the task of caring for the body, but it also has to find its way back to the intelligible world, whence it came.[87] Like Plato (*Timaeus* 87C), Plotinus thinks man to be a *synamphoteron* (compound) of soul and body (*Enn.* I, I). This means that the mortal body, is the only possible body and belongs to the nature of man. The mortality of the human body is un-related to the fall of the soul in his opinion, for according to Plotinus, only an embodied soul can sin. Man's body is not some-thing which has to be restored at the end of time. As a matter of fact there is no end of time in Plotinian thought. Time belongs to the visible world, which is part of the eternal process of emanation (*Enn.* III, 7, 12; *Enn.* VI, 9, 9).

In contrast, Makrina considers the mortality of man's present body caused by the fall. In her opinion, man had a spiritual and apathes body before the fall (*De anima et resurrectione*, ch. 18, 4).

In Makrina's view this spiritual and apathes body will be re-stored to the soul at the day of resurrection. In Plato's *Timaeus* the mortality of man's body also belongs to the nature of man and is made by the visible gods, whereas man's soul is made by the Demiurgos Himself. Man is a synamphoteron, a compound of soul and body. However, man's body is mortal, whereas his soul except for its lowest part, the "threptikon" is immortal (*Timaeus* 69a-70a). Man's task is to live in this world (*Timaeus* 41d8-42d1). Man may escape a new incarnation eventually, when he has lived many lives in the body well. Makrina clearly departs from Plato in her conviction that the human body will be resurrected and restored in a special way at the end of time:

Then you will see this bodily garment which is now dissolved by death woven again of the same elements, not according to its present crass and heavy construction, but with the thread resewn into something more fine and delicate (*De anima et resurrectione*).

Resurrection is a fundamentally Christian thought and Makrina bases herself on the Holy Scripture in this matter, as we shall make clear below.

2. *Makrina and the Porphyryian View*

A point of view regarding the visible world and the intermediary position of soul, comparable to Plotinus' view is found in the Neoplatonic writer, Porphyry.[88] Porphyry did not consider corporeal things[89] bad although he thought it necessary for the soul to flee from all corporeal things in order to reach its real destiny in the world above.[90] Human beings have to think of God as being present at all their works and deeds, watching them.[91] God is the cause of all good things, while humans are the cause of moral evil.[92] Plotinus thought sin to be the consequence of man's yielding too much to things that are inferior to the soul by his own free will. According to Plotinus (*Enn.* I, I, 12) who follows Plato (*Timaeus* 41a-d), at man's birth an other kind of soul to which the terrible pathe belong, is added to the higher intellectual soul (nous) of man. So the human soul becomes a compound. It is this compound, that *can* sin (*Enn.* II, I, 5, 1. 18-23), whereas man's higher soul, which is also considered man's *real self* always stays unaffected. Porphyry explicitly says that the cause of great sins should not be sought in the body, but in the soul. He considers virtue the only way to God.[93] Striving after pleasure is completely incompatible with love of God. Man has to get rid of the "pathe" (*De Abstinentia* I, 33-35) and refrain from all sensations which could stimulate them. Like Plotinus (*Enn.* VI, 4, 16 and II, 9) Porphyry thinks that the human soul can be reincarnated after death. However, he explicitly rebukes the concept of Plato's *Timaeus* that a human soul could be reincarnated in an animal-body, in *De regressu animae*.[94] During his life on earth, man has to find spiritual wealth within himself and exercise his mind, for the mind of a wise man (or woman) is a temple of God and God is the only thing a wise man (or woman) needs.[95] So a wise man establishes the "homoiosis theooi" for himself. In *Kata Christianoon* (= *Against the Christians*),[96] and in *De regressu animae*,[97] Porphyry opposes the Christian doctrine of the resurrection of the flesh. In Porphyry's view, the concept of resurrection contradicts the concept of the eternity of this world. However, he says that the soul of the good man will never descend again. Since perfect wisdom is not found in this life below, the life after death has to be perfected by God.

3. *Makrina and the Tradition of Philo of Alexandria*

Philo of Alexandria, known for his influence on Patristic thought, brought a new element into the history of philosophy, i.e., revelation. A Hellenistic Jew, Philo was bred in the Greek Platonic and Stoic philosophy of his age, and tried to conciliate Judaism and Platonism.[98] Philo deals with man's creation in *De opificio mundi* (= *On the Creation*) and elsewhere, but his interpretation of the image-doctrine in *Gen.* I, 26 is complicated and sometimes misunderstood. In some passages,[99] Philo speaks of woman as inferior to man, calling her the cause of all worldly evil[100] while not denying that she is also made in God's image.[101] Man's rational soul, which is a copy of the Divine Logos (Reason), is asexual.[102] The basic sexual male-female polarity belongs to the realm of the visible world of creation, to which the sense-perceptible man belongs (*De op. mundi* 133). God created the incorporeal Ideas first in the causal order, then the visible world and its belongings, except for man (*De op. mundi* 129-134). The creation of sense-perceptible man, mentioned in *De op. mundi* 134, must be understood in light of *Leg. All.* II, 12-13. Here generic man must potentially belong to the sexual categories male and female, and, in the causal order must precede the creation of Adam. The creation of genera occurred causally prior to the creation of the earthly sense-perceptible man (*De op. mundi* 134). Philo does not deal with the question of when and how Adam's female coutnerpart was actually created. He deals with the Genesis-story in an exclusively allegorical way, in *Leg. All.* (*On the allegorial Interpretation*) II, 19-52. It seems, however, highly probable that Eve was created in a way analogous to the creation of Adam. Earthly man is either male or female. The sexuality of a human being belongs to the realm of its corporality, and to that of the irrational soul which a human being shares with other animals. It is the a-sexual rational soul that makes a human being really human. Theoretically, Philo does not deny that man and woman are both endowed with rational souls and (according to this fact) are both made "in the image of God". Nevertheless, Philo considers actual woman inferior to man and woman to be the cause of all evil in this world (*Quaest. in Gen.* II, 45; I, 37). Philo is the first philosopher, who gave a philosophical interpretation of *Gen.* I, 26. He is at the base of the long tradition of various commentaries on this subject. Also his explanation of moral evil in this world is founded on *Genesis*. He deals with the problem of evil in *De op. mundi* 24, 72-75 (edition Cohn Wendeland I, p. 24-25). Vice and virtue have their dwelling-place in mind and reason of man. Like Plato Philo is convinced that God cannot be the Creator of any kind of evil. Therefore he ascribes vice in man to fellow-workers of God, the Creator. The plural "let us make men" in the Genesis-story of creation makes it possible for him to do so. In spite of the fact that a human being is made accessible to vice Philo stresses the fact that the human (rational) soul is made by God Himself a copy of the eternal Logos (*De op. mundi* 48, 139, C.W. I, p. 48-49) and breathed into man. Therefore this rational soul is – in the first man at least – perfect (see also above). Philo, interpreting *Genesis* in an allegorical way, explains the fall as the fall of the intelligence (nous) seduced by the senses and mentions the ways by which intelligence can return to its original state. Then we have to suppress all responsiveness to the pull of the senses and withdraw from the sensible world. Philo's ethic inclines to a world denying asceticism (*De Vita Mosis* = *Moses* II, 68; *Leg. All.* II, 30; *De Fuga et Inventione* = *On Flight and Finding* 50), such in spite of the fact that God who cannot be the cause of any evil, created the sensible world by His will and goodness (*De op. mundi* 17, 20; *Conf.* 114). In Philo's view this visible world is not eternal, but it is made imperishable by God's goodness (*De Decalogo* = *On the Decalogue* 58; *De Aeternitate mundi* = *On the Eternity of the World* 18ff; *Heres* 24b). The aim of man's life on earth is to practize virtue in dealing with one's neighbours. This is the unification with God (*De Vita Mosis* II, 107-108). After this the soul may go the way of inwardness in order to reach the deification, which is an unbroken union with God in love. The soul that yearns with an intense erôs for God, will achieve its fulfilment in this way.

4. *Makrina and the Reincarnation Doctrines*

Makrina deals with the different doctrines of reincarnation, known among Greek philosophers (*De an. et ress.* ch. 14, paragraph 3). She rebukes them all, for all those doctrines imply a cyclic movement of souls between heaven and earth and this movement on its turn presupposes the fall of a soul as the cause of the coming into existence of an earthly being. Makrina thinks the latter to be in contradiction with the goodness of God and His providence. If man's existence were caused by sin, he would be unfit for virtue. Makrina explicitly rejects (*De an. et ress.* ch. 14, paragraph 4) the idea that rational souls of human beings are sometimes reincarnated into animal-bodies and plants as a kind of punishment for their sins. Plato (*Rep.* 620a-d) held that a human soul could be reincarnated into an animal-body, while Plotinus did not explicitly exclude the possibility of the reincarnation of human souls into animal-bodies and plants (*Enn.* II, 9, 6; IV, 3, 9).[103] According to both Plato and Plotinus, a human soul could obviously lose its rational character as a consequence of its evil actions and be reincarnated in a lower being. As we have seen above, Porphyry did not accept this doctrine, but held that a human soul can never lose its rational character. Consequently, he rejects reincarnation in animal-bodies, in *De regressu animae*.[104] Later Proclus takes a comparable position (*In Rempubl.* II, p. 312, 1. 10-14; 312, 7-12) in this matter.

Makrina is especially opposed to the reincarnation of human souls into plants and animals. In her opinion, this would destroy the distinction between man and animal (*De an. et resurr.* ch. 14, 3). In her view, a cyclic movement of human souls is also out of the question for such a movement implies a mingling of good and evil (*De an. et resurr.* ch. 14, 4 and 5). In Makrina's interpretation, cyclic movement of human souls begins in heaven and is caused by a fall of the soul.[105] Makrina criticizes this idea because it would require that sin were the cause of earthly human existence (*De an. et resurr.* ch. 14, 6). Moreover, since heaven is considered immutable by the gentiles, it is inexplicable how the fall of a soul could occur (*De an. et resurr.* ch. 14, 5 and 6). Makrina does not name those she criticizes but when she rejects the doctrine that the fall of a soul in heaven could be the cause of earthly human life, she is clearly rejecting Origen who thought that the fall of purely intelligible and free beings caused embodied human life on earth (*De Principiis* ii, 1, 1-2).[106] In Makrina's opinion, soul and body are created together by the will of God. Souls do not come into existence before the bodies (*De an. et resurr.* ch. 15, 3). Both soul and body come into existence at conception. This means that for Makrina, the soul is present in the sperm from which a living being proceeds. When mankind has reached its fulfilment, the process of coming into being and passing away will end. At the end of time, on the day of the resurrection,[107] mankind will partake in eternal life in soul and in body. At the day of resurrection, the mortal human body will be restored to the immortality which it possessed before the fall. In the view of Makrina and Gregory, the mortality of man's body is a consequence of the fall. However, the fact that man has a body has nothing to do with the fall at all. On the contrary, to have a body belongs to man's nature (*De an. et resurr.* ch. 18, 2). The difference with Origen in this respect is clear. The concept of a spiritual body at the resurrection found in Origen (*De Princ.* III, VI; II, X, 1-2, 3) does not exclude the possibility that this spiritual body will also disappear (*De Princ.* II, III, 2-3, Jerome, *Ep. ad Avitum* 5). Makrina mainly bases her views on resurrection on Scripture. In her opinion (*De anima et resurrectione* ch. 16) Psalms 103, 117, 27 and others favour the resurrection of the body. At the end of time, the whole universe will be restored by the Spirit of God. In Psalm 103, Makrina finds evidence for the doctrine of the apokatastasis (restoration of all things), also defended by Gregory in the *Oratio Catechetica* ch. 26. Makrina thinks the restoration of human life to be part of this restoration of all things.[108]

The end of the dialogue between Makrina and Gregory is a defense of the Christian doctrine of resurrection. Most of the evidence is drawn from the Holy Scripture. Makrina knows how to refute the arguments of the adversaries of which Gregory reminds her. The end of the dialogue is theologically interesting. Many of the ideas expressed by Gregory in his *De opificio hominis (= On the creation of man)* are also found in the dialogue *On the soul and resurrection* defended by his great sister Makrina. She and that dialogue deserve a more extended treatment than we could give in this essay. We have merely tried to draw our reader's attention to a fourth-century woman, well bred and gifted with a sharp mind for philosophical thinking. Clearly, Makrina belongs among those women in the ancient world who actually occupied themselves with philosophy.

NOTES

1. Gregory wrote *"De vita Macrinae"* after his sister's death, which occurred in 380.
2. *P.G.* = *Patrologia Graeca.* Migne, Patrologiae cursus completus, series Graeca.
3. See F. van der Meer and G. Bartelink in the Introduction of their Dutch translation of *"De vita Macrinae"*, Antwerpen 1971. The Dutch translation followed the Greek text edited by W. Jaeger, Leyden 1952.
4. *P.G.* (= *Patrologia Graeca*) 46; English translation by W.K. Lowther Clarke, London 1916.
5. *Timaeus* 69c5 sq.
6. The thought that the uncomposite is indestructible is also found in *Phaedo* 78c1-79a11.
7. See E.R. Dodds, *Pagan and Christian in an Age of anxiety*, Belfast 1963. See also. G. Quispel in *Gnosis als Weltreligion*, Zürich 1951.
8. Plato considered the visible world a perceptible god, in *Timaeus* 92c. (God is the Good, which is beyond the Ideas according to Plato.) The soul has an intermediate position between the intelligible and the sensible world according to Platonic thinkers and even according to later Stoics influenced by Platonism. Cf. Xenocrates in Simplicius, in *Arist. De Anima* I, 2/404b27, p. 30, Hayduck (fr. 64H); Posidonius in Plutarchus, *De Proc. Animae in Timaeum* 22, p. 1023c; Seneca, *Ep.* 92 "Prima pars hominis est ipsa virtus: huic committitur inutilis caro et fluida, receptandis tantum cibis habilis, ut ait Posidonius"; Plotinus, *Enn.* IV, 8, 7, 1-14; *Enn.* VI, 2, 22, 28-35 (éd. Bréhier).
9. Iamblichus included.
10. Porphyry, *Sententiae* (Stob. III, 3, p. 89); Plotinus, *Enn.* I, 2, 4, 1, 5-7.
11. *Ep. ad Markellam* (Nauck, pp. 283-287), in C.J. de Vogel, *Greek Philosophy* III,, 1444, Leyden 1964.
12. Cf. Epictetus, *Dissertationes* IV, I, 91-94, 97-104 (ed. Schenkl, Leipzig 1916).
13. Basilides, fr. 1 (Volker, Quellen, p. 38).
14. Cf. Numenius in Chalcidius in *Timaeum*, 295-299.

15. Cf. Irenaeus *Adv. Haer.* I, ch. VIII, (*P.G.* 7), English translation in ante-Nicene Christian Library, edited by E. Roberts and James Donalson, Edinburgh 1868.

16. See St. Augustine, *Tractatus in Evangelium Joh.* I, 14 and IX, 2. (Oeuvres de Saint Augustine, Homilies sur l'évangile de Saint Jean I-XVI, Desclée de Brouwer, Brugge 1964, p. 158, n. 6 and p. 507, n. 64.)

17. See G. Quispel in *Gnosis als Weltreligion*, Zürich 1951.

18. Cf. Didache VI, 2 where poverty and enkrateia are praised as virtues, which could make man perfect; see further Tatianus in Clemens Alexandrinus, *Strom.* III, 12; and Hippolytus of Rome, *Philos.* VIII, 20, who were even against marriage. See also Clem. *Alex. Strom.* V, 94, 3 and further Pastor Hermas, *Visio* I, 1-29, where in heaven Rhoda accuses Hermas of the fact that he has desired her.

19. German scholars use the theological term "Naheerwartung" to refer to this phenomenon.

20. See St. Paul's first letter to the Corinthians ch. 1; St. John, *Revelations* 14, 4: "... and see they were virgins."

21. G. Quispel *Gnosis als Weltreligion*, Zürich 1951.

22. Cf. Johannes Leopoldt: *Das Evangelium nach Thomas*, Berlin 1967, pp. 76-77.

23. Πάθη (pathe) is the plural of Πάθος (pathos). τὸ πάθος means incident, accident; πάθος of the soul means "emotion", "passion", but also "sensation", "experience", "feeling", "suffering". The substantive pathos is connected with the verb πάσχειν (paschein) = to experience, to suffer.

24. Makrina opposes Aristotle's concept of the soul as the *entelecheia* of the body.

25. *Dan.* 9, 23; *Prov.* 9, 10; 2 *Cor.* 7, 10.

26. *Sur l'origine de l'homme, Hom.* I, ch. 18, éd. Sources Chrétiennes, 160, p. 213.

27. *Op. cit.*, ch. 20 and 23.

28. See also *Paedagogus* II, I, 9, 12.

29. The creation of man in the image and likeness of God in *Gen.* I, 26 is explained by Clemens in *Strom.* V, 14, 94. Clemens, like St. Paul in I *Cor.* I, 15 and II *Cor.* 4, calls the Logos (Christ) the real image of God. Man's natural mind is the image of the image fo God. This holds for man and woman.

30. Eve was associated with evil in gnostic tradition. See Epiphanius, *Pan.* 45, 2, 1. For a more detailed description of this concept see L. Ginzburg in *The Legends of the Jews*, Philadelphia 1946.

31. See for instance Joh. Chrysostomus, *Patrologia Graeca* 15, 218 (hom. in quosdam locos N.T.); Tertullian, *De feminis velandis* VIII, *Patrologia Latina* 2, 948 sq. (Migne, Patrologiae cursus completus, series Latina.)

32. C. Quispel points to the rabbinical subordination of women in "Makarius, das Thomas Evangelium und das Lied von der Perle", Leyden 1967, p. 32, n. 2.

33. *De vita cont.* (= De vita contemplativa = On the contemplative Life); *Quod. omn. prob. lib.* 75, 84 (= Quod Omnis Probus Liber sit = Every good man is free). (English translation in Loeb Classical Library.)

34. See for instance *St. John* 4, 1-7, where Jesus speaks to the Samaritan woman. See also the gnostic *Gospel of St. Thomas*, Sentence 114, where Petrus does not agree that Jesus speaks to women. Jesus is reproached for speaking to women in the *Gospel of Mary* and in the *Pistis Sophia.*

35. See Herbert Danby, *The Mishnah* translated from Hebrew, with Introduction and brief Explanatory Notes, Oxford 1933, p. 446. See also Strack-Billerbeck, *Kommentar zum N.T. aus Talmud und Midrash*, p. 438.

36. See Tertullian, *De baptismo*, ch. 17. See K. Holzey in *Die Theklaakten, Münster* 1905.

37. *Mansi* II, 1099-1106.

38. Women had the right to baptize until the fourth century, but lost it afterwards. (*Mansi* III, 952 *Stat. Eccl. Antiq. Canones*). See also H. Huls in his Dissertation, University of Utrecht, 1952.

39. Gregory Thaumaturgos was a great admirer of the Virgin Mary. He had three apparitions of her (Gregory of Nyssa in *Vita Greg. Thaum.*, *P.G.* 46, 893). Mary manifested herself to him not only as a holy, but also as a rather "active" person, occupying herself with Church matters. It is not unthinkable that this picture of Mary influenced the three Capadocians and Makrina as well in their attitude towards women.

40. Compare Philo in *Mos.* II, 16; Gregory of Nyssa in *De virginitate* ch. V, (Sources Chrétiennes, no. 119, Paris 1966).

41. See for instance *Gen. Hom.* I, 13 sq. (*Patrologia Graeca*, 12, 155C).

42. Cf. *De Principiis* (*Patrologia Graeca*, XI, 333) and *Comm. in Joann.* II, 3 (*Patrologia Graeca*, 14, 1, 3).

43. "Eikoon" is an image, which participates in its original, either in a spiritual or a non-spiritual way. See Plato *Timaeus* 92c. The Logos was still subordinated to God the Father before the Council of Nicea.

44. Origen forbids women to speak or prophesize at church meetings. Origène *Fragments sur la Première aux Corinthiens* 75 (Journal of Theological Studies 10, 41-42). See also C.H. Turner in Journal of Theological Studies 10, 270-276.

45. See for instance Athanasius *De incarnatione* (*Patrologia Graeca* 25, 20c); Cyril of Alexandria, *Dial. Trin.* (*Patrologia Graeca* 75, 1089) for the "image-doctrine".

46. See Didyme l'Aveugle, *Sur la Genèse* I, 26-28, 62-64, p. 158, éd. Sources Chrétiennes, 233, Lyon (France) 1976.

47. *Sur la Genèse* 58, p. 150.

48. *Dialexis.* (Montanistou kai Orthodoxou Dialexis, Greek text and French translation edited by Pierre de Labirolle, 1913).

49. Cf. Tertullian in *Adversus Marcionem*, 4. (*Patrologia Latina* II, 288); *De resurrectione carnis* = On the Resurrection of the Flesh 6, *Patrologia Latina* II, 802). However, Tertullian did not always have consistent opinions about Christian doctrine: he denied that woman was a human being

in her own right in *De feminis velandis* ch. VIII, *Patrologia Latina* II, 110. He thinks that St. Paul in I *Cor.* XI, 2, 7 can be explained in favour of his doctrine in this passage.

50. *De habitu virginum* ch. 15 (*Patrologia Latina* IV, 454).
51. Cyprian *De hab. virg.* ch. 4 (*Patrologia Latina* IV, 454).
52. This seems to be a common Jewish view. See L. Ginzberg, *op. cit.*, Vol. V, n. 22 and 23.
53. See H.C. Graaff, *L'image de Dieu et la structure de l'âme d'après les Pères Grecs* in Supplément de la Vie spirituelle, tome 5, nr. 20, 5 février 1952.
54. *In Gen. Hom.* VII, 4, *Patrologia Graeca* 53, 70-76.
55. *Patrologia Graeca* 51, 230-231.
56. Cf. *Quaestio* XX in *Gen.*, ed. Schultze, Vol. I, 24-29, *Patrologia Graeca* 33, 1561 ff. Man is originally created in God's image, woman is not.
57. See R.C. Graaff, *op. cit.*
58. *De Paradiso* I, XI, 50 (*Patrologia Latina* 14, p. 280).
59. *Op. cit.*, p. 299.
60. Ambrosius could never reconcile his doctrine of woman's inferiority with his doctrine of the human soul, which was influenced by Neoplatonic thinking.
61. Treatise *Hexaemeron* = *On the six days* ch. 6 (*Patrologia Latina* 14, p. 258).
62. John Chrysostom, (Johannes Chrysostomus) is an exception in this matter, cf. *Hom.* 4, *In Matth., Patrologia Graeca* 57, 16.
63. Cf. Justinus Martyr, *Dialogus cum Tryphone*, (*Patrologia Graeca* 6, 705); Irenaeus, *Adversus Haereses* 3, 21, *Patrologia Graeca* 7, 945-963; Augustin, *Sermo* 232, ch. 2; Epiphanius, *Adv. Haer.* 78, 18; Ephraim, *De Azymis* 6, 7 (Lamy I, 539; Beck 34).
64. See A. Haman in *Ichthus, La Philosophie passe au Christ*, Literature Chrétienne, Paris 1954.
65. See G. Söll in *Handbuch der Dogmengeschichte*, Band III, fasc. 4, *Mariologie*, Herder-Verlag, Freiburg 1978.
66. The expression "theotokos" was avoided in the Antiochene School, probably under influence of the more general doctrine about women. John Chrysostom explicitly states Mary's virginity *ante et post partum, Patrologia Graeca* 57, 16 sq., but he does not seem to have a very high opinion of Mary in *In Matth. Hom.* 4 and 44, (*ibid.*).
67. See the *Homilia on the State of the Mother of God*, read on the Council of Ephesus by Theodotus of Ancyra; *Acta Conc. Eph.*, ed. Galand, tome IX, p. 450.
68. See also Epiphanius *Adv. Haer.* 79, ch. 4 and 5.
69. The "virgines Christi" were honoured in the old Church, even by the most misogynist writers. Their choice of an ascetic life was considered an act of high morality.
70. See also *Ep.* 128; *Ep.* 57; *Ep.* 108.

71. See Sulpicius Severus *Dialogus adv. Pelagium* I, 17 and F.A. Lehner in *Die Marienverehrung in den ersten Jahrhunderten*, 2, Stuttgart 1886, p. 34 sq. See also *Handbuch der Marienkunde*, herausgegeben von W. Beinert und H. Petri, Regensburg 1984.

72. See for instance Ephraim *Hymni of Sermones* 18, 12-20 (*La.* III). Athanasius *De incarnatione, Patrologia Graeca* 26, 996; Gregory of Nazianzus *Ep.* 101, *Patrologia Graeca* 37, 77-180.

73. They seem to have overlooked those passages in the gospel, where Mary is not passive at all. See for instance *Luke* 2, 18 (Mary reproaches her young son in the presence of silent Joseph) and *St. John* 2, 2 (Mary makes an active effort to get help for the people who are short of wine at the wedding in Canaan).

74. Gregory of Nyssa gives us a more active picture of Mary, when he calls her the new Eve (*In Cant. Canticorum*).

75. See for instance Ambrosius *De virginitate*, (*Patrologia Latina* 16, 319).

76. See Th. Camélot in *Virgines Christi* in *La Vie Spirituelle*, Paris 1944 and in *La nouvelle Eve*, Études Mariales, 1934. See further Lébon in *L'apostolicité de la meditation Mariale, Recherches de Théologie ancienne et mediévale*, 1930.

77. R. Laurentin in *Marie et l'anthropologie chrétienne de la femme*, (in Nouvelle Révue Theologique 89 (1967) pp. 485-515) criticizes the fact that in spite of their worship of Mary the authorities of the Roman Catholic Church did not promote women in social and cultural life.

78. See H. Chadwick, *The Early Church*, London 1978, p. 81; see further Epihanius of Salamis in his treatise *Adversus Imagines* (372), who stresses the point of God's spirituality and that of the Saints.

79. See also Kari Börresen in *The Patristic Use of Female Metaphors Describing God*, published in the Acta of the Eighth Conference of Patristic Studies, Oxford 1979.

80. See Basil in *De structura hominis* ch. 8 (*L'origine de l'homme*, Sources Chrétiennes, n. 160).

81. See Annemarie La Bonnadière, *Chrétiennes des premiers siècles*, Paris 1957.

82. This passage slightly reminds us of Plato's *Symposium.*

83. See C.J. de Vogel in *Plotinus' Image of Man*, in *Images of Man in Ancient and Medieval Thought*, Leuven 1976.

84. See for instance *Enn.* II, 9, 14, where Plotinus opposes the Gnostics, who needed more than one principle to explain the world of visible things.

85. See *Enn.* III, 9, 3. *Hylè* or sensible matter is $\mu\grave{\eta}$ $\check{o}\nu$ (me) in Plotinus' view. Hylè is "what does not belong to being anymore". It is not the total annihilation of being, which is called $o\grave{\upsilon}\kappa$ $\check{o}\nu$ (ouk on), non-being. The *hylè* ($\mu\grave{\eta}$ $\check{o}\nu$) is non-substantial evil.

86. See *Enn.* II, 9, 13.

87. Cf. *Enn.* V, 1, 1; *Enn.* VI.

88. Cf. Augustinus, *De civitate Dei* X, 29, 2, *Patrologia Latina* 41, 308.

89. Cf. *Ep. ad Markellam* 28 (Nauck, p. 292, 293).

90. Cf. *Ep. ad Markellam* 7 sq. (Nauck, p. 278 sq.).

91. *Ad. Markellam* 24 (Nauck, p. 289).

92. *Ad. Markellam* 12 (Nauck, p. 282).

93. *Ad. Markellam* 14-19 (Nauck, pp. 283-287).

94. For the reconstruction of *De regressu animae*, see Joseph Bidez in *Vie de Porphyre, le philosophe néo-platonicien, Recueil des travaux publiés par la Faculté de philologie et lettres de l'université de Gand*, Vol. 43 (1913). Bidez based his reconstruction in a large way on quotations in Augustine's writings.

95. *Adv. Markellam* 7-11 (Nauck, p. 278 sq.).

96. See A. von Harnack in *Porphyrius, Gegen die Christen*, Berlin 1916.

97. See Augustin, *Sermo* 242, 7, *Patrologia Latina* 38, 1137.

98. *De opificio mundi* (*On the Creation*) II, 7-9; VI, 24.

99. See *Spec. Leg.* (On the special Laws Books) I, 200-201. *Quaest. in Gen.* (*Questions on Genesis*) I, 25; *Quaest. in Ex.* (, 7.

100. *Quaestiones in Gen.* I, 45 and I, 37.

101. See R.A. Baer Jr. in *Philo's Use of the Categories Male and Female*, Leyden 1970.

102. *De op. mundi* 146 (English translation *On the Creation of the World* in Loeb Classical Library).

103. See H. Dörrie, *Kaiserzeitliche Kontroversen zur Lehre von der Seelenwanderung*, in *Hermes* 85, 1957, p. 414 sq. Dörrie also points to the fact that Plotinus' doctrine on reincarnation is not homogeneous and liable to variations.

104. Porphyry held reincarnation in animals possible in his treatise *De antro nympharum.*

105. Makrina obviously simplifies things here. Compare Plato's and Plotinus' doctrine on the soul (see above).

106. See Origen in *De Principiis* = *On First Principles*, English translation by H. de Lubac, ed. by G.W. Butterworth, New York 1966.

107. Gregory defends the same doctrine in the *Oratio Catechetica* and *De opificio hominis*, ch. 16. Man belongs to two worlds from the beginning in his opinion.

108. Makrina also borrows an argument from the reincarnation-doctrines of the Gentiles for the restoration of bodily human life. The philosophy of the Gentiles makes it highly probable that the soul will receive a new body (*De an. et ress.* ch. 14, 2).

9. Hypatia of Alexandria

MARY ELLEN WAITHE

Fourth century Alexandria was the western world's center of scientific, philosophic, and other intellectual achievement. Christianity was gaining as much political and intellectual power as the old pagan religions were losing, and Alexandria was the site of tremendous social, political, religious, and academic turmoil. Nevertheless, the Alexandria of Hypatia's era held its place as the leading center for advanced scholarship. Its Museum was the center of mathematics and science where Ptolemy's successors merged physics, mathematics, and philosophy into an applied natural philosophy, mechanics, creating precision scientific instruments which tested metaphysical and cosmological theories. Alexandria's Library housed thousands of volumes of scholarly readings, including the works of the great pagan philosophers: Plato, Xenophon, and Aristotle. Seven centuries before Hypatia's birth, Ptolemy Soter established Alexandria as an intellectual community. The passage of seven centuries witnessed some of the most significant events of western civilization: the decline of Greece, the development of Jewish and Arabic intellectualism, the birth of Christianity, the expansion and christianization of the Roman Empire, and finally, Roman Christian persecution of Jews and pagans, including teachers of pagan philosophy. Most famous among such teachers was Hypatia.

I. BIOGRAPHY

Hypatia's birth is usually dated at *circa* 370-375.[1] However, Hoche[2] notes that following the Suda *Lexicon s.v.* Damascius, we might assume that 375 is the correct date. Hoche reports that Malleus and Wernsdorf favor *circa* 350. She lived during paganism's last stand against the encroaching Christian religion and in a sense personally represented the conflict between pagan Greek science, philosophy, and mathematics, on the one hand, and the Christian religious and political empire on the other. Scientific neo-Platonism was flourishing when Hypatia was born. Under Plotinus it acquired some of the trappings of mystery religion and theodicy. The problems of knowledge of the One, the nature of intelligence, and of the soul, and the possibility of evil and of providence formed portions of Plotinian metaphysics, cosmology, and religion, influencing the teachings of Porphyry. The latter remained a staunchly pagan anti-Christian philosopher, although a critic of the magical, theurgic aspects of Egyptian religion. There is no record of Hypatia's early education, although most assume that she was initially instructed by her father who taught mathematics and astronomy at the Museum. But since there is no mention that Theon was trained in philosophy, and since Hypatia was known to have taught philosophy in Alexandria, we must assume that at least her training in philosophy was received from philosophers of the neo-Platonic school at Alexandria, unless she was self-educated. Although the Suda *Lexicon* suggests that Hypatia had studied philosophy in Athens, I agree with Hoche's analysis that it is doubtful that this was the case. Hoche assumes instead that she was educated by mathematicians at the Museum in Alexandria and by other scholars (presumably philosophers at the Library) there.[3] The Suda had written that the heads of the city of Athens visited Hypatia at Athens. This would have meant that she was a visitor of reknown when and if she went there, and not a student. But Hoche claims that the reference to Hypatia "that the heads of the city came to see her" is likely to be meant as an analogy to the way that great philosophers were treated by public figures in Athens who came to visit them. Like the philosophers of Athens, Hypatia was visited by the heads of the city of Alexandria.

Hoche[4] argues convincingly that Hypatia probably assumed the direction of the neo-Platonic school of Plotinus. Her appointment came near the year 400 when she was 25 or 30 years old. Hoche notes that while it was common in neo-Platonism for the outstanding pupil to inherit the position of the teacher, the comment of the *Suda* that she taught and was paid by public funds lends support to Wernsdorf's assumption[5] that Hypatia was appointed to the position by officials of Alexandria and that she was paid for it. According to Hoche, this would indeed be without precedence in any of the philosophical schools. He says that consequently her appointment must have been a unique and exceptional honor, all the more so when we consider that women were not routinely elected to paid public office. The unusualness of Hypatia's position appears all the more significant when we consider that the government of Alexandria was Christian and Hypatia was a pagan. Hoche suggests that since appointments to the Museum were made by the Emperor or his representatives, Hypatia must have been paid out of Museum funds even though there is no record of her membership in that institution. Its last known member was her father Theon.

So much of what has been written about Hypatia has centered around thinly veiled discussions of her sexual activity and her marital status. Various historians have acclaimed[6] or disclaimed[7] her chastity and modesty. For example, Thomas Lewis notes that:[8]

> She had a confident audacious way of Address, that she could brazen it out, and appear without any concern in a publick Assembly of Men, for ... she was esteemed by all for her incomparable modesty. ... *Suidas* is wrapt-up in the *Modesty* of this Lady, and as a Specimen, tells us of a handsome young Spark who went to School to her, and had such a Platonic Opinion of her Vertue, that he courted her for his WH---; but She, either from a dislike to his Person, or perhaps being pre-engag'd to Orestes the Praefect of the City, (whom she would often call upon at his own House) would not admit of his Addresses. The Gallant still thought his Amour Practicable, and continu'd his Importunity; but, she, as a Lady of Honour remained inflexible; and at last, without attempting to reason with him like a Platoness, made use of a Stratagem to put an end to the Courtship which I believe the most common Prostitute in Venice would blush at: It is so gross an Argument, and a Conviction so Obscene and

Odius, that I shall ... not stain my Paper or offend the Reader with the Translation.

The story as the Suda *Lexicon* tells it, is that pursued by a student in whom her only interest was discussing philosophy, Hypatia finally ended the harassment by flinging the 5th century equivalent of a used sanitary napkin at him, exclaiming that the joys of sex rather than those of philosophy were what was on the student's mind. According to Toland:[9]

> ... one of her own Schollars made warm love to her, whom she endeavor'd to cure of his passion by the precepts of Philosophy ... the Spark vehemently soliciting her ... at a time when she happen'd to be under an indisposition ordinary to her sex: she took a handkerchef, of which she had been making some use on that occasion, and throwing it in his face said: *This is what you love, young fool, and not anything that's beautiful.* For the PLATONIC philosophers held goodness, wisdom, virtue, and other such things, as by reason of their intrinsic worth are desireable for their own sakes, to be the onely real Beauties of whose divine symmetry, charms, and perfection, the most superlative that appear in Bodies are but faint resemblances. This is the right notion of PLATONIC LOVE. Wherefore HYPATIA'S procedure might very well put a student of philosophy at Alexandria to the blush and quite cure him too.

Orestes, mentioned above by Lewis, was the Praefect of the City of Alexandria, and frequently sought Hypatia's advice on philosophical and political issues. Orestes was involved in a political power play with Cyril, the Bishop of Alexandria. According to Socrates Scholasticus, a contemporary of Hypatia, Cyril apparently hired/ inspired a group of Nitrian monks who:[10]

> ... pull her out of her chariot: they hail her into the Church called Caesarium: they stripped her stark naked: they raze the skin and rend the flesh of her body with sharp shells, until the breath departed out of her body: they quarter her body: they bring her quarters unto a place called Cinaron and burn them to ashes.

II. TEACHING

Our information about Hypatia's teaching activities comes from a number of sources, including some of her most famous students. According to Damascius, she taught geometry and mathematics. Philostogorius tells us that she excelled her father Theon in mathematics — and Theon was the Museum's most famous mathematician! Hesychius tells us that she was an excellent astronomer — as was her father. Her reknown in these fields is confirmed in the letters of her pupil Synesius, who was almost exclusively educated by Hypatia. According to Synesius' letters[11] Hypatia taught the works of Plato, and Aristotle, as well as neo-Platonism and its "mysteries," astronomy, mechanics, and mathematics. We know that Synesius learned Plotinian neo-Platonism, an eclectic "pagan" religious philosophy opposed to Christian philosophy, from Hypatia. This philosophy formed an integral part of the intellectual transition from pagan Greek philosophy to Christianity. It was Synesius' study of Plotinus under Hypatia that caused Synesius to become a Christian and later a bishop of the Church at Ptolemais. According to Synesius' letters, not only was Hypatia viewed as the greatest then-living exponent of Platonic and Aristotelian philosophy, neo-Platonism, and mathematics, but her students came from afar to study under her. From the tone of Synesius' letter in 395 to Herculianus,[12] both young men had travelled from Cyrene to Alexandria to study with:[13]

> ... a person so renowned, her reputation seemed literally incredible. We have seen and heard for ourselves she who honorably presides over the mysteries of philosophy.

By the year 393 Synesius was Hypatia's pupil, having come from Pentapolis to study with the already-famous philosopher who (if Hoche's and others' estimates of her date of birth are correct)[14] was barely 23 years old herself. At about the time that Synesius went to Alexandria to study under Hypatia, the emperor Theodosius forbade pagan cult practices in Egypt, and there was widespread turmoil and rioting between pagans and Christians there. The popular pagan and Christian belief in magic and mystical powers continued to dominate western culture and philosophic thought. Even though paganism was being suppressed a strong belief in the divination of the future, and of the will of god through the interpretation of dreams persisted. Synesius reflected this hybrid Graeco-Christian epistemology in his works *De Insomnis*[15] and *Dion.*[16]

In 404 Synesius sent both works to Hypatia, who had by this time been appointed head of the neo-Platonic school at Alexandria. In his letter, Synesius asks for Hypatia's comments on his two books. He straightforwardly remarks that since *De Insomnis* was itself a product of divine revelation, he will publish it no matter what Hypatia thinks of it. We cannot assume therefore from Synesius' letter that Hypatia's epistemological views precluded a belief that divine revelation was a source of knowledge; rather it appears that she would not have argued with his basic premise. Synesius' letter does state that he will not publish *Dion* until Hypatia has commented on it and given it her approval.[17] *Dion* was published, so we must assume that Hypatia did agree with its thesis and gave it her approval.

Dion is in part a defense of philosophy against rhetoricians who styled themselves as philosophers. In it Synesius speaks in defense of the neo-Platonism taught by Hypatia. In its mixture of mysticism and cynicism, God is not only supreme, but One, and unknowable in any direct way by man. From the transcendent One emanates a universal *Nous* whose innate ideas are the pseudo-platonic forms, Ideas of sensory knowledge. From *Nous* itself emanates Matter, the essence of the material universe and the immediate cause of the universe and its sentient beings. Matter is evil. *Nous* is holy. But since man is partly material and part spiritual/rational, man is part evil, part holy. Through self-discipline and a cynic subjugation of the senses man can become capable of receiving direct revelation of divine truth from the universal *Nous*. This philosophy of religion/epistemology espoused by Hypatia and Synesius was clearly compatible both with Hypatia's paganism and with Synesius' Christianity.

According to the Suda *Lexicon*, Hypatia wrote a Commentary on Diophantus' *Arithmeticorum*, authored an Astronomical Canon which formed part of her Commentary on Ptolemy's *Syntaxis Mathematica*, and wrote a Commentary on the *Conic Sections* of Apollonius Pergaeus. The Suda mistakenly reported that all works by Hypatia had been lost, and later scholars attributed this to the burning of the Library in Alexandria. However, there is convincing evidence that the Commentary on Diophantus' *Arithmeticorum* has survived, interpolated in part into the original text. Hypatia's Commentary on Book III of Ptolemy's *Syntaxis Mathematica* and its accompanying Astronomical Canon has unquestionably survived intact. (See below, *Works.*)

We know that Hypatia taught the works of the great pagan philosophers Plato, Aristotle, Pythagoras, Xenophon, the Cynics, perhaps the Stoa, and their successors and commentators including Plotinus. Since she was interested in mathematics and the sciences, her teaching may have focused on those of the ancients' writings which concerned metaphysics, cosmology, and epistemology rather than their ethical and political philosophy. It is also likely that she taught Diophantus' *Arithmeticorum*, a work of algebraic theorems. According to two mutually independent sources, Paul Tannery, the nineteenth-century French historian of mathematics, and the Abbé Rome, the twentieth-century Belgian historian of astronomy, Hypatia frequently used an idiosyncratic method of division in the sexagesimal system to test mathematical theorems. Tannery had apparently not known of the survival of Hypatia's Commentary on Ptolemy's *Syntaxis Mathematica*. Rome was apparently unaware of Tannery's conclusion that Hypatia's Commentary on Diophantus' *Arithmeticorum* had survived interpolated into the original. Yet both scholars have noted, as an apparent Hypatian trademark, the use of the sexagesimal system to check mathematical theorems and calculations. This "trademark" seems to have aided both scholars in distinguishing Hypatia's Commentaries from the body of the work commented on and into which later copyists had incorporated her writings. In addition to teaching algebraic and astronomical theory, Hypatia undoubtedly also taught geometry, particularly the solid geometry of Apollonius Pergaeus' *Conic Sections*. Although *Conic Sections* survives, it appears that Hypatia's Commentary to it does not — unless it is so successfully incorporated into the original text as to be indistinguishable. According to Tannery, this is what happened with her Commentary on Diophantus.

It is easy to see how Hypatia's expertise in philosophy formed the natural foundation for what was eventually to become her primary intellectual pursuit, astronomy. Like Theon, Hypatia was a mathematician and astronomer. In the early 5th century, astronomy was the most scientific of philosophical enterprises. Scientists and mathematicians sought to understand and apply Aristotelian metaphysics, physics, and cosmology, and Platonic epistemology to the visible universe using the theorems of the mathematician, the theories of the geometor, and the scientific instruments of the astronomer and geographer (Ptolemy, for example, was both) as a means of learning answers to fundamental philosophical questions: Who are we, what is our place in the order of things, what is the nature of god, of good and of evil? For Hypatia and intellectuals of her era, metaphysics and cosmology lead to mathematics, astronomy, geometry, and physics, and through them to answers to the great religious, social and political questions of the time.

III. WORKS

According to the Suda *Lexicon*, Hypatia was the author of three works, a commentary on Diophantus of Alexandria's *Arithmeticorum*, a commentary on Ptolemy's *Syntaxis Mathematica*, and a commentary on Apollonius Pergaeus' *Conic Sections*. And although the Suda reports that all three books perished, at least two, the commentaries on Ptolemy and on Diophantus, have survived. The commentary on Pergaeus' geometric theories may have survived, but I have been unsuccessful in locating it. However, several promising avenues of research remain to be explored before we can be justified in concluding that it has in fact perished.

1. *Commentary on Diophantus'* Arithmeticorum

In Plato's *Gorgias*[18] 451 b-d, Socrates distinguishes arithmetic from mere calculation, noting that arithmetic investigates "the odd and the even, however great their respective numbers might be," whereas calculation "investigates how the odd and the even are related both to themselves and to each other in regard to number." In Diophantus the distinction between abstract numbers as odd and even (arithmetic) and the relationship between specific numbers (calculation) is sometimes lost, in part because his calculations take an abstract form. Hypatia's introduction of some new problems and of some alternative solutions to Diophantus' original problems helps clarify the abstractness, the arithmetic nature, of Diophantus's contributions to algebraic theory. The absence of a notation to represent more than one unknown quantity in a given problem meant that neither Hypatia nor Diophantus had a convenient way to denote different unknowns and to eliminate all but one of them in the course of solving a problem. For this reason, problems which would otherwise contain an indeterminate equation with several unknowns, are instead represented for example, by an assumption that the smaller number is 3, the largest number 10, with the indeterminate number being called the "sought" or "unknown." The effect of this assumption is to make the problem *appear* to be one having a determinate solution — a puzzle rather than a principle, theorem, corrolary, etc. Hypatia's contribution is frequently to demonstrate the generality and indeterminateness of the problem by substituting for the assumed unknowns numeric values which are themselves unrelated in that they are not multiples, powers, surds, fractions, or square roots of the originals. Hypatia's genius in demonstrating that Diophantus' *Arithmeticorum* was, as Socrates would have said, arithmetic rather than calculation, certainly contributed to the preservation of that work.

According to Paul Tannery[19] one of the recensions of Diophantus' text contained some scholia by one or more ancient commentators even though the copyist had apparently attempted to identify and omit all such scholia. He identifies some alternative solutions and a number of new problems by Hypatia (and possibly by some later, unidentified scholiasts) which were admitted to the manuscript as though they were part of the original text. In Tannery's Introduction, the new problems are identified as "II. 1-7, 17, 18, etc." Tannery's text contains what may be clues as to the problems included in the "etc." but without clearer evidence as to which of these other problems were likely written by Hypatia, I do not feel justified in including them here. Examination of Tannery's multi-volumed *Memoires Scientifiques* yields no clues to identifying those problems.

Translation of the Text[20]

Materials in [square brackets] supplied.

> Book II. Throughout, the assumed ratio of larger to smaller number is assumed to be 2:1.
> II.I. To find two numbers such that their sum is in a given ratio to the sum of their squares. Given that their sums are to the sum of their squares as 1/10. Assume the smaller = x, the larger = 2x; the sum of these = 3x and the square [of the sum of] these [latter] is $5x^2$. Then it should be [the case that] 3x is 1/10 x $5x^2$. Therefore $30x = 5x^2$ making x = 6.
> Thus the smaller = 6, the larger = 12, and the problem is solved.
> II.II. To find two numbers such that their difference is in a given ratio to the difference of their squares. Given that their differences are to the difference of their squares as 1/6. Assume the smaller = x; the larger 2x; their difference is x, and the square of [the sums of the latter number, 2x and] this difference [x] is $3x^2$. Then it should be [the case that] x is 1/6 x $3x^2$. Therefore $6x = 3x^2$ which makes x = 2.
> Thus the smaller = 2, the larger = 4, and the problem is solved.
> II.III. To find two numbers such that their product is in a given ratio to their sum or [vel] to their difference.
> (a) Given in the first place that their product is 6 times their sum. Given that the [numbers] sought are x and 2x; ... in the given ratio. Their product is $2x^2$; their sum 3x; then it should be [the case that] $2x^2$ is 6 times 3x. Therefore $18x = 2x^2$ for every x; therefore 18 = 2x and making x = 9. The first = 9, the second = 18, and the problem is solved. [Their product, 162, is 6 times their sum, and 18:9 = 2:1.]
> (b) If it is given that their product is 6 times their difference, then on the other hand their product is $2x^2$, their difference is x, and in contrast, $6x = 2x^2$ whence x = 3. The first [number] = 3, the second = 6 and the problem is solved. [6 - 3 = 3; 6 x 3 = 18. Their product is 6 times their difference. And 6:3 = 2:1.]

II.IV. To find two numbers such that the sum of their squares is in a given ratio to their difference. Given that the sum of their squares is 10-fold their difference. Assume in return that one = x, the other = 2x. Then it should be [the case that] the sum of their squares is $5x^2$, their difference is x, thus $5x^2$ is 10 times x. Therefore, $5x^2$ = 10x, making x = 2.

Thus the first should be 2, the second 4 and the problem is solved.

II.V. To find two numbers such that the difference between their squares is in a given ratio to their sum. Assume that the difference of their squares is 6-fold their sum. Assume in return that one is x, the other, 2x. The difference in their squares is $3x^2$, their sum is 3x; (it must be the case that $3x^2$ is 6-fold 3x).

Therefore $3x^2$ = 18x and makes x = 6, and the proof is evident. [x = 6, 2x = 12; 6^2 = 36, 12^2 = 144, 144 - 36 = 108; 6 + 12 = 18, 18 x 6 = 108.]

II.VI. To find two numbers having a given difference and such that the difference of their squares is larger by a given amount than the difference between the two numbers. The square of the differences of [the numbers] must be less than the sum of the same difference [i.e., the difference of the numbers] and the given [difference] between the differences of the squares and of [the numbers] themselves. Let it be assumed now that the difference of [the numbers] themselves is two and let the difference of the squares of the numbers themselves exceed the difference of the numbers themselves by 20 units. Let the smaller = x; the larger should be = x + 2 and the differences between them = 2, the differences of their squares is 4x + 4. 4x + 4 must be two units greater than 20; ... 4x + 4 = 22 making x = 4½. The smaller [number] is = 4½, the larger = 6½, and the proposition is completed. [x = smaller, y = larger; y - x = 2.

$$(y^2 - x^2) - (y - x) \quad = 20$$
$$(y^2 - x^2) \quad\quad\quad = 22$$
$$((x + 2)^2 \quad\quad - x^2) = 22$$
$$((x^2 + 4x + 4) - x^2) = 22$$

$$4x + 4 \qquad\qquad = 22$$
$$4x \qquad\qquad\qquad = 18]$$

II.VII. To find two numbers such that the difference of their squares is greater by a given number than a given ratio of the difference between them. Let it be assumed that the difference between their squares is 3-fold the difference between them plus 10. The square of the difference between them [the numbers] must be less than 3-fold their difference plus the given 10. Let the difference between them be 2 and the smaller $= x$; therefore the larger will be $= x + 2$. $4x + 4$ must be 3-fold 2 and to this 10 is added. Therefore, $3 \times 2 + 10 = 4x + 4$. $3 \times 2 + 10 = 16$ which is equal to $4x + 4$, making $x = 3$. Making the smaller number $= 3$; the larger -5 and the problem is solved.

II.XVII. To find three numbers such that if each were to give to the subsequent a given fractional part of itself together with a given number, each having given and taken is equal. Assume that x_1 [gives to] x_2 1/5 of itself plus 6, and the latter (x_2) [gives to] x_3 1/6 of itself plus 7, x_3 to x_1 [gives] 1/7 of itself plus 8. Let $x_1 = 5x$ and similarly $x_2 = 6x$. When x_2, has received $x + 6$ from x_1, it becomes $7x + 6$, and if x_2 gives x_3 1/6 of itself (which is x) and 7, it $[x_2]$ becomes $6x - 1$. But when x_1 has given 1/5 of itself and 6, it becomes $4x - 6$. And when this $[x_1]$ has from x_3 taken 1/7 and 8, must become $6x -1$. But $4x -6$ when added to $2x +5$ makes $6x -1$. Therefore $2x + 5 = 1/7x_3 + 8$. If from $2x + 5$ 8 is subtracted there remains $2x -3 = 1/7x_3$; therefore $x_3 = 14x -21$. Next, this one $[x_3]$ from x_2 has received 1/6 and 7, and given of itself [to x_1] 1/7 and 8, it becomes $6x -1$. But when $[x_3 = 14x -21]$ gives 1/7 of itself and 8, it becomes $12x -26$, and when from x_2 it accepts 1/6 of x_2 and 7 $[x + 7]$ it $[x_3]$ becomes $13x -19$. This must be equal to $6x -1$, making $x = 18/7$. $x_1 = 90/7$, $x_2 = 108/7$, $x_3 = 105/7$ and so the proposition is complete.

Experts have been in disagreement over which books of Diophantus' *Arithmeticorum* may be missing and what those missing books might have contained. We know from the Suda *Lexicon* that Hypatia was famous for her commentary on this work. We know from Tannery[21] that the Hypatian recension of the *Arithmeticorum* is apparently the oldest and most genuine copy of that manuscript. To my knowledge, Tannery is the only scholar to have meticulously traced all known copies of the early manuscripts of the *Arithmeticorum*. His conclusion is that Hypatia's commentary was limited to the first six books of Diophantus' work and that her commentary copy of the original text was the only copy of it to survive. The Hypatian recension contains only six books, whereas the original was reputed to have contained seven more.

Tannery gives his theory of the survival of Hypatia's commentary in the Introduction to Volume II. According to him, perhaps only one exemplar of Hypatia's recension of the text survived. He calles this exemplar (a) and suggests that it is the copy seen by Michael Psellus (1018-1078). Tannery finds no trace of (a) after the fall of Constantinople in 1204. But in the meantime, he hypothesizes, during the 8th-9th centuries, another copy of (a) was made. He calls this copy Alpha. Alpha has also been lost, but it apparently contained some scholia by one or more ancient commentators even though the copyist had attempted to omit all scholia. The result is that this archetype, Alpha, contains what Tannery identifies as some alternative solutions and a number of new problems by Hypatia (and possibly by some scholiasts following her — but this cannot be ascertained). These alternative solutions and new problems were admitted to the text as though they were part of the original.

The best and earliest copy of the lost archetype Alpha is Madrid's Matritensis 48, written in the 13th century. Before Matritensis 48 (which Tannery calls A) was spoiled by erasures and corrections, the manuscript known as Vaticanus Graecus 191 was copied from it. Matritensis apparently had been at the Vatican or elsewhere in Rome for a considerable period towards the last half of the 15th century while Vaticanus Graecus 191 was copied from it. From this latter copy, Vaticanus Graecus 304 was copied at the beginning of the 16th century. Vaticanus Graecus 304 served as the archetype for five manuscripts, including the last four books of Parisinus 2379, copied by Ioannes Hydruntinus after 1545.

The first two books of Parisinus 2379 descended from Alpha and its model (a), but via a different route. Following the fall of Constantinople in 1204, exemplar (a), seen by Psellus, was lost. But Alpha been copied from (a) during the 8th or 9th centuries. Tannery assumes that Alpha was the archetype manuscript from

RECENSIONS OF HYPATIA'S COMMENTARY ON DIOPHANTUS' *ARITHMETICORUM*

(a) Exemplar seen by Michael Psellus in the 11th century but lost by 1204.

ALPHA, copied from (a) during the 8th or 9th centuries.

Pre-Planudean Class

Madrid: Matritensis 48, Tannery's "A," written in the 13th century.

↓

Vaticanus Graecus 191, copied from Matritensis 48, late 15th century.

↓

Vaticanus Graecus 304, copied from Vaticanus Graecus 191, early 16th century, became archetype for at least five manuscripts: Oxonianum Baroccianum 166, Urbinas Graecus 74, Neopolitanus IIIc 17, Parisinus 2378, and the last four books of Parisinus 2379.

↓

Parisinus 2379 (last four books only) copied by Ioannes Hydruntinus, not earlier than 1545.

Planudean Class

Lost 14th century MS, of which 10 leaves are extant in Ambrosianus Et 157 sup.

↓

Marcianus 308, copied in the early 15h century from lost 14th century manuscript. Owned by Cardinal Bessarion. Seen by Regiomontanus in Venice during 1464.

→ Ambrosianus 91 sup. is copied from Ambrosianus Et 157 sup. and Marcianus 308, for Mendoza in 1545.

→ Vaticanus Graecus 200 is copied from Ambrosianus Et 157 sup. and Marcianus 308, for Mendoza, 1545.

↓

Parisinus 2379, books one and two copied from Vaticanus Graecus 200.

which Maximus Planudes[22] who lived *circa* 1260-1330, developed his own commentary on Books I and II. This 14th century Planudean manuscript is lost with the exception of 10 leaves known as Ambrosianus et 157 sup., and the manuscript Marcianus 308, owned by Cardinal Bessarion and seen by Regiomontanus in Venice in 1464.[23] From those manuscripts, Ambrosianus 91 sup. and Vaticanus Graecus 200 were copied by the same copyist, for Mendoza in 1545. It is from Vaticanus Graecus 200 that the first two books of Parisinus 2379 were copied. Parisinus 2379 thus represents a hybrid copied from two families or classes of recensions of the lost Hypatian original: the first, or pre-Planudean class, and the Planudean class. Students of Greek mathematics and ancient astronomy will want to consult not only Tannery's established Greek text (with latin facing) of Diophantus' *Arithmeticorum* containing the above commentary problems, but will also want to consult Abbé A. Rome's Greek text of Hypatia's revision of Theon's Commentary on Ptolemy's *Syntaxis Mathematica*, in search of evidence of what may well be Hypatia's academic signature. In Tannery's Introduction, he suggests that Michael Psellus' remarks at the beginning of the letter describing the "Egyptian method" of Diophantus were copied wholesale from a manuscript of Diophantus which contained an "ancient and systematic commentary" which Tannery believes to have been authored by Hypatia. This "Egyptian method" involved using an abacus-like instrument and the sexagesimal system. Hypatia used the sexagesimal system to refine some of Diophantus' algebraic laws. In her Commentary on Book III of Ptolemy's *Syntaxis Mathematica* she uses an idiosyncratic method of division in the sexagesimal system to criticize Ptolemy's theories about the retrograde movement of planets. Rome notes her distinctive use of the sexegesimal system to provide far more accurate results than were achieved by previous scholars in a way that was quicker for making computations on an abacus. Rome also notes that this possible "signature" of Hypatia's is completely absent from Books I & II of Theon's Commentary, but appears in Book III (which Theon attributes to Hypatia) and occasionally in later books. This suggests that her Commentary may have extended beyond Book III.

2. *Commentary to Book III of Ptolemy's* Syntaxis Mathematica

Pappus, and Hypatia's father Theon were the two most famous and important commentators on Ptolemy's *Syntaxis Mathematica*. This book is also sometimes known as the *Almageste*, its Arabic nickname (*Al* = the, *mageste* = greatest) for Ptolemy's greatest work. While Hypatia's fame as a refiner of Ptolemaic astronomy was frequently recounted by historians including Socrates Scholasticus,[24] Fabricus,[25] and Suda,[26] it has been mistakenly assumed that her work did not itself survive. Yet other works from the Alexandrinian academic community of the late 4th century/ early 5th century have survived including numerous copies of Theon's Commentaries on Ptolemy's *Syntaxis Mathematica*, and the Astronomical Tables (probably by Hypatia) which made previous calculations of astronomical events based on Ptolemaic theory completely obsolete. Tannery[27] notes that:

> ... in repeating [Fabricus'] claim [that Hypatia's Commentary on Ptolemy was lost] historians of mathematics failed to consider a two-fold unlikelihood; that, on the one hand, in an era of commentators such an original work as the new *Astronomical Tables* appeared; and, that on the other hand, a work that was so important as to immediately supercede that of Ptolemy [Hypatia's Commentary] disappeared without a trace.

While Tannery apparently concludes that the Astronomical Tables were authored by Hypatia, another scholar, J.F. Montulca notes[28] the survival of

> ... the third book of the commentary on *Almageste*, which her father Theon expressly attributes to [Hypatia].

It appears to be the case that Theon was working on his Commentary to Ptolemy's *Syntaxis Mathematica* and asked Hypatia to review the manuscript. Hypatia realized that her father's comments on Book III raised numerous conceptual, methodological, and mathematical issues, which neither Theon nor Ptolemy had addressed. In working out her analysis of those issues, Hypatia recomputed the mathematical values of the celestial events described by the ancient astronomers including Ptolemy. The *Astronomical Tables* is the work product of that exercise. Her Commentary to Book III (and perhaps to subsequent books) fleshes out her analysis of the philosophical and mathematical issues suggested to her by Theon's original Commentary. In developing that analysis, the Commentary became truly her own. Hence, Theon's attribution of it to her and its inclusion with his own Commentary.

Tannery was apparently unaware of the recension referred to by Montulca in which Theon not only acknowledges Hypatia's contribution to the whole work, but attributes Book III to her. In the late 18th or early 19th century, Abbé Nicolas Halma found the only edition of Theon's Commentary which contained Book III by Hypatia. This edition came from the di Medici collection and is listed as Medici 28.18. In his translation of Book I of Theon's Commentary[29] Halma notes that the genuine Book III, i.e., the only edition containing Hypatia's Commentary, was to be found in the Codex of the 10th century. It appears that Halma either died or ran out of funds prior to translating and establishing the text of Hypatia's Commentary. However, he did publish her *Astronomical Tables* which prefaced the Commentary. Nearly a century following Halma, Abbé A. Rome was to locate the edition mentioned by Halma. In the interim, Montulca would mention Halma's comment that Theon expressly attributed the book to Hypatia.

Theon's attribution of Book III to Hypatia is contained in the following phrase:

’Εκδόσεως παραναγνωσθείσης τῇ φιλοσόφῳ θυγατρί μου ‘Υπατίᾳ

While Halma and Montulca took this to read that Theon "attributed" the Commentary on Book III to Hypatia, Rome has variously taken it to mean "by Theon and Hypatia," "edited," "reviewed," or "re-written" by Hypatia. He speculates:[30]

As the third book had been reviewed by Hypatia.... It is difficult to say what the intervention consisted in. ... [O]ne can well imagine Theon touching up Pappus [Pappus' Com-

mentary to Ptolemy's *Syntaxis Mathematica*] to the point
that the commentary he completed was his own work; and
Hypatia beginning to undertake the same kind of thing with
her father's work and during his life time. Was her revision
only of Book 3? Sir Thomas L. Heath seems to say so in the
account he made of the second volume of this [Rome's
edition of the commentaries to Ptolemy's Book I and II]
work in *Classical Review* in 1938. He was perhaps brought to
that opinion by note 1 on p. 317 above (volume 2).

We wouldn't dare to give a categorical statement: books 1
and 2 are known in the original edition, the 3rd in the
Hypatian edition; but after (book 3) we find no further
mention of the editor. This could be interpreted in two ways:
the original edition or the revised edition [of the succeeding
books is by Hypatia]. The disappearance of the 3rd book
from all the manuscripts excepting L [Medici 28.18] tends to
make us believe that the revision was made only on the 3rd
book....

On the other hand it is very curious that the method of
sexagesimal division taught by book 1 is different from that
recommended by the 3rd book, which is much easier if one
uses an abacus. But this procedure of the 3rd book reappears
in the 4th and the 9th. If other things of this sort had appeared, we would dare to say that the entire end of the work
has come to us in the Hypatian revised edition. But a solitary
indicator cannot support such a conviction.

Hypatia's Commentary on Book III of Ptolemy's *Syntaxis Mathematica* takes up pages 807-942 of Rome's third volume. A modern
language translation has not yet been made. The work is a chal-
lenge to translators because understanding it requires not only a
knowledge of 5th-century Alexandrinian Greek, but a thorough
knowledge of the early editions of Ptolemy's works as well as
knowledge of ancient Egyptian mathematics and astronomy. In
spite of these challenges, brief descriptions can be given of parts of
it, and its potential significance can be explored.

Hypatia begins with a thirty-six page chapter containing a
recapitulation of the two preceeding books and an analysis of the
history of solar astronomy to her day. She describes the then

current use of the definition of the tropical year which is the starting point for calculations about the movement of the sun. (Readers will remember that the sun was at that time believed to revolve around the earth.) The tropical year is the time that it takes the sun to return to the same equinox: less than 365¼ days. The sidereal year is the period of return to the same fixed star and is longer than the tropical year. Hypatia next considers Ptolemy's theory of the precession of equinoxes. This is a theory about why the point on the earth at which an equinoctial day begins is not constant. For each successive equinox, vernal and autumnal, the point at which the day of the equinox begins moves slightly westward, necessitating a calendrical adjustment as the precession reaches full circle. This makes the length of the year 365 days plus a fraction. The precession of equinoxes theory would tend to require that one assume that both the sun and the moon accelerate their speeds as they circumscribe the earth. Thus the theory has as a result a commitment to the view that the sun and moon rotate erratically.

For the most part, Hypatia's rethinking of her father's Commentary clarifies and places in context Ptolemy's theory of solar movement, the lengths of the year, day, seasons, etc. And while her comments frequently have the air of criticism about them, they also contain many simple technical corrections to applications of Ptolemaic theory. Some of these corrections apparently resulted from her philosophical analysis of Ptolemy's methodological and conceptual errors. For example, she questions whether some of the difficulties with Ptolemy's theories about the precise time and location of the equinoxes are attributable to his having taken into account only the tropical and not the sidereal year. Ptolemy's calculations of the times and locations of equinoxes become increasingly inaccurate for centuries long preceeding and following his own lifetime, suggesting that the theories are observation-dependent, rather than observation-confirmed. Rome[31] notes that her observations are interesting because they raise the question of observing both the rising of stars that coincide with the sunrise, and, the Sothic year. (The Sothic year is the time it takes the star Sirius to return to the same celestial location: 365 days, 6 hours, varying minutes. The precise minute of its return is repeated only at intervals of 1460 Sothic years.) Since the Sothic year is Sirius' sidereal year, allowing for predictable changes in the length of sidereal years might, if factored into calculations of the vernal and autumnal equinoxes, yield more accurate calculations for equinoctial years remote in time from Ptolemaic observations of equinoxes.

From the perspective of the 20th century, one of the major shortcomings of Ptolemaic theory concerns a theory Ptolemy borrowed from Hipparchus: the theory of "eccentrics." Hipparchus thought that apparent anomalies observed in the movements of the sun and the moon could be explained if it were the case that the earth suddenly displaced itself. This displacement would, Hipparchus thought, account for changes in the apparent orbital velocity of the sun and the moon. Hipparchus' displacement theory necessitated a corollary, the so-called theory of the "precession of equinoxes" which Ptolemy thought accounted for the apparent retro-grade movement of planets. These and related theories which supported the geocentric view of the universe required continuous orbital displacement of the sun and of the planets. In Book III, Hypatia claims that it is impossible for the sun to pass through the same point on the deferent as it does on the eccentric. In her view, the two movements of the sun could not be so well synchronized, so she reconstructs Ptolemy's "proof."

Hypatia's commentary on Book III of Ptolemy's *Syntaxis Mathematica* can best be appreciated by putting that work in its historical context. Ptolemy had more or less perfected ancient astronomy. The geometrical design of the heavens as observed by astronomers more or less corresponded to the state of the art of geometric theory. Ptolemy explained discrepancies between theory and astronomical observations by adopting the simplest hypothesis that would account for both the theory and the observation. The earth remained the center of the universe until Nicolas Copernicus deduced that the sun was its center. Since it is the location of the earth relative to the sun, and the relative motions of both that distinguish Copernican from Ptolemaic theory, we might inquire whether Copernicus read Hypatia's comments on Book III, and whether her methodological criticisms of Ptolemy and of Hipparchus concerning the motions of the sun influenced Copernicus' own thinking.

When Copernicus went to Italy to study astronomy, he attempted to learn all that he could about the ancient astronomers, and in particular about Ptolemy. He read Ptolemy's commentators closely. If he did not in fact read what the nineteenth-century mathematician/astronomer Delambre described as "the most important and the most unusual [commentary on Ptolemy] that survives of the Greeks" [Theon's commentary containing Hypatia's commentary], Copernicus came within a hair's breadth of doing so. The young doctoral candidate was travelling through Florence at the very time that the *Medici 28.18* was in the library of Laurenzo di Medici. Is it possible that he passed through Florence but did not stop at the library of one of the most famous collectors of ancient texts in Italy? Could he possibly not have read Hypatia?

We can trace the history of *Medici 28.18*, the only copy of Theon's Commentary to contain Book III by Hypatia. By 1534[32] the library of Laurenzo di Medici listed manuscripts 28.18, 2390, 2396 and 2398 among its holdings. Angelo Poliziano (Politian) lived from 1454-1494 and spent his early adulthood as a tutor in the home of Laurenzo de Medici. By age 30 Politian was already a famous classicist in the di Medici library. Poliziano made marginal notes in 28.18, probably during the period *circa* 1480-1490. We know that in 1492 Jean Lascaris (1445-*circa* 1534), a Constantinople-born humanist, returned to Turkey in the employ of Laurenzo di Medici. Among the manuscripts he obtained from Franciscus, Attar of Cyprus in Constantinople was 2398, an early copy of Theon's *Commentary*, but missing Hypatia's revision of Book III. Mss. 2398 is consistent with 28.18, 2390, 2396 and other manuscripts, but only 28.18 contains the Hypatian Book III.

According to Rome[33] 2398 can be dated by its red ink and its square oncial letters to the 7th and 8th centuries. Halma's *Almageste de Ptolemée* (on spine),[34] claims that the model from which 2398 was copied should be dated to the 6th century because the manuscript lacks certain characteristics which were common only from that time onwards, viz., punctuation, page enumeration, chapter headings, and, spacing between words. Since 2398 is consistent with 28.18 (the only copy containing the Hypatian edition) and with 2390, 2396 and others, these manuscripts are considered by Halma and Rome to derive from the same earlier archetype.[35]

RECENSIONS OF HYPATIA'S COMMENTARY ON PTOLEMY'S
SYNTAXIS MATHEMATICA

6th century	Model from which 2398 was copied. Model lacks characteristics of post-6th century mss., notably, punctuation, page enumeration, chapter headings, and spacing between words.
7th-8th centuries	2398 is dated by Rome to this period due to its red ink and oncial letters. 2398 is consistent with 28.18 (Hypatian edition), 2390, 2396 and other copies of Theon's commentary.
prior to 1490	Poliziano, classicist at the di Medici library, makes marginal notes in 28.18, (Hypatian edition), probably during the period 1480-1490.
1492	Jean Lascaris, in the employ of Laurenzo di Medici, purchases 2398 and other mss. from Franciscus, Attar of Turkey. 2398 is consistent with 28.18 (Hypatian edition), 2390, 2396 and other mss.
1534	Library of Laurenzo di Medici lists mss. 28.18, 2390, 2396 and 2398 among its holdings.

But if these manuscripts all derive from the same ancient 6th century archetype, why does only one contain Book III? The most attractive hypothesis is that Theon completed his Commentary and submitted the work, which may be identified as *a*, to Hypatia for review. When she reviewed her father's comments on Book III, something happened. Perhaps she recognized conceptual, methodological and mathematical problems concerning the motions of the sun that had not been taken into account by either Theon or Ptolemy. Perhaps Theon's students were anxious to continue working with him and perhaps a copy of their teacher's original commentary *minus the troublesome Book III* was made. There would then have existed two copies of Theon's text, α containing, and β missing, Book III. When Hypatia completed her commentary on Book III, Theon wrote the acknowledgement of Hypatia's authorship and it was substituted by him for his own Commentary on Book III. In the meantime Theon's students made copies of β. These copies were the models for 2390, 2396, 2398 and 25 other copies of Theon's Commentary. If multiple recensions of α were made, only one appears to have survived. It should be noted that one of the recensions of β, 2396, mentions that Hypatia revised Book III. Perhaps Theon made this notation in β after several copies had been made to indicate that β was an incomplete edition which Hypatia was in the process of revising. No doubt there are other possible explanations for the survival of only one copy of Hypatia's Commentary when so many copies of her father's Commentary survived.

3. *Other Works*

The Suda *Lexicon,*[36] Fabricus in *Bibliotheca Graecorum,*[37] and Socrates Scholasticus in *Historiae Ecclesiasticae*[38] all mention that Hypatia authored a commentary on Apollonius of Perga's *Conic Sections*. This Commentary appears to be the only one of the three Hypatian writings reported lost which has actually failed to survive. Edmund Halley, the 17th century British astronomer, collected the ancient Latin and Arabic versions of *Conic Sections* in an attempt to reconstruct the original and to separate scholia and commentary from the original text. This was apparently an insurmountable task, at least with respect to identifying the Hypatian commentary, for although Halley's text lists Hypatia's commentary among its contents, there exists only a title page, without additional text. I have not been successful in locating the materials that Halley was working from, but there appears to be little reason to hope that Hypatia's commentary on Apollonius' *Conic Sections* has in fact survived.

Two scientific devices are sometimes attributed to Hypatia's invention. The first, a planisphere, or "astrolabe" was requested by her pupil, Synesius *circa* 397-401. This item was a three-dimensional celestial map executed in silver. It was given by Synesius to Paeonius, a Count[39] at the Emperor's court in Constantinople. (The Synesius-Paeonius connection may account for the survival of Hypatia's commentaries on Ptolemy and Diophantus. The reader will recall that the Ptolemy commentary is consistent with manuscripts purchased in Constantinople for the Medici Library, and that an early exemplar of the Diophantus commentary seen by Psellus, was lost after the fall of Constantinople. To be sure, the connection between Synesius and Paeonius on the one hand, and the survival of the commentaries on the other, is at best, speculative.) There is a record of Synesius sending the astrolabe to Paeonius.[40] In 404, Synesius writes to Hypatia, sending her a copy of the letter to Paeonius with which the gift had been enclosed, and notes that the letter was written during his ambassadorial period.[41]

In 402, Hypatia receives a letter from the ailing Synesius giving a brief description of what he calls a hydroscope.[42] This is a scientific instrument which was then in common use, although Hypatia is often credited with its invention. French mathematician Pierre de Fermat reconstructed a sketch of the instrument Synesius describes. According to Fermat, it is a hydrometer, used to determine the specific gravity of liquids.[43] Tannery surmises that the

> instrument was used to determine the weights of different liquids used by the ill; since Medical Science was agreed that lighter fluids were best.[44]

The device worked by inserting it cone-down into liquid. The liquid enters the "flute-like" tube through the "notches" or perforations, sinking it more or less according to the specific gravity of the liquid. By counting notches, the comparative weights of different liquids can be measured.[45]

SUMMARY

Born into the intellectual community established by Ptolemy Soter, Hypatia was to become the most famous commentator on the work of Ptolemy Claudius until Copernicus, more than eleven centuries later. Until her commentaries on Ptolemy's astronomy and Diophantus' mathematics can be evaluated, and until the historical record of Copernicus' study of Ptolemy's commentators can be completed, her influence on modern science and mathematics cannot be completely described. Much scholarly investigation of her writings remains to be done, yet, her influence on the histories of philosophy, astronomy, and mathematics is unquestionable. She taught a metaphysics and epistemology that were compatible with paganism and Christianity alike. She mastered philosophy including the writings of Plato, Aristotle, Pythagoras, Xenophon and others. Philosophy provided her with the theoretical underpinnings she used to evaluate the most powerful algebraic, geometric and astronomical theories of her era. She was a towering intellect, reknown before she was thirty in intellectual communities as far from her native Alexandria as Libya and Turkey. Living in an intellectual environment from which women were almost always excluded, she earned an unprecedented appointment to head a paid, public office, the school of Plotinus. The Roman government persecuted pagans and Jews, yet for fifteen years it would pay the pagan Hypatia the unique and exceptional honor of leading that prestigious institution. Living in a time of great social, religious, scientific, and philosophic unheaval, Hypatia would meet an early and horrible death. And, although she was known as the greatest philosopher of her day, her teachings and writings would be virtually ignored by historians of philosophy for nearly fifteen hundred years.

NOTES

1. Socrates Scholasticus, *Ecclesiastical History*, Book 7, p. 13f. Book 8, p. 9.
2. Hoche, R., "Hypatia, die Tochter Theons," *Philologus* 15 (1860): 439.
3. Hoche, *op. cit.*, 441.
4. *Op. cit.*
5. Wernsdorf, J.C. *Hypatia, philosopha Alexandrina*, dissertation Vitembergae (1747, 1748).
6. Toland, J. *Hypatia: or, the History ...*, London (1720).
7. Lewis, Thomas, "The History of Hypatia, a most impudent schoolmistress of Alexandria..." in *Tetradymus* London: Bickerton, (1721).
8. *Op. cit.*, 8-9.
9. *Op. cit.*, 123.

10. Freemantle, Anne, *A Treasury of Early Christianity*, New York: Viking (1953), p. 380.
11. Synesii Epistolae in *Epistolographi Graeci*, R. Hercher, Paris: Didot (1873), and *Letters of Synesius*, A. Fitzgerald, London: Oxford University Press (1926).
12. According to the dating given by Druon in his *Oeuvres de Synesius, Evêque de Ptolemais...* Paris: Hachette (1878), Epistle IV.
13. *Op. cit.* translation mine.
14. See Gardner, Alice, *The Fathers for English Readers: Synesius of Cyrene* New York: Young (1886), p. 177.
15. *Op. cit.*
16. *Ibid.*
17. *Ibid.*, Epistle 63.
18. Woodhead translation in *The Collected Dialogues of Plato*, Edith Hamilton and Huntington Cairns, eds., Princeton: Princeton University Press (1961).
19. *Diophanti Alexandrini Opera Omnia*, Lipsiae: Teubneri (1893-1895), in his Introduction to Volume II.
20. Translation by Lloyd S. Waithe from the Latin text by Paul Tannery of *Hypatia's Commentary on Diophantus' Arithmeticorum.*
21. *Op. cit.*, volumes I, II.
22. Compiler of the Greek Anthology and of Aesop's *Fables.*
23. For a concurrent history of Hypatia's Commentary on Ptolemy's *Syntaxis Mathematica*, see the following section.
24. Socrates Scholasticus. *Historiae Ecclesiasticae.*
25. Fabricus, *Bibliotheca Graecorum*, s.v. "Hypatia."
26. Suda, *Lexicon* s.v. "Hypatia."
27. Tannery, Paul, "L'Article de Suidas sur Hypatia," *Annales de la Faculté des Lettres de Bordeaux*, 1880, p. 199. Translation mine.
28. Montulca, J.F. *Histoire des Mathématiques* (nouvelle tirage), Paris: Librarie Scientifique et Technique, (1960), p. 332.
29. Halma, Nicolas. *Almageste de Ptolemée* (on spine) *Commentaires de Theon d'Alexandrie sur le premier Livre de la Composition Mathématique de Ptolemée. Traduit pour la premiere fois du grec en français sur les mss. de la Bibliotheque du Roi, par M. l'abbé Halma*, Paris (1821).
30. *Op. cit.*
31. *Op. cit.*, p. 851, n. 1.
32. *Index Bibliothecae Medicae*, Florence (1882).
33. "Le Troisieme Livre des Commentaires sur l'Almageste par Theon et Hypatie," *Annales de la Société Scientifique de Bruxelles*, v. 46, p. 4.
34. *Op. cit.*, p. lxvj.
35. Halma's *Theon et Hypatie, Commentaires de Theon d'Alexandrie sur le 3e Livre de l'Almageste de Ptolemée*, contains only the revised calculations of Ptolemy's *Handy Tables.*
36. s.v. "Hypatia."
37. *Op. cit.*

38. *Op. cit.*
39. Gardner, Alice, The Fathers for English Readers: Synesius of Cyrene, N.Y.: Young (1886), p. 177.
40. A. Fitzgerald: *Letters of Synesius* (Oxford University Press) 1926, p. 258.
41. *Op. cit.*. Epistle 63.
42. *Op. cit.*, Epistle 52.
43. Fermat, Pierre de , in *Journal des Sçavans*, 20 Mars, 1679.
44. Paul Tannery, *Oeuvres de fermat*, Paris (1841), V. 1, appendix, p. 363.
45. W.S. Crawford, *Synesius the Hellene* London: Rivingtons, p. 150.

10. Arete, Asclepigenia, Axiothea, Cleobulina, Hipparchia, and Lasthenia

MARY ELLEN WAITHE

There are some ancient women philosophers about whom very little is known other than their names. Frequently, these were members of one of the philosophic sects, and they either left no written philosophy, or their writings, and specific information about those writings has been lost. In most cases, the record is very sketchy, and most of our knowledge about these philosophers comes from general information about the philosophic communities of which they were a part, from knowledge of their teachers, or of their students. While little is known about their personal achievements, they can be described as having been part of a philosophic community. They are mentioned here to stimulate further research about them. Many ancient philosophic communities admitted women as active, participating, philosophers and, in some cases as leaders of philosophic schools. This chapter introduces the reader to some of those philosophers.

I. ARETE OF CYRENE

Arete of Cyrene was the daughter of Aristippus, head of the Cyrenaic school, and was his successor in that school. Cyrene was what we now know as the northeastern area of Libya. Arete's father was a student and friend of Socrates and was present at Socrates' death. The school which he founded was one of the earliest proponents of hedonism.

Mozans,[1] refers to Boccacio's *De Laudibus Mulierum* as the source of information about Arete's professional life:

A History of Women Philosophers / Volume 1, ed. by Mary Ellen Waithe
©*Martinus Nijhoff Publishers, Dordrecht – Printed in the Netherlands*

... she is said to have publicly taught natural and moral philosophy in the schools and academies of Attica for thirty-five years, to have written forty books, and to have counted among her pupils one hundred and ten philosophers. She was so highly esteemed by her countrymen that they inscribed on her tomb an epitaph which declared that she was the splendor of Greece and possessed the beauty of Helen, the virtue of Thirma, the pen of Aristippus, the soul of Socrates and the tongue of Homer.

According to Diogenes Laertius:[2]

Now the pupils of Aristippus were his own daughter Arete, and Aethiops of Ptolemais, and Antipater of Cyrene. Arete had for her pupil the Aristippus who was surnamed *metrodidactos*, whose disciple was Theodorus the athiest....

Arete's role as successor to her father in the hedonistic school is noted by Strabo,[3] Clement of Alexandria,[4] and Eusebius[5] (265-339 A.D.) in a book generally attributed to Plutarch (2nd century, A.D.) and referred to, although not by name, by Themistius.[6]

Arete's father is not believed to have written any philosophic doctrines. Those Cyrenaic doctrines which have survived are believed to have been recorded by Arete's son, Aristippus the Younger. Since the son was nicknamed "metrodidactus" (mother-taught), we may speculate which parts of the Cyrenaic moral philosophy to attribute to the grandfather, which to Arete, his pupil, and which to the son who was, in turn, her pupil. While we have no direct access to her individual views, we can examine those of the sect or cult which she headed, assuming that she shared its general philosophic perspective.

The Cyrenaics held ethics, knowledge of what is good and evil for the family and society, to be the essence of philosophy. The elder Aristippus was criticized by Aristotle[7] as having ignored mathematics and physics because they do not inquire into the good and evil. Ritter,[8] basing himself on Laertius and Sextus Empiricus comments on Aristotle's claim:

This, however, so far as it applies to the ancient Cyrenaics [among whom we would include Arete of Cyrene] in general, is somewhat of an exaggeration; for not only are we told that they applied themselves to the study of logic and its practical utility, but we also know, on formal testimony, that they did not wholly neglect physical researches. They divided, for instance, all philosophy into five parts — the doctrine of Desire and Aversion — Affects and Actions — Causes, and Proofs; the fourth related to the physical, and the fifth to logical science, both however were, it is true, subordinate to the ethical, as is clear from the fact of their calling science in general ethics.

The Cyrenaics argued that reason was insignificant unless it was viewed as that which teaches a person to avoid things that interfere with pleasure. They held that pleasure was the sole criterion of morality, and was therefore the ultimate goal of life. Pleasure did not consist in the absence of pain. Rather, pain and pleasure were both emotions, and the absence of either was inactivity or rest in the soul. Pleasure and pain are both, therefore, motions of the soul. Life itself was a sum of motions of the soul. There was, however, no perfect rest of the soul, merely imperceptable motion. Pleasure was a gentle motion of the soul, pain a violent excitement of the soul.

1. *Pain and Pleasure*

As a violent excitement of the soul, pain deprived the individual of the conditions of calm reflectiveness which were necessary for consciousness of the pleasant. All states of extreme excitement (pleasant as well as painful) deprive the individual of the ability to calmly reflect on and thus enjoy the pleasant. Arete would have considered excessively exciting pleasures incompatible with true pleasure, because the vehemence of the excitement precluded true enjoyment.

Cyrenaics held that pleasure was more than the sensual corporeal gratification experienced by the body; rather it was the mental perception of that gratification, whether the object of gratification is real, or an artistic imitation of the real. They viewed thought to be the consciousness of present sensations, thus, humans can use certain common linguistic expressions or terms, but those terms necessarily refer to disparate objects, namely, the separate perceptions and appearances or instantiations of those terms as the present sensory experiences of each individual's mind.

2. *Virtue and Hedonism*

Individuals' minds and souls must be independent of pleasure and not controlled by the hope for and desire of it, or by the fear and loathing of pain. The Cyrenaics defined the good for individuals as independence. Arete's school held that virtuous action was whatever action that was a mean to a pleasant end. Insofar as the practice of what others called virtue required the absence of pleasure, or required the presence of pain, "virtue" in its usual sense was undesirable and unethical. But insofar as a practice was pleasant it was correctly called "virtuous." Independence cannot be found by subjecting and controlling all pleasures, but by not desiring pleasures that one does not already have. All pleasures are similar and equivalent. Consequently, pain is best avoided by maintaining complete indifference to all pleasures other than that which one is in the present state of enjoyment of. This version of ethical hedonism, of which Arete was a proponent, is quite different than a doctrine for profligate living. Although hedonist philosophy challenged popular conceptions of virtue, Epicureanism, one of the largest philosophic sects of the ancient world had its foundations in the Cyrenaic school.[9]

3. *Hedonistic Moral Psychology*

The philosophic community which Arete eventually headed maintained a moral psychology which taught the uselessness of envy, passion, fear, and superstition. Consideration of loss of past pleasures, or of the possibility of failing to achieve future pleasures, only diminishes the present moment by poisoning it with fear, hope, and disappointment. Cyrenaic hedonism required individuals to be completely adaptable to all of life's disappointments and setbacks. The philosophy of which Arete was a proponent focussed on an individual's ability to obtain enjoyment in every situation. Individuals must direct their energies to maximizing the enjoyment of their current circumstances, not regretting the loss of past pleasures, as well as not entertaining hopeful anticipation of future joys. Since the future was unreliable, one could not rationally seek one's good through attempting to live a life that was on balance happy; rather, one had to direct one's energies and attention to finding happiness and enjoyment in each moment as it presented itself.

We can well imagine the difficulties of living in such a philosophic community. One never received sympathy or support in times of sorrow and disappointment. Expressions of negative emotions evidenced a breach of faith in the doctrine. Change, even in the most quotidienne circumstances, was undesirable. And although we may not ever know precisely what her contribution to philosophic hedonism consists of, we do know that Arete of Cyrene figures among those ancient women who studied and taught philosophy, and who lived this philosophy as head of a philosophic community.

II. ASCLEPIGENIA OF ATHENS

1. *Background*

Asclepigenia, a younger contemporary of Hypatia, lived at Athens and taught in the neo-Platonic school there. The school was headed by her father, Plutarch ("the Younger") of Athens (c. 350-430) and differed greatly from the scientific school of Hypatia at Alexandria. Plutarch's philosophy was syncretic, i.e., it attempted to unify the principles of Platonic and Aristotelian philosophies with seemingly opposing principles of pagan theurgy and magic. Asclepigenia was part of this new syncretism. With her brother, Hierius, and her colleague, Syrianus, she inherited the direction of the neo-Platonic Academy upon the death of her father in 430. Her most famous pupil, Proclus, was later to become one of its ablest exponents.

Asclepigenia lived during a period of religious and political turmoil which had some of its origins in philosophical disputes. Christianity was widespread and enjoyed great, if not overwhelming, political influence. Yet this was an evolving religion of uncertain philosophical perspective which was at the same time assimilating various elements of paganism, particularly Greek philosophy. The comparatively new Christian doctrine was evolving a character distinct from the religious implications of the neo-Platonic metaphysics taught in Plutarch's Academy, it was subject to philosophical criticism from that school. Ordinary pagans acknowledged fate as a potentially influenceable factor of personal and national destiny. Christians, on the other hand, were characterized by their acceptance of tragedy, suffering, disease, and death. If they could only endure, even welcome those otherwise undesirable experiences, consolation, in the form of salvation was promised. In contrast to the increasingly popular Christian philosophy, the metaphysics, cosmology, and religion which Ascelpigenia taught attempted to understand causes, to predict what the gods or fates would create, and to work magic and theurgy to intercede with those gods and fates to produce the desired outcomes. Pagan philosophers like Asclepigenia believed that the fates were potentially changeable provided one had a clear understanding of metaphysics and cosmology, and of magic and theurgy. The former told one how the fates influenced events; while the latter told one how to influence the fates.

2. *Metaphysics and Magic*

The Plutarchian philosophy taught by Asclepigenia was concerned with seeking the the greatest good. Dissatisfaction with life's fates required action. Philosophers who had mastered the secret principles of Platonic and Aristotelian metaphysics which controlled the universe, could act upon those principles by working magic. The neo-Platonic, ante-Plotinian schools of philosophy represented by Hypatia at Alexandria and Asclepigenia at Athens, taught a metaphysics which defined the One as that which is greater than Being, Intelligence, or Cause. Plotinus had taught that the One emanates a kind of image which reflects itself and thereby becomes Nous or Intelligence. Metaphysics was related not only to religion but to ethics insofar as the practice of virtue was understood as the way to the contemplation of the Absolute. The philosopher can do this by introspectively analyzing the way in which the soul turns to the intellect in retracing and discovering its own nature.[10] Understanding oneself permits contemplation of the metaphysical truths about Intelligence, Being, Cause, and the Absolute. In the Alexandrinian school of Hypatia, this path towards contemplation of the Absolute had become largely mathematical and scientific, whereas, the Athenian school, with Asclepigenia perhaps the foremost exponent of the theurgical aspects of pagan philosophy, tended more toward mysticism, magic, and contemplation of the mysteries of Platonic and Aristotelian metaphysics.

3. *Plotinus, Plutarch, Proclus*

Where a philosopher has left no written doctrines, it is possible to learn much about her by studying the philosophy espoused by her teachers and by her pupils. The Athenian school to which Asclepigenia belonged was a successor to the Platonic Academy as influenced by Plotinus. Like Plotinus, Plutarch the Younger and by extension, Asclepigenia, held that there were five realms of Reality: the One, Intelligence, Matter, Soul, and Nature. They believed that each soul had a divine part. Plotinus held that the Soul and Intelligence were transcendent metaphysical enitities as well as immanent human entities. Intelligence is the true self, but the true self can only be found when Intelligence is exercised through contemplation of the nature of the self. It is this introspective contemplation that is the source of true human happiness. The One is the source of an emanative process, the first step of which produces Intelligence (Nous). Mystical union with the One is the ultimate goal of Intelligence, and hence of contemplative introspection.

According to Marinus' *Life of Proclus* XVIII-XXIX, Asclepigenia taught the theurgical aspects of Aristotelian and Platonic philosophy to Proclus. In Proclus we see a refinement and extension of Plotinian emanative processes. Proclus' emanative processes are not merely "vertical" like those of Plotinus, but also "horizontal." The first vertically derived member of each hypostasis engenders a series of monads of the same hypostasis. Like Plotinus, Proclus maintained that the emanative process began with the One, but unlike Plotinus, he held that the One does not directly emanate Intelligence (Nous), but that "henads," identified with the highest polytheistic pagan dieties, and a kind of Platonic ideal number, are horizontally interposed between the One and Intelligence. Asclepigenia's influence on Proclus can be seen in the way that neo-Platonic metaphysics accommodates pagan religion by hierarchically ordering all of the polytheistic pagan dieties into a comprehensive metaphysical system. Mystical union with the One was the ultimate human goal, achievable only through a syncretism of Plotinian metaphysics, and, magic and theurgy. For it was magic and theurgy which gave the philosopher access to the pagan dieties that figures so prominently in the higher stages of mystical and metaphysical knowledge.

Unlike Plotinus, Proclus held that there is a particular aspect of soul which is higher than Intelligence and which makes such union with the One possible. Proclus also departed from Plotinus in that he did not consider matter, with which the emanative descent terminates, to be evil. According to A.J. Festugière:[11]

> Proclus was essentially a man of *logos*, a dialectician, the last of the great representatives of greek dialectic, ... a rationalist. But this rationalist was a platonic rationalist. In the platonic tradition, *logos* or discursive reason, did not exclude *nous*, or thought, or even that which underlies thought, that precise essence of the human being, that which is properly the instrument through which we attach ourselves to the Divine.

In his *Life of Proclus*[12] Marinus notes:

> As I said before, as a result of this work he [Proclus] obtained the higher and more perfect theurgical virtues and no longer remained on the level of the merely intellectual virtues. Therefore he did not live according to just one of the two divine characteristics, but both: by means of his mind alone he aspired towards what was higher, and by means of a not merely social but rather providential attention he cared for those things which were lower. He went to Chaldaic gatherings and (prayer) meetings, employed divine silent tops for strophalemancy, and in general practiced various things of this kind. He learned their significance and use from Asclepi-

genia, the daughter of Plutarch; for she alone had preserved from (her grandfather) Nestorius, and through the intermediary of her father, the knowledge of the (religious) orgies and the whole theurgic science.

The precise, well-defined levels of the Asclepigenian theurgic program are designed to lead the philosopher into and through the mysteries that are beyond the scope of metaphysics alone. These steps, as outlined by Proclus are:

(1) a life of purging one's consciousness so that one becomes freed of the senses,
(2) an illumination, consisting of climbing a ladder towards greater and greater levels of abstraction,
(3) unification with the One.

According to Festugière,[13] the purification of the soul and mind is accomplished through philosophy, the pursuit of knowledge of truth and virtue. But the purification of the body requires theurgy (the orgiastic rites). The enlightened body is one which experiences a mystical escape from its physical materiality. For Asclepigenia and her pupil, Proclus, knowledge of the One is a cognitive (philosophical), mystical (psychological), and physical (magical) experience. As such, knowledge of the One is not possible by divorcing the philosophical from the psychological and magical/theurgical.

III.   AXIOTHEA OF PHILESIA

This 4th century B.C. woman was a student of Plato, and later, of Speusippus. Themistius says[14] that after Axiothea read the *Republic* she travelled from Arcadia to Athens and became a follower of Plato. What is interesting is that according to Dicaearchus[15] she had to dress like a man to gain admittance to Plato's lectures. Alice Swift-Riginos[16] comments:

Coupled with the notice that Axiothea dressed as a man the story of her conversion has an ironical twist: inspired by the very dialogue which maintains the equality of women with men as potential members of the guardian class, Axiothea apparently had to disguise her sex ... to be accepted in the circle of Plato's students. And although Themistius gives the anecdote as an example of the protreptic force of the *Republic*, the story has another point as well — the discrepancy between Plato's written doctrines and his actual practices. Dicaearchus may not have known the story of Axiothea's conversion, but surely by the mention of the fact that she was dressed as a man Dicaearchus was alluding to this discrepancy and was not ... merely pointing out the eccentricity of Plato's character as reflected by the pupils he attracted.

IV.   CLEOBULINA OF RHODES

Until recently, the study of rhetoric was considered an important area of philosophical inquiry. Very little is known about Cleobulina, so it is not clear whether she should be considered a rhetorician, and hence a philosopher. According to Diogenes Laertius[17] Cleobulina was the daughter of Cleobulus, one of the Seven "Wise Men." She would therefore have lived *circa* 570 B.C. She is mentioned by Cratinus in his play *Cleobulinae*, and an example of her rhetoric is quoted twice by Aristotle. In *Poetics*[18] he says:

> But a whole statement in such terms will be either a riddle or a barbarism, a riddle, if made up of metaphors, a barbarism, if made up of strange words. The very nature indeed of a riddle is this, to describe a fact in an impossible combination of words (which cannot be done with real names for things, but can be with their metaphorical substitutes) e.g. "I saw a man glue brass on another with fire," (Cleobulina) and the like.

Aristotle quotes a verse form of this same riddle in his *Rhetoric*[19] and cites it as an example of an enigma:

A man I once beheld, (and wondering view'd,)
Who, on another, brass with fire had glued.

According to Menage[20] this refers to the medical application of cupping. In this operation, a vacuum is created to draw blood to the skin's surface. This riddle which Aristotle so admired that he twice quoted Cleobulina, preserving her fame as a rhetorician, may be solved if you assume that you have a brass, bell-shaped object, with a hole located on the dome of the bell, such that the interior of the hole was located higher on the dome of the bell than was the exterior of the hole. Insert a lit candle (the size of the hole) through the hole so that the flame is inside the dome of the brass. The wax would melt and drip downward through the hole, sealing it. If this brass were placed on the skin, while the candle was lit, the fire would consume the available oxygen. This would create a vacuum, thereby gluing the brass to the body with fire.

Plutarch reports Thales' praise of Cleobulina as a "wise and far-famed" woman with "a statesman's mind," who influenced her father to rule Rhodes more fairly.[21]

V. HIPPARCHIA THE CYNIC

Our information about Hipparchia comes from Laertius. She is also mentioned by Clement of Alexandria,[22] Antipater of Sidon,[23] and the Suda.[24] Laertius informs us that she threatened to commit suicide if her parents did not permit her to marry Crates, who, out of respect for them, tried to dissuade her. According to Laertius:

> ... at last, as he could not persuade her, he rose up, and placing all his furniture before her, he said, 'this is the bridegroom whom you are choosing, and this is the whole of his property; consider these facts, for it will not be possible for you to become his partner, if you do not also apply yourself to the same studies. and conform to the same habits that he does.'

Hipparchia assumed the Cynic garb, and lived the Cynic life with Crates. This was a hard life, memorialized in an epigram by Antipater:[25]

> I, Hipparchia, have not followed the habits of the female sex, but with manly courage, the strong dogs [Cynics]. I have not wanted the jewel on the cloak nor bindings for my feet, nor headties scented with ointment; rather a stick, barefeet and whatever coverings cling to my limbs, and hard ground instead of a bed. A life such as mine is preferable to that of the Menalian maid, since hunting is not as worthwhile as seeking wisdom.

As difficult as living the Cynic life was, it is clear that at least one male philosopher criticized Hipparchia for doing so. Theodorus criticized her undomestic habits, and Laertius reports that she attacked him with this piece of sophistry:

> What Theodorus could not be called wrong for doing, that same thing Hipparchia ought not to be called wrong for doing. But Theodorus does no wrong when he beats himself; therefore Hipparchia does no wrong when she beats Theodorus. He made no reply to what she said, but only pulled her clothes about; but Hipparchia was neither offended nor ashamed, as many a woman would have been; but when he said to her: 'Who is the woman who has left the shuttle so near the warp?'

Laertius records her reply:

> I, Theodorus, am that person, but do I appear to you to have come to a wrong decision, if I devote that time to philosophy, which I otherwise should have spent at the loom?

VI. LASTHENIA OF MANTINEA

Diogenes Laertius[26] mentions Lasthenia of Mantinea in connection with Axiothea of Philesia as a student of Speusippus. According to Laertius, Dionysius writing to Speusippus says "and one may learn philosophy too from your female disciple from Arcadia...." Because Lasthenia was a pupil of Speusippus, Plato's nephew and successor, it is sometimes assumed that she was a colleague of Axiothea of Philesia and, like her, Plato's student.

NOTES

1. Mozans, *Woman in Science*, Appleton (1913), 197-199.
2. Laertius, Diogenes, s.v. Life of Aristippus, II, 72, 86.
3. Strabo, *Geography*, XVII 3, 22, ed. Kramer.
4. Clement of Alexandria, *Stromates*, IV, XIX 122, 1.
5. Eusebius of Caesarea, *Preparatio Evangelica*, XIV 18.32.764a, (Oxford, 1913).
6. Themistius, *Orationes*, XXI, 244, ed. Dindorf.
7. Aristotle, *Metaphysics* 3, 2.
8. Ritter, Heinrich, *The History of Ancient Philosophy*, Volume II, Oxford: Talboys (1938), p. 88.
9. See: Grote, George. *Plato and Other Companions of Socrates*, Volume III, London: Murray, (1867) XXXVII, p. 554.
10. This is reminiscent of Aesara of Lucania's description of "following the tracks within oneself."
11. Festugière, *Études de Philosophie Grecque*.
12. Rosàn, *Philosophy of Procus*, XXVII.
13. *Op. cit.*, 585-596.
14. *Orations* 23.295C, ed. Dindorf.
15. Dicaearchus, Fragment 44, ed. Wehrli.
16. Swift-Riginos, Alice, *Platonica*, Leiden: Brill (1976), p. 185.
17. Laertius, Diogenes, *Lives of the Eminent Philosophers*, s.v. Cleobulus.
18. Aristotle, *Poetics*, 1458a24.
19. Aristotle, *Rhetoric*, III, ii, 12. (1405b).
20. Menage, Gilles, *The History of Women Philosophers*, Beatrice H. Zedler, transl. Lanham, MD: University Press of America (1984), p. 5.
21. Plutarch, *Septem Sapientium Convivium* in *Moralia*, 2, #148. Babbitt transl. London: William Heinemann (1949).
22. Clement of Alexandria, *Stromates*, IV.19.
23. Antipater of Sidon, *Anthology*, III, 12, 52.
24. Suda, *Lexicon*, s.v. "Hipparchia."
25. *Loc. cit.*
26. *Op. cit.* s.v. "Plato," III.46, 317, and s.v. Speusippus, IV, 2, 375.

Bibliography

In addition to works cited in this volume, this bibliography contains references to works that will be of interest to readers.

Aelius Spartianus. *Scriptores Historiae Augustae*. Translated by David Magie. London: William Heinemann; New York: G.P. Putnam's Sons, 1921.

Allen, Sr. Prudence. *The Concept of Woman*. Montreal: Eden Press, 1985.

Ambrosius. *De Paradiso*, in Migne, *Patrologia Latina*, 14.

—— *Hexaëmeron (On the Six Days)*, in Migne, *Patrologia Latina*, 14.

—— *De virginitate (On Virginity)*, in Migne, *Patrologia Latina*, 16.

Anderson, Graham. "Putting Pressure on Plutarch: Philostratus' Epistle 73." *Classical Philology* 72, January 1977, 43-45.

Antipater, Lucius. *Die Fragmenta*. Leipzig: Teubner, 1879.

Anton, John. "The Secret of Plato's *Symposium*." *Southern Journal of Philosophy*: XII: 3 (1974): 278.

Archytas. *Pseudo-Archytae Fragmenta*. Edited by J. Nolle. Diss. Monast. Tubingen 1914.

Aristotle. *The Basic Works of Aristotle*. Edited by R. McKeon. New York: Random House 1941.

Athanasius. *De incarnatione*, in Migne, *Patrologia Graeca*, 25, 26.

Athenaeus. *Diepnosophists*. Translated by C.D. Yonge, London: Bohn, 1907.

—— Translated by G.B.Gulick, Cambridge: Harvard University Press; London: William Heinemann, 1951.

Augustin. *Sermo* 232, in Migne, *Patrologia Latina*, 38.

—— *de Civitate Dei*, in Migne, *Patrologia Latina*, 41. Text and translation in the edition of Desclée de Brouwer, Brugge, 1957.

Augustine. *Tractatus in Evangelium, Johanni* in Desclée de Brouwer. *Oeuvres de Saint Augustine, Homilies sur l'évangile de Saint Jean I-XVI*. Brugge, 1964.

Bader, Clarisse. *La Femme Grêcque*, Paris: Didier et Cie., 1872.

Baer, Jr., R.A. *Philo's Use of the Categories Male and Female*. Leyden, 1970.

Bakhtin, M.M. "Discourse in the Novel," *The Dialogic Imagination*. J.M. Holquist and C. Emerson, translators. Austin: University of Texas Press, 1980.

Balsdon, J.P.V.D. *Roman Women: Their History and Habits*. New York: John Day, Co., 1963.

Basil the Great. *Sur l'Origine de l'homme*. Edition Sources Chrétiennes, no. 160, Paris, 1970.

Basilides. *Fragment I* Volker, *Quellen*, p. 38.

Bentley, Richard. *Dissertation Upon Phalaris*. London: H. Morlock & J. Hartley, 1699.

Bidez, Joseph. *Vie de Porphyre, le philosophe neoplatonicien, Receuil de travaux publiés par la Faculté de philologie et lettres de l'université de Gand*, Vol. 43, 1913.

Birley, Anthony. *Septimius Severus: The African Emperor*. London: Eyre & Spottiswoode, 1971.

Bloedow, Edmund F. "Aspasia and the 'Mystery' of the Menexenos," *Wiener Studien* (Zeitschrift für Klassiche Philologie und Patristic) Neu Folge. 9 (1975): 32-48.

Borresen, Kari. *The Patristic Use of Female Metaphors Describing God*. In Acta of the Eighth Conference of Patristic Studies, Oxford, 1979.

Bowersock, G.W. *Greek Sophists in the Roman Empire*. Oxford: Clarendon Press, 1969.

Brandwood, Leonard. *A Word Index to Plato*. Leeds: W.S. Maney & Son, Ltd. 1976.

Bréhier, Emile. *The Hellenistic and Roman Age*. Translated by Wade Baskin. Chicago and London: University of Chicago Press, 1965.

Burkert, Walter. *Lore and Science in Ancient Pythagoreanism*. Translated by Edwin L. Minar, Jr., Cambridge: Harvard University Press, 1972.

Burnet, John. *Early Greek Philosophy* 4th edition. London: Adam & Charles Black, 1930.

Bury, John. *A History of Greece to the Death of Alexander the Great*, 2nd edition. London: MacMillan & Co., 1929.

Bury, Richard de. *Histoire Abregée des Philosophes et des Femmes Célèbres*. Paris: Monory, 1773.

Bury, Robert G. *The Symposium of Plato*, 2nd edition. Cambridge: 1932.

Cacoullos, Ann. "The Doctrine of Eros in Plato," *Diotima* (Athens); 1 (1973): 84.

Cambridge Ancient History. Cambridge: Cambridge University Press. 1st edition, 1923-1934.

Camélot, P.Th. *Virgines Christi*, in La Vie Spirituelle, Paris, 1944.

— *La nouvelle Eve*, Études Mariales, 1934.

Campbell, James M. *The Influence of the Second Sophistic on the Style of the Sermons of St. Basil the Great*. Washington, D.C.: Catholic University of America, 1922.

Chadwick, H. *The Early Church*. London, 1978.

Cicero, M. Tullius. *De Oratore*. Loeb Classical Library, Cambridge: Harvard University Press, 1948.

Clarke, M.L. *Higher Education in the Ancient World*. Albuquerque, N.M.: University of New Mexico Press, 1971.

Clement of Alexandria. *Clement d'Alexandrie, les Stromates*. Paris: Editions du Cerf, 1951-4.

— *Stromateis*. O. Stählin, editor. Akademie-Verlag, Berlin, 1960.

— *Paedagogus*. Editors C. Mondésert, A. Plassart. Sources Chrétiennes 2, Paris, 1961.

Copleston, Frederick. *A History of Philosophy: Volume I Greece and Rome*. Garden City, N.Y.: Image Books, 1962.

Crawford, W.S. *Synesius the Hellene*. London: Rivingtons, 1901.

Cyprian. *De habitu virginum*, in Migne, *Patrologia Latina*, IV.

Cyril of Alexandria. *Dialogus I de Sancta et Consubstantiali Trinitate*, in Migne, *Patrologia Graeca*, 75.

"D." Mme Jeanne. "Hypatie la Philosophe," *Revue Contemporaine*. Ser. 2, V. 69, 1969.

Danby, Herbert. *The Mishna translated from the Hebrew, with Introduction and brief Explanatory Notes*. Oxford, 1933.

Delatte, Armand. *Études sur la Littérature Pythagoricienne*. Paris: Bibliotheque de l'Ecole des Hautes Études, 217. 1915.

Delatte, Louis. "Les Traités de la Royaute d'Écphante, Diotgène et Sthenidas," *Bibliotheque de la Faculté de Philosophie et Lettres de l'Université de Liège*, Vol. 97, 1942.

Delling, G. *Paulus Stellung zu Frau und Ehe*. Stuttgart, 1931.

Dicaearchus. Wehrli, F. Editor. Basel: B. Schwabe & Co., 1944.

Didot, Ambroise. *Bibliotheque Grêcque, avec Traduction Latine en Regard, V. II*. Paris: Firmin, 1839-90.

Didyme l'Aveugle. *Sur la Genèse I*. Sources Chrétiennes, no. 233. Lyon: 1976.

Didymus, the Blind. *Dialexis Montanistae et orthodoxi*, Pierre Labriolle, editor. (Greek text and French translation), in Bulletin d'ancienne littérature et d'archéologie chrétienne, 1913.

Diels, Hermann. *Doxographi Graeci*. Berlin (no publisher given), 1879.

Dio. *Dio's Roman History*. Translated by E. Cary. London: William Heinemann; New York: G.P. Putnam's Sons, 1927.

Diodorus Siculus. *Bibliothecae Historica*. Recension: Peter Wesseling. London: Oxford, 1956-7.

Diodorus of Tarsus. *Questio XX in Genesin* edition Schultze, Vol. I, 24-29; in Migne, *Patrologia Graeca*, 33, p. 1561.

Dodds, E.R. *Pagan and Christian in an Age of Anxiety*. Belfast, 1963.

Dörrie, H. "Kaiserzeitliche Kontroversen zur Lehre von der Seelenwanderung" in *Hermes* 85, 1957.

Dover, K.J. "The Date of Plato's Symposium," *Phronesis* 10 (1965).

Druon, H.V.M. *Oeuvres de Synesius, Évêque de Ptolemais*. Paris: Hachette, 1878.

Edinger, H.G., transl. *Thucydides, the Speeches of Pericles*. New York: Ungar, 1979.

Ephraim, the Syrian. *De Azymis*, Lamy I, 539; Beck, 34.

— *Hymni and Sermones*, Th.J. Lamy, editor, 1882/1902.

— *Hymni* 2-7 (on virginity) French translation by François Graffin in *L'Orient Syrien*, 1961.

Epictetus. *Dissertationes*, H. Schenkl, editor, Leipzig, 1916.

Epiphanius of Salamis. *Panarion or Adversus Haereses*, in Migne, *Patrologia Graeca*, 41/42.

— *Adversus Imagines*, in Migne, *Patrologia Graeca*, 41/42.

Erde, Edmund L. "Comedy and Tragedy and Philosophy in the *Symposium*: An Ethical Vision," *Southwestern Journal of Philosophy*: 7 (1976): 161.

Estiènne, Henri. *Lettres de Theano Fille de la Sagesse Pythagoricienne*. Bound following his *Diogenes Laerce ... de vitis*. Geneva: 1570.

Eusebius of Caesarea. *Preparatio Evangelica*. Oxford: Oxford Univesity Press, 1913.

Evrard, Etiènne. "A Quel Titre Hypatie Ensèigna-t-elle la philosophie?" *Revue des Études Grêcques*, XC, (1977), 69-74.

Fabricus. *Bibliotheca Graeca*. Hamburg: Bohn, 1790-1809.

Ferguson, John. *The Religions of the Roman Empire*. Ithaca, N.Y.: Cornell University Press, 1970.

Fermat, Pierre de. Untitled report in *Journal des Sçavans*, 20 Mars, 1679.

Festugière, A.M.J. *Études de Philosophie Grêcque*. Paris: J. Vrin, 1972.

Fitzgerald, A. *Letters of Synesius*. London: Oxford University Press, 1926.

Fohalle, René. "La Langue d'un Texte 'Dorien' ...," *Étrennes de linguistique offèrtes par quelques amis a Emile Benvéniste*. Paris: Geuthner 1928.

Freeman, Kathleen. *Ancilla to the Pre-Socratic Philosophers*. Oxford: Basil Blackwell, 1948.

Freemantle, Anne. *A Treasury of Early Christianity*. New York: Viking, 1953.

Friedlander, Paul. *Plato*. Two Volumes. Hans Meyerhoff translation. New York: Pantheon, 1958; Princeton: Bollingen, 1964.

Gardner, Alice. *The Fathers for English Readers: Synesius of Cyrene*. New York: Young, 1886.

Gibbon, Edward. *The Decline and Fall of the Roman Empire*. London & Toronto: J.M. Dent; New York: E.P. Dutton, 1910.

Ginzburg, L. *The Legends of the Jews*. Philadelphia, 1946.

Gold, Barbara K. "A Question of Genre: Plato's *Symposium* as Novel," *MLN*: 95 (1980): 1353.

Gollob, Eduard. "Eine wiedergefundener Diophantuscodex," *Zeitschrift für Mathematic und Physik*, XLIV no. 2, (1899) 137-40.

Gomme, A.W. *Essays in Greek History and Literature*. Oxford: Basil Blackwell, 1937.

Gorman, Peter. *Pythagoras, A Life*. Boston: Routledge & Kegan Paul, 1979.

Graaff, H.C. "L'image de Dieu et la structure de l'âme d'après les Pères Grêcs," *Supplément de la Vie Spirituelle*, tome 5 nr. 20, 5 février, 1952.

Greene, W.C., ed. *Scholia Platonica*, Haverford: American Philological Association, 1938.

Gregory of Nazianz. *Epistles*, in Migne, *Patrologia Graeca*, 37.

Gregory of Nyssa. "De Vita Macrinae," F. van der Meer and G. Bartelink, translation (Dutch), Antwerpen, 1971, from the Greek text edited by W. Jaeger, Leyden, 1952. English translation by W.K. Lowther Clarke, London, 1916.

— *De Anima et Resurrectione*, in Migne, *Patrologia Graeca*, 46. German translation in Bibliothek der Kirchenväter.

— *Vita Gregorii Thaumaturgi*, in Migne, *Patrologia Graeca*, 46.

— *De Virginitate*. Sources Chrétiennes, no. 119, Paris, 1966.

— *In Canticum Canticorum*, text edited by Werner Jaeger and H. Langerbeck, Leyden, 1960.

— *Oratio Catechetica*, in Migne, *Patrologia Graeca*. German translation by Joseph Bardell, Stuttgart, 1971.

— *De opificio Hominis*, in Migne, *Patrologia Graeca*, 44.

Grote, George. *Plato and the Other Companions of Socrates*. London: Murray, 1867.

Gruppe, O.F. *Über die Fragmente des Archytas und der alteren Pythagoreer*. Berlin: Eine Preisschrift, 1840.

Hackforth, R. "Immortality in Plato's Symposium," *Classical Review* LXIV (1950): 43.

Halley, Edmund. *Apollonius Pergaeus Conic Sections*. Oxford: (no publisher given) 1710.

Halma, Nicolas B. Almagèste de Ptolemée (on spine), *Commentaires de Theon d'Alexandrie sur le premier Livre de la Composition Mathématique de Ptolemée. Traduit pour la premier fois de grèc en français sur les mss. de la Bibliotheque du Roi, par M. L'Abbé Halma et suivi les notes de M. Delambre*. Paris: Merlin, 1821.

— *Theon et Hypatie, Commentaires de Theon d'Alexandrie sur le 3e Livre de l'Almageste de Ptolemée*. Paris: Merlin, 1820.

Haman, A.T. *Ichthus, La Philosophie passé au Christ*. Litérature Chrétienne, Paris, 1954.

Harris, B.F. "Apollonius of Tyana: Fact and Fiction," *The Journal of Religious History*, 5: (1969) 189-199.

Heath, Thomas, *Greek Astronomy*. Oxford: Clarendon Press, 1932.

— *A History of Greek Mathematics*. Oxford: Clarendon Press, 1921.

— *Diophantus of Alexandria*. New York: Dolphin, 1960.

— Review of A. Rome, *Classical Review*, 1938.

Hedengrahn, Peter. *Exercitium Academicum Mulieres Philosophantes Leviter Adumbrans*. Upsaliae, 1700.

Hercher, Richard. *Epistolographi Graeci*. Paris: Didot, 1873.

Herodian of Antioch. *History of the Roman Empire from the Death of Marcus Aurelius to the Accession of Gordian III.* Translated by Edward C. Echols. Berkeley & Los Angeles: University of California Press, 1961.

Hoche, Richard. "Hypatia, die Tochter Theons," *Philologus* 15, (1860): 435-474.

Holzey, K. *Die Theklaakten.* Münster, 1905.

Huby, Pamela. "The Menexenus Reconsidered," *Phronesis*: 2: (1957): 104.

Jamblichus. [sic.] *De Vita Pythagoras.* Translated by Holstenni & Ritterschussi, 1707; and by Deubner, L. Leipzig, 1937.

Iamblichus. *Life of Pythagoras.* Translated by Thomas Taylor. London: John W. Watkins 1965 reprint of 1818 edition.

Index Bibliothecae Medicae. Florence, 1882.

Irenaeus. *Adversus Haereses*, in Migne, *Patrologia Graeca*, 7. English translation by E. Roberts and James Donaldson, Edinburgh: Ante Nicene Christian Library, 1868.

Jahn, Otto. "Socrate et Diôtime, Bas-Relief de Bronze." *Annales de l'institut Archéologique*, XIII: (1841).

— *Platonis Symposium.* Bonnae, 1875.

Jerphagnon, Lucien. *Vivre et Philosopher sous les Césars.* Toulouse: Edouard Privat, 1980.

Joel, Karl. *Die Frauen in der Philosophie.* Hamburg: Verlagsanstalt und Druckerei, 1896.

John Crysostom. (Johannus Chrysostomus) "Homilia in quosdam locos N.T.," in Migne, *Patrologia Graeca*, 51.

— *In Genesin Homiliae*, in Migne, *Patrologia Graeca, 53.*

— "Hom. 4, In Matth.", in Migne, *Patrologia Graeca*, 57, 16.

Jowett, Benjamin. *The Dialogues of Plato*, 2nd revised ed. Oxford: Clarendon Press, 1875.

Justinus Martyr. *Dialogus cum Tryphone*, in Migne, Patrologia Graeca, 6.

— *Dialogue avec Tryphon.* Text and French translation by G. Archambault, Paris, 1909.

Kelson, Hans. "Platonic Love," *American Imago*: 3: 1-2 (April, 1942): 75.

Kennedy, George. *The Art of Rhetoric in the Roman World: 300 B.C.-A.D. 300.* Princeton, N.J.: Princeton University Press, 1972.

Kranz, Walther. "Diotima," *Die Antike* 2: (1926): 313.

— "Diotima von Mantinea," *Hermes*, 61: (1926): 437-447.

Lacombrade, Christian. *Synesius de Cyrene.* Paris: Société d'Édition "Les Belles Lettres," 1951.

Laertius, Diogenes. *Lives of the Eminent Philosophers.* Cambridge: Harvard University Press, 1942.

la Bonnadière, Annemarie. *Chrétiennes des premiers siècles.* Paris, 1957.

Lampropoulou, S. "Hypatia philosophe Alexandrine," *Athenai, Bibliopholeion*, I.v.29. 1977.

Laurentin, R. *Marie et l'anthropologie chrétienne de la femme* in *Nouvelle Revue Theologique* 89 (1967), 484-515.

Lebon. *L'apostolicité de la méditation Mariale, Recherches de Théologie ancienne et mediévale*, 1930.

Lehner, F.A. *Die Marienverehrung in den ersten Jahrhunderten*. Stuttgart, 1886.

Leopoldt, Johannes. *Das Evangelium nach Thomas*. Berlin, 1967.

Levinson, R.B. *In Defense of Plato*, Cambridge: Harvard University Press, 1953.

Lewis, Thomas. *The History of Hypatia, a most impudent Schoolmistress of Alexandria...* London: Bickerton, 1921.

Ligier, Hermann. *De Hypatia Philosopha et Eclectismi Alexandrini Fine* (thesis) Bibliotheque Universitaire des Lettres, 1879.

Luce, J.V. "Immortality in Plato's Symposium: A Reply," *Classical Review* 61 (NS 2) 1952: 137.

Mansi, Stat. Eccl. Antiq. Canones, 952.

Marinus of Flavia Neopolis. *Life of Proclus*, English translation. (no translator and no publisher given) London, 1792.

Martial. *Epigrams*. Translated by W.A.C. Ker. Cambridge: Harvard University Press, 1968.

Maximus Tyrius. *Dissertation*. Translated by Thomas Taylor. London: C. Whittingham, 1804.

McCabe, Joseph. *The Empresses of Rome*. New York: Henry Holt & Co., 1911.

Mead, G.R.S. *Apollonius of Tyana: The Philosopher-Reformer of the First Century A.D.* London and Benares: Theosophical Publishing Co., 1901.

Menage, Gilles. *Historia Mulierum Philosopharum*. Lugduni: Apud Anissonios, Joan. Posuel, & Claudium Rigaud, 1690.

— *The History of Women Philosophers*. Beatrice H. Zedler, translator. Lanham, MD.: University Press of America, 1984.

Méridier, L. *Plato*. Paris: Société d'édition "Les Belles Lettres," 1920.

Meunier, Mario. *Femmes Pythagoriciennes, Fragments et Lettres*. Paris: L'Artisan du Livre, 1932.

Meyer, Wolfgang A. *Hypatia von Alexandria*. Heidelberg: Georg Weiss, 1886.

Migne. *Patrologiae Cursus Completus, Series Graeca, Series Latina*. Paris: Garnieri Fratres, 1844-1890.

Mingazzini, Paolino. "Su Duo Oggetti in Terracotta Raffiguranti Socrate," *La Parole del Passato: Rivista di Studi Antichi*, XXV: (1970): 351-358.

Montulca, J.F. *Histoire des Mathématiques*. Nouvelle tirage, Paris: Librarie Scièntifique et Technique, 1960.

Mozans, (pseud. for) Zahm, J.A. *Woman in Science*. New York: Appleton, 1913.

Murphy, Gerard J. *The Reign of the Emperor L. Septimius Severus from the Evidence of the Inscriptions.* Jersey City, New Jersey: St. Peters College Press, 1945.

Nagy, Blaise. "The Naming of Athenian Girls: A Case in Point," *Classical Journal*: LXXIV (1979): 360-364.

Neumann, Harry. "Diotima's Concept of Love," *American Journal of Philology*: 86: (1965): 38.

Nolle, J., ed. *Ps.-Archytae Fragmenta.* Tubingen: Diss. Monast. 1914.

Oppian. *Cynegetica.* Tr. A.W. Mair. London: William Heinemann; New York: Putnam, 1928.

Orellius, J. Conrad. *Opuscula Graecorum Veterum.* Lipsiae: Weidmann, 1821.

Origen. *Gen Hom.*, in Migne, *Patrologia Graeca*, XII.

— *De Principiis*, in Migne, *Patrologia Graeca*, XI.

— *On First Principles.* English translation by H. de Lubac, G.W. Butterworth, editor. New York, 1966.

— *Comm. in Joann.*, in Migne, *Patrologia Graeca*, XIV.

Origen. Origène, *Fragments sur la Première aux Corinthiens 75. Journal of Theological Studies* 10.

Owens, Joseph. *A History of Ancient Western Philosophy.* New York: Appleton-Century-Crofts, 1959.

Parker, H.M.D., Warmington, B.H. *A History of the Roman World from A.D. 138 to 337.* New York: Macmillan, 1958.

Pedersen, O. *A Survey of the Almagest.* Odense: Odense Universitetsforlag, 1974.

Penella, Robert J. *The Letters of Apollonius of Tyana: A Critical Text with Prolegomena, Translation and Commentary.* Leiden: E.J. Brill, 1979.

Perowne, Stewart. *The Caesars' Wives.* London, Sydney, Auckland, Toronto: Hodder and Stoughton, 1974.

Philo Alexandrinus. *De vita Contemplativa.* Text edited by Cohn and Wendland. English translation in Loeb Classical Library.

— *Quod Omnis Probus Liber sit.* Text edited by Cohn and Wendland. English translation in Loeb Classical Library.

— *De vita Mosis.* Text edited by Cohn and Wendland, Berlin, 1896. English translation in the Loeb Classical Library.

— *De Fuga et Inventione.* Text edited by Cohn and Wendland. English translation in the Loeb Classical Library.

— *De Aeternitate mundi.* Text edited by Cohn and Wendland. English translation in the Loeb Classical Library.

— *De Decalogo.* Text edited by Cohn and Wendland. English translation in the Loeb Classical Library.

— *De Opificio Mundi.* Text edited by Cohn and Wendland. English translation in the Loeb Classical Library.

— *Specialibus Legibus.* English translation in the Loeb Classical Library.

— *Quaestiones et Solutiones in Genesin.* English translation in the Loeb Classical Library.

— *Quaestiones et Solutiones in Exodum.* Text edited by Cohn and Wendland, Berlin, 1898. English translation in the Loeb Classical Library.

Philostratus. *Letters* in *Letters of Alciphron, Aelian, and Philostratus.* Translated by A.R. Benner and Francis H. Fobes. Cambridge: Harvard University Press, London: William Heinemann, 1949.

— *The Life of Apollonius of Tyana.* Translated by F.C. Conybeare. London: William Heinemann, New York: Macmillan, 1912. Two volumes.

— *Life of Apollonius.* Translated by C.P. Jones. Edited and abridged by G.W. Bowersock. Middlesex, England: Penguin Books, 1970.

— *The Lives of the Sophists.* Translated by W.C. Wright. London: William Heinemann; New York: G.P. Putnam's Sons, 1922.

Platnauer, Maurice. *The Life and Reign of the Emperor Lucius Septimius Severus.* Westport, Conn.: Greenwood Press, 1970. (reprint of 1918 edition.)

Plato. *The Collected Dialogues of Plato.* Edited by Edith Hamilton and Huntington Cairns. Princeton: Princeton University Press, 1961.

— *Timaeus.* Text edited by John Burnett, Oxford, 1902, reprinted 1954.

Plotinus. *Ennead.* Bréhier edition.

Plutarch. *The Lives of the Noble Grecians and Romans.* Translated by J. Dryden. New York: Modern Library. (no publication date given: reprint of 1864 edition.)

— *Septem Sapientium Convivium* in *Moralia*; Volume 2, Babbit translation. London: William Heinemann, 1949.

Plutarchus. *De Procreatione Animae in Timaeum*, Bernadakis edition, Leipzig: Teubner-Verlag, 1888-1896.

Poestion, J.C. *Griechische Dichterinnen; Griechische Philosophinnen.* Bremen: H. Fischer, 1882.

Porphyry. *Sententiae.* In Stobaeus, III.

— *Sententiae.* B. Mommert, editor. Leipzig, 1907.

— *Sententiae.* E. Lamberz, editor. Leipzig: Teubner-Verlag, 1975.

— *Ad Markellam.* Nauck edition, pp. 283-287; partly in de Vogel, C.J., *Greek Philosophy III*, Leyden, 1964.

— *De antro Nympharum.* Edited by R.M. van Goens, Utrecht, 1765. (Dutch translation by C. Verhoeven, Baarn, 1984.)

— *De antro Nympharum (The Cave of the Nymphs in the Odysee).* English translation by Seminar Classics, State University of New York. Arethusa, 1969.

— *Kata Christianoon (Gegen die Christen).* A. von Harnack, editor and translator, Berlin, 1916.

Preston, Harriet W. and Dodge, Louise. "A Pupil of Hypatia," *Atlantic Monthly* 75, (1895), 371-382.

Proclus. *Commentary on Plato's Timeaus.* Translated by Thomas Taylor. London: 1820.

— *Commentaire sur le Timée.* Editor J. Vrin. Paris, 1966-1970.

— *Commentary on Plato's Republic*, in *The Six Books of Proclus* (no translator given) London: Valpy, 1816).

Quispel, G. *Gnosis als Weltreligion*. Zürich, 1951.
— *Makarius, das Thomas Evangelium und das Lied von der Perle*, Leyden, 1967.

Rebiere, Alfonse. *Les Femmes dans la Science*, 2ième edition, Paris: Nony, 1897.
Révielle, Jean. *La Religion à Rome sous les Sévères*. Paris: E. Leroux, 1886.
Ritter, Heinrich. *The History of Ancient Philosophy*. Oxford: Talboys, 1938.
Rome, A. "Le Troisième Livre des Commentaires sur l'Almageste par Theon et Hypatie," *Annales de la Société Scientifique de Bruxelles*, V. 46, (1926): 1-14.
— "Observations d'Equinoxes et de Solstices dans le Chapitre 1 du livre 3 du Commentaire sur l'Almageste par Theon d'Alexandrie," *Annales de la Société Scientifique de Bruxelles*, Vol. 57 (1937): 213-236. (premier partie), and Vol. 58 (1938): 6-26. (second partie).
— *Commentaires de Pappus et de Theon d'Alexandrie sur l'Almageste, Tome III., Theon d'Alexandrie Commentaire sur les Livres 3 et 4 de l'Almageste, Studi e Testi*, 106, Citta del Vaticano: Biblioteca Apostolica Vaticana (1943).
— "The Calculation of an Eclipse of the Sun according to Theon of Alexandria," *Proceedings of the International Congress of Mathematicians* (1950) Vol. 1.
Rosàn, L.J. *The Philosophy of Proclus*. New York, 1949.
Rosen, Stanley. *Plato's Symposium*. New Haven: Yale University Press, 1968.
Ryle, Gilbert. *Plato's Progress*. Cambridge: Cambridge University Press, 1966.

Simon, Jules. *Histoire de l'Ecole d'Alexandrie*. Paris: Joubert, 1845.
Socrates Scholasticus. *Historiae Ecclesiasticae*. London: H.B. Bohn, 1853.
Soll, G. *Handbuch der Dogmengeschichte*, Band III, fasc. 4, *Mariologie*, Herder-Verlag, Freiburg, 1978.
Stobaeus. *Eclogae Physicae Dialecticae et Ethicae* bound with *Florilegium*. O.P. Hense, translator. Berlin: Apud Weidmannas, 1884-1912.
— *Florilegium*. A. Meineke editor, Leipzig: B.G. Teubner, 1855-1857.
Strabo. *Geography*, H.L. Jones, translator. London: Heinemann, 1917-1932.
Strack-Billerbeck. *Kommentar zum N.T. aus Talmud und Midrash.*
Suidae [sic.] Suda. *Lexicon*. Stuttgart: B.G. Teubneri, 1967-1971.
Sulpicius Severus. *Dialogue adv. Palagium.*
Swift-Riginos, Alice. *Platonica*, Leiden: Brill, 1976.

Tannery, Paul. *Diophanti Alexandrini Opera Omnia*. Two volumes. Lipsiae: Teubneri, 1893-1895.
— "L'Article de Suidas sur Hypatia," *Annales de la Faculté des Lettres de Bordeaux*, 1880.

— *Oeuvres de Fermat*. Paris: Gauthier-Villars et fils, 1841-6.

— *Mémoires Scientifiques*. Toulouse (published privately), 1912.

Taylor, A.E. *Socrates*. Westport, CT: Greenwood Press, 1975. Reprint of 1951 Beacon Press edition.

— *Plato, the Man and his Work*. London: Methuen, 1978. Reprint of 1926 edition.

— *Plato's Biography of Socrates*. London: H. Milford for the British Academy, 1917.

Taylor, Thomas. *Political Fragments of Stobaeus*, Chiswick, England: privately published, 1822.

— *Iamblichus' Life of Pythagoras*. London: A.J. Valpy, 1818.

Tertullian. *De Baptismo*. Migne, *Patrologia Latina*, II.

— *Adversus Marcionem (Against Marcion)*, in Migne, *Patrologia Latina*, II. Text and English Translation by Ernest Evans, Oxford, 1972.

— *De resurrectione (On the Resurrection of the Flesh)*, in Migne, *Patrologia Latina*, II.

— *De feminis velandis*, in Migne, *Patrologia Latina*, II.

Themistius. *Themistii Orationes quae supersunt, recensuit H. Schenkl*. G. Downey, editor. Leipzig: B.G. Teubner, 1965-1974.

— *Orationes*. G. Dindorf, editor. Leipzig: C. Cnobloch, 1832.

Theodoret, J.A. *Iamblichus of Chalcis, De Vita Pythagoras*. Heidelberg (no publisher given), 1598.

Theodotus of Ancyra. *Homilia on the State of the Mother of God*, in *Acta* of the *Council Ephesus*, Galand edition, tome IX.

Thesleff, Holger. "Pythagorean Texts of the Hellenistic Period," *Acta Academiae Aböensis, Humanoira*. Series A, Vol. 30, 1, (1965).

— "An Introduction to the Pythagorean Texts of the Hellenistic Period," *Acta Academiae Aböensis, Humanoira*. Series A, Volume XXV: 1: (1961).

Thucydides. *The Peloponnesian Wars*. Thomas Hobbes translation, edited by David Grene. Ann Arbor: The University of Michigan Press, 1959.

— *Thucydides, the Speeches of Pericles*. H.G. Edinger, translator. New York: Ungar, 1979.

Tihon, Anne. "Le calcul de l'éclipse de Soleil du 16 juin 364 p.C. et le "Petit Commentaire" de Theon," *Institute Historique Belge de Rome*, V. 46-47 (1976-1977).

Toland, J. *Hypatia, or the History...* in *Tetradymus*. London: J. Brotherton, 1720.

Turton, Godfrey. *The Syrian Princesses: The Women Who Ruled Rome A.D. 193-235*. London: Cassell & Co., 1974.

Usener, H. "Fasti Theonis Alexandrini," in *Monumenta Germania Historia*, V. 13, Thom. Mommsen, editor, *Chronica Minora*, IV-VII (1899). Berlin: Apud Weidmannas.

Vacherot, Etienne. *Histoire Critique de l'école d'Alexandrie*, Paris: Ladrange, 1846-1851.

Vlastos, Gregory. *Platonic Studies*. Princeton: Princeton University Press, 1981.

de Vogel, C.J. *Greek Philosophy*, III. Leiden, 1964.

— *Plotinus' Image of Man*, in *Symbolae*, Leuven, 1976.

Von Harnack. *Porphyrius, gegen die Christen.*

Warner, Martin. "Love, Self and Plato's *Symposium*," *Philosophical Quarterly*, 29: (1979): 329-339.

Wernsdorf, J.Chr. *Dissertatio Academica de Hypatia, philosopha Alexandrina.* (Vitembergae) 1747, 1748. 18 pages.

Wieland, C.M. *Works* (Oeuvres Completes) Goeschen edition, Duisbourg (1791).

Williams, Mary Gilmore. "Studies in the Lives of the Roman Empresses: Julia Domna," *American Journal of Archaeology*: 6 (1902).

Wolff, J.Chr. *Mulierum Graecarum Quae Oratione Prosae Usae Sunt Fragmenta et Elogia Graece et Latina.* London: 1739.

Xenocrates. Simplicius, in *Arist. De Anima*. Hayduck edition.

Xenophon. *Memorabilia*. 2nd edition, Oxford: Clarendon, 1901.

— *Symposium*. London: Heinemann, 1922.

— *Hellenica.* J. Irving Manatt, editor. Boston: Ginn, 1901.

Zahm, J.A. *Woman in Science*. New York: Appleton, 1913.

Zeller, Eduard. *Philosophie der Griechen*. 4th edition, Leipzig: R.R. Reisland, 1902.

— *Plato and the Older Academy*. London: 1888.

Index

Kallikratidas, father of Phintys of Sparta, 26, 71
Kallisto, letter from Theano II, 47-52

Laertius, Diogenes, 59, 206-209
Lascaris, Jean, 189
Lasthenia of Mantinea, 83, 92, 208-209
law, nature of, 22-23, 37, 56-57
love
—, of children, 41-43
—, of parents, 34, 38
—, of spouse, 43-47
Lucian, 105
Lysippus, 104

magic, 201-205
Makrina, 7, 101-121
—, on the unity and immortality of the soul, 140-141
Makrina the Old, 139, 150
Marcella, 142
Marcus Aurelius, 117
Marius Maximus, 124
marriage, duties of women
—, Christian view of, 147-152
—, Jewish view, 148-149
—, Theano I and, 14
—, Theano II and, 29-31
—, Perictione I and, 32-38
—, Phintys and, 27-31
mathematics, 60, 67, 169, 173, 176-180, 186, 198
matter, 143, 174, 203
Maximus Tyrius, 106
medical ethics, 53-54
di Medici, 185, 186, 189, 190
medicine, philosophy of, 24-25
men, virtues of, 27, 28
Menage, Gilles, 207
metaphysics,
—, in Hypatia, 169, 176
—, in Asclepigenia, 202-205
metrodidactus, see Aristippus the Younger

Milo, 15
mind, 20-22, 24
Moderatus of Gades, 129
moderation (see also temperance), as virtue of women
—, letter of Myia, 15-17
—, in Phintys of Sparta's *On the Moderation of Women*, 26-31
—, in Theano II, 47 ff
moral philosophy
—, Aesara of Lucania and, 19-26
—, Arete of Cyrene and, 197-200
—, Julia Domna, and, 129 ff
—, Perictione I and, 32-39
—, Phintys of Sparta and, 26-31
—, Theano I and, 14-15
—, Theano II and, 41-45
moral psychology
—, Aesara of Lucania and, 20-21, 24
—, Arete of Cyrene and, 200-201
—, Theano II and, 41-43
music, 48, 52, 54, 56
Myia, 5, 11, 15
—, letter to Phyllis, 15-17
mysticism, 147-149, 173-174, 203-205

natural law theory, in Aesara, 19-23
nature, in Asclepigenia, 203
neo-Platonism, 132, 141 ff, 169, 170, 173-174, 201 ff
neo-pythagoreanism, 59 ff, 129
Nero, 129
Nestorius, 205
Nous, 142, 146, 160, 174, 203, 204
number
—, Arignote on, 12
—, Theano I on, 12-13
Numenius, 143
numismatics, 103-104, 117, 122

One, the, 169, 202-205
Oppian, 123
Origen, 150 ff, 162